A BASEBALL WINTER

A BASEBALL

CONTRIBUTORS Peter Pascarelli · Tim Tucker · Terry Pluto

Marty Noble · Ross Newhan

The Off-Season Life

WINTER

of the

Summer Game

EDITED BY TERRY PLUTO AND JEFFREY NEUMAN

MACMILLAN PUBLISHING COMPANY   NEW YORK

COLLIER MACMILLAN PUBLISHERS   LONDON

Macmillan Publishing Company
866 Third Avenue, New York, N.Y. 10022
Collier Macmillan Canada, Inc.

Library of Congress Cataloging-in-Publication Data
Main entry under title:

A baseball winter.

Includes index.
1. Baseball—United States—Management.   I. Pluto,
Terry, 1955–   .   II. Neuman, Jeffrey.   III. Pascarelli,
Peter.
GV875.7.B37   1986   796.357'0973   85-20938
ISBN 0-02-597760-1

Macmillan books are available at special discounts for bulk purchases
for sales promotions, premiums, fund-raising, or educational use.
For details, contact:
Special Sales Director
Macmillan Publishing Company
866 Third Avenue
New York, N.Y. 10022

10 9 8 7 6 5 4 3 2 1

Designed by Jack Meserole

Printed in the United States of America

Contents

Acknowledgments

A Baseball Winter has been a labor of love, but a labor nonetheless. It is unlike any other baseball book we've ever seen, in its focus on the backstage aspects of the game: contract negotiations, trade talks, in short, the game as it is played off the field. The offseason of 1984–85 was in many ways a typical offseason, and the five teams we've examined represent a broad spectrum of personalities and philosophies. Taken together, they tell us a great deal about the state of the business and the state of the game.

We would like to thank, first and foremost, Peter Pascarelli, Tim Tucker, Marty Noble, and Ross Newhan. Their writing and reporting brought to life the somewhat odd notion of an offseason diary. Thanks also to Henry Aaron, Gerry Fraley, Wayne Minshew, Chris Mortensen, John Mullen, Sheldon Ocker, Al Thornwell, George Wieser, and Bucky Woy.

At Macmillan, thanks go to Charlie Hayward and Greg Hamlin, who were supportive of this unusual project from the start; to Dominick Anfuso, who made many insightful comments and provided much needed encouragement; and to Emily Posner, for tolerating intermittent editorial rages. Thanks, also, to Dr. Judith Benstein, for her aid and comfort above and beyond the call.

And to Gabe Paul, for being such a good sport.

—Terry Pluto and Jeffrey Neuman

About the Contributors

Terry Pluto spent several years on the baseball beat covering the Baltimore Orioles and Cleveland Indians. He is now on the staff of the *Akron Beacon-Journal,* and writes a regular column for *Baseball America*.

Peter Pascarelli was born and raised in Boston, where his summer jobs included selling hot dogs in Sections 1 through 4 of Fenway Park. A graduate of the University of Massachusetts, he has worked for the *Rochester Democrat and Chronicle, The News American* in Baltimore, and the *Dallas Times Herald*. He is currently the baseball writer for *The Philadelphia Inquirer*. He lives in Corona Del Mar, California and Philadelphia with his wife Elizabeth and her three children, Robyn, David, and Patrick.

Tim Tucker is assistant sports editor of *The Atlanta Journal* and *The Atlanta Constitution*. He previously covered the Atlanta Braves for five years, winning three national Associated Press Sports Editors awards for writing and reporting on the beat. He also was twice named Georgia Sportswriter of the Year by the National Association of Sportswriters and Sportscasters. He is a native of Commerce, Georgia , and a journalism graduate of the University of Georgia.

Ross Newhan has been a baseball writer for twenty-five years, starting at the *Long Beach Press-Telegram* (Calif.) in 1961. He has covered the Angels and Dodgers for the *Los Angeles Times* since 1968. He has twice been president of the Los Angeles–Anaheim chapter of the Baseball Writers Association of America, and a member of the board of directors of the national association. He attended Long Beach State College, and now lives in Anaheim with his wife, Connie, and their children Sara and David.

Marty Noble has been on the baseball beat in the New York area since 1974, first for *The Record* (Hackensack, N.J.) until 1980, and currently for the Long Island newspaper *Newsday,* for whom he covers the Mets and Yankees. He lives in Waldwick, New Jersey with his wife, Yvette, and their daughter, Carolyn.

Prologue

DETROIT—Ron Roenicke takes a two-step lead off first. In the Tigers' dugout, everyone is on their feet, and have been since Kirk Gibson's homer in the eighth gave them an 8–4 lead. The noise of the crowd is deafening as Willie Hernandez kicks at the rubber, takes the sign from Lance Parrish, and goes into the set position. He glances at Roenicke, rocks back, uncoils, and fires. The fastball to Tony Gwynn is up and in; Gwynn, swinging late, slices the ball down the left-field line. Larry Herndon, playing Gwynn deep in straightaway left, takes off at the crack of the bat, and catches the ball in full stride two steps from the foul line. The Tigers pour onto the field, surrounding Hernandez just to the left of the mound. They are World Champions.

In the Tigers clubhouse the champagne flows, and the talk is of dynasty. In the Padres clubhouse the words vary, but the lament is the traditional one: wait till next year.

But nobody's waiting. Back in the old days (remember 1974?) a baseball club had absolute control over its destiny. Its players were under contract, and stayed there forever. When it signed a young player and put him into its farm system, he was theirs until they decided they'd had enough of him. "Play me or trade me" was just an empty threat. And a $100,000 salary was the sign of a true star.

Free agency changed all that. Today, players can, after sufficient time in the majors, sell their services to the highest bidder, demand that they be traded, and specify which teams they're willing to be traded to. In the modern age, the phrases "no-trade clause" and "deferred payment" seem to come up far more often than "cut-off man" or "high hard one." And the duration and terms of a player's contract often have more effect on a team's ability to trade him than his range in the field or ability to hit the curveball.

The planning that goes into building a champion is more complicated than ever before. But plan you must. And so, long before the last batted ball of the season settled into Herndon's glove, preparations for the following season were already well underway. . . .

⅃ _Clearing the Decks_

September 27

PHILADELPHIA—The Philadelphia Country Club is one of those tweedy bastions of proper snootiness that embody the popular image of Philadelphia's famed Main Line. It isn't the kind of place you expect to see tobacco-chewing baseball types hacking their way through 18 holes of golf.

But baseball has become more buttoned-down in recent years. Sunflower seeds have largely replaced chewing tobacco. And nouveau riche millionaires with subscriptions to _The Wall Street Journal_ have supplanted the hard-bitten, unpolished types of yesteryear. So it isn't outlandish for Philadelphia Phillies president Bill Giles to invite his manager, coaching staff, and top scouts to an outing at the club on the last off-day of the 1984 season.

This is supposed to be a fun day without baseball decisions hovering in the background. But Giles greets his baseball people at the first tee in a crisis atmosphere. The Phillies have long ago plummeted out of the pennant race. They are in the midst of finishing the season's final month with an abysmal nine-game losing streak. The future of manager Paul Owens is openly being questioned. Home attendance has dropped for the third straight year, continuing a slide of over 700,000 in the last five years. And the baseball judgments of Giles and his brain trust are under fire after trades with the Detroit Tigers and the Chicago Cubs helped make the Tigers and Cubs division champions.

3

So this outing has become more than a day of golf, cocktails, dinner, and a late-night billiards game back at Giles's home. It is the beginning of an agonizing weekend of decision-making.

"We tried not to talk baseball a whole lot," Giles would later recall. "But it was there all the time. This was a hard weekend for all of us. We had some decisions, and I wasn't sure until the end which way we'd go. But we tried to relax."

Things got so relaxed that one coach drove his golf cart over a ball washer. Everyone marveled at the golfing style of the Phillies' legendary one-handed scout Hugh Alexander. The pool game later resulted in Owens's taking a bundle out of the pockets of the others. It turned out to be the last game Owens would win as manager of the Phillies.

September 29

PHILADELPHIA—Giles's Veterans Stadium office is heavy on wood paneling, mahogany tables and desks, and high-backed leather chairs. Baseball memorabilia dot the walls, but the dominant artifact is a large oil painting of Giles's father, Warren.

The elder Giles weaned his son on baseball. He owned the Cincinnati Reds for several years before becoming president of the National League. Giles still talks of childhood memories, like seeing his father weep for the first time after the Reds defeated the Detroit Tigers in the 1940 World Series.

Warren Giles's baseball, however, bears little resemblance to the business his son now operates. Baseball's brave new world has made the game a high-risk, high-profile, expensive exercise in marketing and entertainment. The stakes are huge, with players' salaries averaging over $300,000 and television contracts that pay each team over $7 million a year.

And as Bill Giles gazes out his office window at his near-empty stadium this final weekend, he is faced with some hard choices.

On the top of the list is what to do about the managerial job. Giles had announced back in July that Owens and his entire coaching staff would return for the 1985 season. Giles owed much to

Owens for rescuing a pennant in 1983 after descending from his front-office job. And though they come from different baseball worlds, Giles and Owens are bound by a loyalty to the Phillies and a joint responsibility for the horde of controversial player moves made since Giles took control of the Phillies in 1982.

Yet as difficult as it might be for Giles to tell Owens he is out as manager, the situation cries for a change. The Phillies never made a semblance of a charge at the first-place Cubs from mid-July on. Players have been whispering about the murky lines of authority in the Phillies' dugout, where Owens is the titular head but where the game decisions are made by coaches John Felske, Claude Osteen, and Dave Bristol.

The awful Phillies finish puts an ugly exclamation point on the rush to judgment. The club has nose-dived in local public opinion. And with an overhead that demands over two million in home attendance just to break even, standing pat could lead to a financial nightmare. So Giles has spent most of the last three days huddling with his various advisors, and he has had intermittent private meetings with Owens.

After a Friday night rainout, the odds still seemed in favor of Owens returning. The 60-year-old manager, called the "Pope" for his resemblance to Pope Pius VI, talked for an hour in his office about the progress made in the final weeks despite the losses. He talked about looking forward to 1985 when he could fully unleash his impressive young players like Juan Samuel, Von Hayes, and Jeff Stone.

But everything changed by this evening. Whether it is Giles wearing down Owens or Owens just recognizing the inevitable, it is evident that the tide has turned. Owens will step down quietly, accept a lofty five-year contract as "assistant to the president" and for the first time in two decades be out of the day-to-day firing line he has been in as farm director, general manager, and manager.

And it is also evident that Giles will stay within his organization by making Felske the new manager. In so doing, Giles bows to the persuasion of his closest front-office advisors, farm director Jim

Baumer and vice-president Tony Siegle. Both worked with Felske years ago in the Milwaukee Brewers organization. Both persuade Giles that Felske is ready for the major-league managerial job. Owens provides the clincher when in a meeting this evening, he is asked by Giles if Felske is ready, and gives his endorsement.

Public relations also has its hand in the Felske decision. Giles initially toyed with the idea of a "name" manager, making a subterranean overture to the legendary Earl Weaver. But he is swung to the position of staying within the organization, not just because of his aides' advice but because of the interest shown in Felske by the Montreal Expos and the Seattle Mariners. Both clubs have asked permission to interview Felske for managerial openings.

After publicly saying a year ago that Felske would be the heir apparent to Owens whenever a change was made, Giles knew how unseemly it would look to then lose Felske to another organization.

By late today, all but the official announcement has been made. That will come tomorrow following a final-day double-header with the last-place Pittsburgh Pirates. But there will still be some last-minute intrigue.

September 30

PHILADELPHIA—Felske has already been told he will be named manager. But the coaching staff is walking on eggs. An hour before the 10 A.M. start (a fittingly weird ending to the whole scenario), Giles summons batting and first-base coach Deron Johnson to the 400-level inner sanctum. With dispatch, Giles tells Johnson he will not be rehired but could remain in the organization in another position.

A stunned Johnson remains in uniform for the first game but then decides to catch an early-afternoon flight back home to California. Explanations are sketchy on why he is the only Phillies coach not to be rehired. There is speculation that he was the coach who drove over the ball washer at the august Philadelphia Country

Club. And perhaps such indiscretions are reason for termination even if the hitters Johnson coached led the National League in batting average and home runs.

At the obligatory press conference it is continually stressed that all this was Owens's idea. Owens expresses happiness at having a job he says is what he always dreamed of having in his last years before retirement. Felske is almost shoved in the background, as the media event quickly becomes more Owens's farewell than Felske's ascent.

But the deed is done. And Giles, exhausted by four days of meetings that often lasted well past midnight, sighs as the press conference breaks up. "At least the decks are cleared, at least we can now start the offseason," he says.

ATLANTA—Before the Atlanta Braves' 162nd game of the season, the manager is packing the items in his office. He isn't packing for the offseason. He is packing for good. There are several boxes stacked neatly in one corner. A few pictures have been taken off the walls.

Joe Torre, the Braves' manager for three years and the most successful manager the team has had since moving to Atlanta, knows that changes are coming. He knows there must be changes in a team that won the National League West in 1982, slipped to second place in 1983, and fell out of contention—and two games under .500—in 1984. He knows the first change will come in the manager's office.

"If it hadn't happened to me before, I wouldn't know," says Torre, fired in 1981 as manager of the New York Mets. "The symptoms are there. The plague is what it's called. You're not getting as many calls; you're not being talked to as much."

Outside the manager's office, in the clubhouse, coach Joe Pignatano is wandering aimlessly, telling players, "We're gone.'" He is referring to himself, Torre, and pitching coaches Rube Walker and Bob Gibson. The players are mostly quiet. They, too, know what surely will happen.

ARLINGTON, TEXAS—The California Angels' imperfect season ends today on a perfect note. It ends in milestone manner as Mike Witt pitches a perfect game against the Texas Rangers at Arlington Stadium.

Witt, a 24-year-old right-hander, who emerges from his fourth major-league season with a career high of 15 wins, registers only the 13th perfect game in big-league history. The win enables the Angels to tie Minnesota for second place in the American League's Western Division, considered to be baseball's worst.

Angels fans expected better, probably none more so than the club's number one fan, owner Gene Autry. The one-time singing cowboy parlayed his movie success and investments in broadcasting and real estate into a sizable fortune. Having made himself a millionaire, he then went on to make millionaires out of many of baseball's top free agents. But his lavish spending has resulted in only moderate success on the field—two divisional titles in the eight years after his first multimillion dollar splurge for Joe Rudi, Don Baylor, and Bobby Grich. Hardly the returns expected from a club whose payroll is perennially among baseball's top three.

The price paid has been an often ignored and consistently underfinanced farm system and a series of field managers obviously expected to produce immediate dividends with the frequently misguided investments of the front office. Bill Rigney, the Angels' first manager, lasted more than eight years. He was fired in May of 1969. There were nine managers over the next 14 years including John McNamara, who replaced Gene Mauch after the 1982 title year.

McNamara's 1983 team, decimated by injuries, finished 22 games under .500 and 29 games out of first. The core of the 1984 team was the same. A year older and similarly susceptible to injury, it was often compared to an all-star team; unfortunately, it was the all-star team from 1976. Reggie Jackson, Rod Carew, Fred Lynn, Doug DeCinces, Bobby Grich, Bob Boone: The names look good in lights, but not under the demanding glare of a 162-game schedule.

McNamara juggled adroitly, got more than could be hoped for

from a suspect pitching staff, and had the Angels only a half game out with ten to play. Then the bats died completely, followed closely by desire. The Angels end the season in apparent need of a heart transplant, their intensity under fire by media and management, the impression being that they have run hard only to the bank.

The Angels are also confronted by a series of characteristic questions as the season ends.

Will McNamara be offered a new contract, and will he accept it?

How can the club sustain its stated desire to go with younger players and build from within when the farm system seems bare and the older, more renowned players are protected by multi-year, no-trade contracts?

Will the seven Angels eligible for free agency—Fred Lynn, Don Aase, Bruce Kison, Rob Wilfong, John Curtis, Craig Swan, and Derrel Thomas—be re-signed or allowed to leave?

The glow from Witt's perfect game lasts only as far as the bus ride to the Dallas-Fort Worth airport. The Angels seem to face a troubled and complex winter.

MONTREAL—For so many years, Mets players regarded the winter as a sort of parole, an earned freedom from the imprisonment of losing. The final days of seasons were, in effect, the final days of their sentences. And as the 162nd game approached, players' anticipation increased. Pat Zachry, in his final season with the Mets, had compared September to Christmas Eve. "You can't wait for it to be over so you can get to the good stuff," Zachry said. Some didn't wait. Frank Taveras left the Mets five days before the scheduled end of the 1980 season to attend the funeral of his grandmother. She had died the previous September, too.

In that way, as well as others, the 1984 Mets differ from their ancestors. There is no rush to the clubhouse exit this final day. Following a last-day defeat against the Expos, the Mets disband. Most are happy to be returning home, but none has longed for the end of this season. Some even want more. "If we had seven more games, we could still catch the Cubs," Hubie Brooks says.

And this time, there is no immediate purge of their memories, either. To the contrary, and for the first time in a long time, there are experiences to save and later savor. "We leave proud," Wally Backman says. "A little disappointed because we know what could have been. But no one's down."

The 1984 Mets have the second-highest win total in the 23-year history of the franchise. On July 27, the Mets stood in first place in the National League East, 4½ games in front. And although they couldn't withstand the Cubs' pursuit and subsequently didn't catch the Cubs, that hardly tainted their image. First place was the last place they were expected to be.

The primary goal of first-year manager Dave Johnson had been to establish three young starting pitchers and the middle of the infield. Mets general manager Frank Cashen had hoped merely for respectability. Instead, the Mets rushed past respectability and won 90 games, the fourth best record in baseball. True, the Phillies and Cardinals had self-destructed and the Expos had executed their annual team dive. And true, the Mets would have gained three places in the standings even if they had won eight fewer games. But races are relative.

Cashen had identified the 1982 season as "a shove backwards," and though the team had improved in 1983, the pace of improvement had left the Mets a half-year behind schedule in Cashen's mind. But in one year of Johnson, Dwight Gooden, and Keith Hernandez, in the fifth year of Cashen's five-year plan, the Mets have caught up with their schedule.

CLEVELAND—This was a year the Cleveland Indians didn't lose 100 games. They didn't end up in last place, they didn't quit in September, and they didn't bore everyone to death. As one of their loyal fans explained, "The Tribe didn't stink too bad this season."

In Cleveland, where the stench of decaying baseball teams has hung over the city since 1959, that's a compliment. This is a team that hasn't won a title since 1954, and even that year ended in tears as the club that won a record-setting 111 games during the regular season was swept by the New York Giants in the World Series. Yes, the New York Giants baseball team . . . it was that long ago.

The last time the Cleveland Indians made a serious run at the pennant was 1959. Only five of their teams have had winning records in the last 25 years, and none of those won more than 87 games. "Considering all that, it's amazing the Indians are still in Cleveland and that anyone shows up to watch them play," said Dave LeFevre.

LeFevre is a big part of the reason for optimism in Cleveland. He is the new owner of the Indians—sort of. The estate of the late F. J. "Steve" O'Neill announced in June that it would sell the team to LeFevre. The O'Neill family owns about 60% of the team. The American League quickly approved the sale. But a lawsuit filed by some minority stockholders in the team has held up the transfer to LeFevre. Even so, most people believe that LeFevre and his close friend, veteran baseball executive Tal Smith, will run the Indians in 1985, signalling the end of the Gabe Paul era in Cleveland.

Paul has emerged as the villain of villains in the Indians' depressing recent past. For all practical purposes, Paul ran the Indians from 1961–72 and then again from 1978 to the present. In those 19 years, Paul's teams had three winning records and one first division finish. Since his return to Cleveland from the New York Yankees in 1978, the Indians have not fared better than sixth place in the seven-team American League East. This explains the "SAVE THE TRIBE, FIRE THE CHIEF," bumper stickers that flooded the Cleveland area in the 1980s.

In those 19 years, Paul hired and fired 10 Indians managers, ran through a dozen pitching coaches, and made what seemed like a million pointless trades. And the more things changed, the more they stayed the same for the Indians. That's when the fans began to realize the fiasco on the field and blamed it on the man making the decisions in the front office.

Paul owns 5% of the Indians. He plans to move permanently

to his winter home in Tampa, Florida and serve as a consultant to the team once the legal snags of the sale are eliminated. That can't happen too soon for most Indian fans.

October 1

ATLANTA—Ted Turner, the owner of the Braves, has asked Torre to be at the Turner Broadcasting System offices at 10 o'clock sharp. Turner did not have to tell Torre the purpose of the visit.

At exactly 10, Torre walks into Turner's sprawling, messy office. He takes a seat across the desk from Turner, casting a glance at the desktop sign which reads, "Lead, follow or get out of the way." Turner begins to ramble in his deep southern drawl.

Turner mentions something about the team's young players not producing enough. He mentions something about "the thinking of the organization." He mentions something about "the progress of the farm system." He appears very uncomfortable.

For 25 minutes, this goes on. Then, Torre gets up to leave. Turner has never said the words "you're fired," but the act nevertheless is done. As Torre moves toward the door, Turner asks if he would like another job—something else with the baseball team, perhaps, or something with Turner Broadcasting, perhaps. Torre asks that they talk about that in a few weeks.

There is no need for desperation. Just two months earlier, Torre had been given a two-year, $450,000 contract extension, and he will continue to be paid by Turner. Less fortunate are the coaches who were fired with him: Pignatano, Walker, Gibson. Their winter surely will be longer and colder.

At the exact time Torre is being fired, Edward Haas is meeting at Atlanta-Fulton County Stadium with several key members of the Braves' front office: general manager John Mullen, executive vice-president Al Thornwell, director of scouting Paul Snyder, and director of player development Hank Aaron. They are talking about the future of the team, about the importance of the young players, about the need for philosophical continuity throughout the organization, and about the press conference that will be held the following afternoon.

At that time, Eddie Haas, after spending most of three decades in the Braves' organization as a player, coach, instructor, and minor-league manager, will be named to replace Joe Torre. Ever since rumors began a month earlier that Torre would be fired, it has been clear that his replacement would be Haas. If the people at this meeting had gotten their way, in fact, Haas would have been made the Braves' manager three years ago instead of Torre. But at that time, Turner listened to his television executives instead of his baseball executives.

The TV executives told Turner he needed someone with more charisma, more name recognition, and more polish than quiet, somber Eddie Haas of Paducah, Kentucky. They told him he needed someone whose name would ring a bell on Madison Avenue. They told him he needed Joe Torre.

But today, Turner listens to his baseball people. And they tell him the same thing as they did three years ago: Eddie Haas, they tell him, should be the manager. Today, the baseball people win out.

On many major decisions within the Braves, the baseball executives and the TV executives have different objectives and different desires. Turner genuinely wants a winning baseball team, but he also wants a baseball team that will draw large ratings—and thus large commercial revenues—on his nationwide Superstation, WTBS. A year ago the TV people wanted Turner to sign free agent Pete Rose. The baseball people did not. The baseball people won that one, too; they are on a roll right now.

October 2

ATLANTA—The media are assembled in the press lounge at Atlanta-Fulton County Stadium when Ted Turner enters the room with a 49-year-old, gray-haired, pipe-smoking man at his side. Turner and Eddie Haas take their places behind a battery of microphones.

"Well," Turner begins, "I don't guess this is any big surprise, but we're here to announce that Eddie Haas is the new manager of the Atlanta Braves." Eddie Haas has wanted this job for a very long time, through all those years in the minor leagues. But the part he could just as easily do without is at hand. Haas, a quiet man who has spent most of his career in obscurity, now must fight the cameras and the questions. Uncomfortably . . . unnaturally. All of this, it is clear, will be an adjustment for him—one to be made gradually, through the winter and spring.

"Eddie's a baseball man," says Aaron, who is standing near the back of the room. "He's such a great evaluator and teacher that his teams invariably play their best ball at the end of the season." Aaron did not have to add that Torre's teams, both in New York and Atlanta, invariably played their worst ball at the end of the season.

Haas had been the manager of the Braves' AAA farm team until mid-July, when he was summoned to the big leagues and installed as Torre's first-base coach. This was an ominous move for Torre. The next manager was being put in place, and the players sensed it. So, with 10 weeks to get a front-row look at the Braves, had Haas made any firm judgments about the team he now would manage?

He thinks about it for a few seconds and then looks up. "Yes," he says. "Dale Murphy has a job."

It appears to please Haas that his inquisitors laugh. The adjustment is beginning.

ANAHEIM—The Angels have seldom given their manager more than a one-year contract, and seldom has a season ended without a measure of uncertainty about the manager's status. The 1984 season is no different.

Retiring general manager Buzzie Bavasi had publicly second-guessed McNamara's choice of pitchers in August, leading to a week of soap opera stories in which first Mike Port met with Gene Autry to discuss the manager's role, and then the media jumped to McNamara's defense, aiming a barrage of criticism at Autry and Bavasi for failing to respond to the team's needs.

The storm subsided, but questions about McNamara's future shadowed the team through the last month of the season. They were intensified by rumors that the Boston Red Sox were interested in McNamara as a successor to retiring manager Ralph Houk.

Autry and Port meet today at Anaheim Stadium to discuss the managerial situation. Autry later tells the media that the blame for the team's disappointing performance lay with his millionaire hitters, that the manager had done a good job under the circumstances and that the 1985 job is McNamara's if he wants it.

McNamara doesn't. He will soon sign a two-year contract to manage the Red Sox. The revolving door in the Angels' managerial office will have to take another spin.

October 8

SAN DIEGO—Some teams make trades only as a last resort, tiptoeing upon such ventures as if walking on a mine field and rarely daring to gamble on a move.

Other teams are a little more willing to venture into trade talks but prefer a hush-hush style, revealing nothing to inquisitors and concealing their intentions as if they were state secrets.

Then there are the Philadelphia Phillies. No clandestine methods are included in their arsenal, no masked intentions or secrets. No one has to wonder if the Phillies are interested in joining the trade market.

Instead, they unleash their front-office pointmen like so many sharks in a feeding frenzy. Phils officials make no effort to hide whom they're talking to and what they're looking for, talking loudly about their intentions with an almost hyperactive openness and flair.

This winter's main goal, at least the stated one, will be to find pitching help. Many factors contributed to Philadelphia's 1984 collapse, but one of the most important was the poor second-half performance by the Phils' bullpen. By trading Willie Hernandez to Detroit in perhaps the worst trade of the previous year, the Phillies lost a dependable performer who bloomed into superstardom with the Tigers. Without Hernandez around, relief ace Al Holland ended up having to carry more of the load. And he tailed off down the stretch, ending the year with a mind-numbing streak of 11 blown leads and ties over the final six weeks.

So relief pitching is the Phils' primary need as perceived at season's end.

It is also clear what the Phils have to offer in exchange for pitching. Their scouts and coaches seemed in general agreement that catcher Bo Diaz, who was injured during most of the 1984 season; shortstop Ivan DeJesus, who had an awful season offensively and defensively; and assorted other spare parts are expendable.

With that game plan, the Phils descended upon the World Series. The Series is annually attended by club executives from all major-league teams, so it becomes the first opportunity for clubs to start feeling out each other about their off-season plans.

Giles, in the season's final-weekend think tank, gave the go-ahead for a quick sweep of the other clubs by his various trade negotiators. The hope was that the Phils could make a quick trading score and accelerate their rebuilding schedule.

So Giles okayed having top scouts Alexander, Ray Shore, and Moose Johnson attend the Series along with himself and his three top front-office aides, Owens, Siegle, and Baumer. They begin their quest tonight, the eve of the Series opener, at a lavish party thrown at lush Balboa Park by the San Diego Padres. Phils representatives attack unsuspecting officials of other clubs over fresh seafood and cocktails.

In sharp contrast to the feverish Phillies are the Mets. Their needs are no less well-defined, and what they have to offer is every bit as clear, but they try to avoid holding their trade talks over a public address system. If at all possible, they keep a low profile, not revealing their intentions unless absolutely necessary. They feel no need for a quick kill here; they are content to plant a few seeds, and in at least one case, fertilize a seed long since planted.

It was October 2, 1983 at Shea Stadium in New York that Frank Cashen had first dared to covet Gary Carter. On that day, the Mets were to apply the finishing touch to their second successive last-place finish. Even so, they swept a double-header from the underachieving Montreal Expos, depriving them of second place.

Cashen sat with John McHale, and recognized the torment in McHale's demeanor. Another season of promise and disappointment. McHale was discomforted enough to indicate the Expos might consider personnel changes. Cashen, seizing the moment, said, "If you're ever going to dismantle, I'd be interested in Gary Carter."

At the time of this first mention of Carter, the Expos would no sooner have dealt their all-star catcher than the Mets would have dealt Darryl Strawberry. Carter was the cornerstone of the Expos' organization, and cornerstones come with unwritten no-trade clauses. Carter was to the Expos what Tom Seaver and Pete Rose had been in their respective first tours with the Mets and Reds: the player most closely associated with the team. A club doesn't casually deal its signature player.

This is not to say a club will never trade its "franchise" either; the Mets traded Seaver in 1977, and the Reds allowed Rose to leave after the 1978 season. Cashen himself had pried Keith Hernandez away from the Cardinals in 1983.

Aware that "untouchables" are an endangered species, Cashen occasionally reiterated his interest in Carter to McHale. He did so at Shea Stadium on September 21. McHale only pointed out Carter's no-trade provision. Cashen found no reason to be encouraged other than the knowledge that his own organization was better equipped to supply the Expos' demands than it had been a year earlier. If McHale only would say, "So make me an offer."

Developments would soon lead McHale to speak those words. Murray Cook had been named Expos general manager and had had the opportunity to evaluate the players, whose unlimited potential and limited success had annually perplexed and frustrated their fans across Canada.

Cook, who earlier in the summer had escaped the Yankees asylum, found deficiencies in the Expos' regular lineup, and concluded that overall improvement could be achieved most readily by trading one of their stars. He made recommendations to his new employer, Charles Bronfman, and immediate superior, McHale. "Carter is the one who would bring the greatest return," he said. Cook was never instructed to "dump" Carter and the gigantic financial obligation of his contract. But the seven-year, $13.1 million contract has become a burden for a franchise with decreasing attendance. Cook was told, "Do what you have to do."

October 9

SAN DIEGO—After the first game of the Series, Jim Baumer is ensconced in the corner of a post-game hospitality suite talking with Milwaukee scout Dee Fondy while John Felske stands nearby. "We've been here two days and I think we've talked to every club in baseball," says Felske with a touch of wonder in his voice. "When Bill Giles and his people want to make a trade, they are unbelievable."

Meanwhile, Hugh Alexander is button-holing his various cronies and confidants, the most notable being a kindred spirit named Jack McKeon, who as general manager of the Padres has earned the nickname "Trader Jack" for his brash willingness to make deal after deal in building San Diego into champions.

"I can't help Hughie with finding a pitcher or a shortstop or a power hitter, the three things he says he's looking for," says McKeon. "But Hughie and me always check with each other. Maybe we can work one of our three-way deals where I throw in something to get another club involved, get Hughie what he needs, and help myself, too. But I think Hughie's a little too anxious to do something right now. Teams don't like to jump this early."

Nevertheless, Alexander and his band press on. They talk most seriously to people from Atlanta, Montreal, the New York Mets,

Milwaukee, and Cincinnati. Tomorrow afternoon, Giles will convene his whole group at a pool-side meeting for an update.

October 10

SAN DIEGO—Brandishing a yellow legal pad that lists all the various equations the Phillies are trying to complete, Giles runs down the options after 48 hours of negotiating. Lo and behold, it seems that Alexander has begun to wedge out a possible deal with Atlanta. The Braves are interested in Diaz and might be willing to relinquish one of two relief pitchers—Donnie Moore or Jeff Dedmon.

"I think we can do something, I really do," declares Alexander. "You know Uncle Hugh; if there's a chance, I'm going to keep on those suckers until I wear them down."

October 11

DETROIT—The scene shifts to Detroit for games three, four, and five of the Series. Joe McIlvaine, the Mets' recently promoted director of player personnel, chats with Red Sox general manager Lou Gorman, the former Mets vice-president, while Frank Cashen presses—gently—for Gary Carter. "What are you going to do with Jim Rice if you can't re-sign him?" McIlvaine asks. Gorman offers no definitive answer. And the Mets exploration ends there.

The Phillies continue their open attempt to make a deal. While other club officials socialize and talk shop only in the most general way, Giles, Shore, Alexander, and Johnson bore in on active negotiations.

But their attempts begin to loom futile as the week wears on. Their talks with Atlanta hit a snag when the Braves become concerned about the condition of Diaz's knee, which was operated upon twice during the season. The Phillies offer to share their medical reports, in an effort to assure the Braves that Diaz is not damaged goods.

October 13

DETROIT—The Phillies are resigned to the fact that aside from possibly laying the groundwork for future talks, their effort for a quick score is a failure.

It is just too early for other clubs to make final trade decisions. And club executives from other clubs admit that they are a little put off by the Phils' aggressiveness. Given Philadelphia's recent track record, many clubs plan to make the Phillies wait and hopefully force the club to dig into its pool of young prospects.

By late evening, the Phillies' contingent is making flight reservations home. And Alexander, Shore, and Johnson, several cocktails into the evening, are beginning to wind down.

They have talked to so many teams for so many hours that they are beginning to lose their equilibrium. A jokester then suggests to Alexander that if he is so desperate to make a trade, he should try to work out a deal with Shore. "Give Snacks (Shore's nickname) Shane Rawley and Jeff Stone, and he might give you Juan Samuel," suggests the observer. "Now that might not be so bad a deal," Alexander replies. A dazed Johnson stands next to the conversation, nodding his head.

Then a light bulb goes off above his head. "Hey, Snacks and Hughie can't make a trade, they work for the same club," declares Johnson.

Thus educated, the final Phils survivors straggle home to trade another day.

Who Owns the Indians?

CLEVELAND—One of the most asked questions in baseball history is being asked again: Who owns the Indians?

The question has hung over the franchise since Bill Veeck sold the Indians in 1949. Even in the glory days of the 1950s, much of which the club spent snapping at the heels of the great Yankees dynasty, the Tribe was passed around like a pair of Salvation Army shoes.

Veeck sold the club to Ellis Ryan. Ryan sold it to Mike Wilson in 1951, and Wilson sold it to William Dayley in 1957. In the 29 years since Veeck purchased the team in 1946, it has been sold eight times, never to a major national corporation or an individual with enormous wealth. The current ownership, headed by the O'Neill family, includes some 54 limited partners, most brought in in a constant search for new capital.

Steve O'Neill bought the team after the 1977 season when the club was on the verge of bankruptcy. Four years later, O'Neill had the team on the block. O'Neill was 72 years old and was searching for a younger owner who would keep the team in Cleveland.

In November of 1980, the Indians announced O'Neill had sold his 60% share of the team to a group headed by Neal Papiano and theater producer James Nederlander. Although the sale had not yet come up for approval at the American League meeting, Papiano and Nederlander acted as though they were in charge, chasing free agents and suggesting trades. They pursued free agent Dave Winfield, offering him a financial package that included a piece of Nederlander's hit play *Annie*. Papiano was also in contact with Gabe Paul at the winter meetings, suggesting the Indians deal for Fred Lynn, who had been placed on the market by Boston.

None of this sat very well with Paul and O'Neill. Two months later, the sale to Nederlander and Papiano was called off. Paul and O'Neill said Nederlander and Papiano failed to come up with the cash when it was due. But other insiders insist Paul killed the deal. While Paul had been promised he could continue as team president and chief executive officer under the new group, he clearly resented their interference in the area of player moves.

To understand the Indians, you must first understand Gabe Paul. He has spent the last 56 years in baseball, beginning when he sold scorecards at the Rochester Red Wings' games. Now 74, Paul is a millionaire. He owns about 5% of the Indians. The team also pays him a salary of $180,000, supplies him with a car, and makes the payments on his condominium in the Cleveland suburb of Lyndhurst. It has been at least 15 years since Paul needed a baseball job financially. Personally, it is another story.

Paul takes a transistor radio with him to bed, turning the dial from one out-of-town baseball game to another. The next day, he relishes telling friends and business associates of some strange happening he heard in a game out of Detroit, Pittsburgh, or elsewhere. He loves to read sports pages from across the country, keeping up on all the baseball gossip. He has been heavily criticized by the Cleveland media, but Paul has never shut off a writer. He may hate the guy, but his office door is always open and there is a smile on his face as he greets reporters. Paul knows he has great powers of persuasion, and believes he can convince anyone of the rightness of his actions. Paul also knows that today's newspaper story is thrown out with tomorrow's trash. Just as there is always another game in baseball, there's always another baseball story. Just as Paul wants to win tomorrow's game, he wants to get tomorrow's story to represent what he thinks. He freely gives out his home phone number and never complains about calls, even if he is awakened at 2 A.M. by a reporter with a preposterous trade rumor.

Despite his talk of retirement, it's hard to imagine Paul out of baseball. Watching the game is his oxygen; talking trades keeps the blood pumping through his veins. Fourteen-to-sixteen-hour work days are normal, and he has been known to have trade discussions on Christmas Eve. He never really takes a vacation. He may be in Florida, Puerto Rico, or California, but he has a phone nearby and is usually talking shop with someone.

The word in Cleveland is that Gabe Paul was a hell of an operator. Few younger baseball fans will believe it, especially those born in Cleveland after 1954, but sooner or later Paul will make the Hall of Fame. One reason is his great success in New York from 1973 to 1977. He successfully kept George Steinbrenner, Billy Martin, and Reggie Jackson from killing each other. Aided by Steinbrenner's bottomless bank account, Paul made solid trades and free agent acquisitions. His final piece of advice to Steinbrenner was to let a free agent pitcher named Mike Torrez go elsewhere and sign another free agent pitcher named Goose Gossage. The New York writers loved Paul for his congeniality as much as for his baseball expertise, and they credited him with building the Yankees. The press in Cleveland also was happy about Paul's success in New York. They always wrote that Gabe Paul would win in Cleveland if only he had a wealthy ownership behind him.

But now there are whispers that Gabe Paul has lost his fastball. There are stories of Paul nearly dozing off during especially long staff meetings or meetings with players' agents. It was far from a regular occurrence, but the stories persisted. When the subject of age came up, Paul challenged anyone to put in his hours and match his zeal. Few people would be willing to try.

New York lawyer and Cleveland native Dave LeFevre has been the most persistent of the prospective owners. "I made my first offer in May of 1983," recalls LeFevre, who often characterizes the sale as moving at a "glacial pace."

In November of 1983, it appeared that LeFevre had lost out to Manhattan real estate tycoon Donald Trump in his bid to buy the team. But the O'Neill group wanted a 15-year guarantee that Trump would keep the team in Cleveland. Trump, who wanted to move the team to the Meadowlands in New Jersey, refused to sign. Exit Trump; LeFevre returned to center stage.

The sale of the team to LeFevre was announced in June, 1984. The price was $41 million, but it could wind up as high as $45 million when all the debts are assumed.

"I've been frustrated and sometimes felt used," says LeFevre. "But making a deal for the Indians is very complicated, more so than for any other team because of the way the ownership has been constructed with all the partners."

When Paul was in Cleveland from 1961–1972, the Indians were probably the most poorly-financed team in the game. Paul's greatest accomplishment in that period was finding new investors willing to kick in a few bucks to keep the team operating in Cleveland. The Indians' ownership consists of a cumbersome collection of 54 limited partners, a direct result of Paul's Dutch Boy efforts to plug all the holes in the franchise. It wasn't Paul's fault; he had to take cash from anywhere he could find it just to make the payroll and pay the stadium rent. Ironically, the proliferation of limited owners would ultimately come back to haunt Paul, blocking the sale to Dave LeFevre he had arranged.

On the field, the 1984 Cleveland Indians lost 87 games. Off the field, they lost only $2 million. By Indians standards, that's a success. What's $2 million when you're used to losing over $4 million a year?

The Tribe drew only 734,279 fans—the lowest attendance in baseball. In a normal year, that would have put them $5 million in the red, as the Indians have to attract about 1.6 million to break even. But the new network television deal worth $1.125 billion paid each team $8 million in 1984, an increase of $3 million over 1983, so the team dropped only $2 million. Almost every other team in baseball finished in the black thanks to the television money.

To get a true picture of the Indians' books, consider the following:

According to a report by the accounting firm of Ernst and Whinney, the Indians lost $10,704,212 from 1981–83: $3.96 million in 1983; $4.2 million in 1982; and $2.5 million in 1981.

Since 1959, the Indians have drawn over 1 million fans only four times, and never more than 1.1 million a season. The average team today draws about 1.7 million fans a season. In three of the last four years, the Tribe has failed to draw 800,000 fans. Their season-ticket base is under 2,200. Most teams sell at least 8,000 season tickets.

So why would Dave LeFevre be willing to pay $41 million for the Cleveland Indians?

"Because I love baseball and I've always loved the Indians," says LeFevre. "I remember rooting for them in the 1954 World Series. I also like the idea of coming in and building a winner. The challenge is great, but the rewards will be immense for the guy who turns the Indians around."

LeFevre was raised in Cleveland, the grandson of the late industrial tycoon, Cyrus Eaton.

"I live in New York because I work in international law and New York is the place for that," says LeFevre. "But I'm a Cleveland guy with deep Cleveland roots.

"This is a great sports town, but it must be offered a good product. People won't go to see a lousy movie and they won't go to see a lousy baseball team. I think it says some good things about the fans that about 800,000 show up to watch a team that has been in last place for most of the last 25 years. Cleveland has the worst inferiority complex of anywhere I've seen and it can be changed."

LeFevre's optimism is grounded in the club's history. In the late 1940s and early 1950s, the Indians usually challenged the Yankees for the American League pennant. The Tribe was one of the game's best draws in that time span; they drew a then-record 2.6 million fans in their pennant-winning year of 1948. And a basically mediocre Cleveland Browns franchise has averaged about 70,000 a game for the last 10 years.

"The town is so hungry for a winner," says LeFevre. "People are just waiting for something good to support."

But after 25 futile seasons, the Indians fans are a tough sell. There have been youth movements, rebuilding movements, veteran movements—but no movement in the standings. That's why the Cleveland fans are hoping, no, praying that Dave LeFevre will quickly take control of the team.

LeFevre wants Tal Smith to run the team, but Smith can't officially do that until LeFevre owns it. Smith is the highly regarded baseball executive who is credited with building the Houston Astros into a winner. He took over the Astros in 1975 when they were 45½ games out of first place. In 1980, Houston won the National League West and Smith was honored as *The Sporting News* Baseball Executive of the Year. Two years later, Smith clashed with chief Astros owner John McMullen; he left the Astros and formed his own baseball consulting firm. He is now a consultant for the Mariners, the Padres, and the Yankees: He evaluates their farm systems, their big-league talent, and anything else the team wants done. Smith also represents a dozen teams in arbitration cases.

While there is no doubt Smith will be in charge of the Indians once the sale is finalized, he has to protect his interests in case LeFevre's efforts fail. Thus, when a newspaper reports that Tal Smith has signed a two-year contract to run the Indians, everyone leaps to deny it.

"It is unequivocally, absolutely untrue," says LeFevre. "We don't even own the club. Anything the Indians do is a function of the current management team. Tal Smith has a consulting contract with Cleveland and he is in contact with the current management."

"A two-year contract for Tal?" asks Gabe Paul. "Where is the toilet paper? That's the best latrine-o-gram I've heard in a long time."

Despite these denials, everyone in baseball knows how strong the bonds connecting Paul, LeFevre, and Smith are. LeFevre's first foray into baseball was in 1973 as a minor investor in George

Steinbrenner's group that bought the Yankees. The president of the Yankees was Gabe Paul. And Paul's assistant and a vice-president with the club was Tal Smith. This is where the relationship began—long before the three men ever imagined that they would be together on the purchase of the Indians.

Smith and Paul are close friends, dating back to 1958, when Paul was general manager of the Cincinnati Reds and Smith was looking for his first baseball job. Paul hired Tal Smith as a secretary for the team's farm department. In 1960, Paul became the general manager of the Houston Astros and he took Smith along as his assistant. Then the two men were together in New York from 1973–1975.

In 1976, Smith went back to Houston, this time as president. In 1979, Smith convinced LeFevre to sell his minor holdings in the Yankees and buy about 15% of the Astros.

"I have a very special friendship with Dave LeFevre," says Smith. "I'll do about anything I can to help him."

Those words excite the downtrodden Indians fans, who hope Tal Smith, a Gabe Paul disciple, will succeed where Paul has failed.

Meanwhile, the Indians try to conduct their daily business. General manager Phil Seghi, farm director Bob Quinn, and manager Pat Corrales are all in the first year of three-year contracts given to them by Gabe Paul in May. While LeFevre and Smith meet with the team's top free agent, Andre Thornton, Patrick O'Neill, nephew of the late Steve O'Neill, is still the club's owner. And Phil Seghi, a man who has mastered the art of saying nothing in a million words or more, makes a brave show of not wondering who's looking over his shoulder.

"All systems are go," says Seghi. "There is no work stoppage. As always, we're trying to put together a team for next year. I'm on the phone all the time. If someone calls with a trade offer, we'll evaluate it. It's business as usual."

But business as usual means bills to pay. O'Neill insists that the team needs $5 million to make up for the losses of the last few years. All of the 54 limited partners are asked to kick in cash to eliminate the deficit—most pass. If an owner fails to pay his share of the cash call, his share in the team decreases. Those who make the highest payments have their shares increase the most.

With a sale to LeFevre in the offing, few of the owners want to pay. Instead, their thoughts are on the money they will receive from the impending sale.

So no one is sure who owns the team. Steve O'Neill, the real owner, has been dead for a year. His nephew wants to sell it. Dave LeFevre wants to buy it, but can't because of legal problems. Gabe Paul is the president, but wants to retire to his winter home in Tampa. And a ballclub that has always been willing to make moves seems paralyzed.

Business as usual, Cleveland style.

3 Hardball

October 15

ST. PETERSBURG, FLORIDA—The name is James Neader. His profession is player agent. He represents Dwight Gooden. He plays hardball.

The Mets' first impression of Jim Neader is that he plays even harder than his client throws, and they don't like his game. It is less than 24 hours after the end of the World Series, and Neader has repulsed and angered the Mets and ignited the offseason with his opening salvo that his client should receive a seven-figure salary in 1985. Commas are not considered figures.

Neader never says "one million dollars," but he talks all around that figure, saying Gooden should be paid with the other top pitchers in the game. The Mets might have been amused if Neader hadn't been so public in his demands.

Neader, apparently unaware of the Mets' passion for privacy, has erred. His tactics of calling for an unprecedented level of pay for a second-year player and threatening a spring training holdout would be bad enough, but to do so publicly as a preface to negotiations . . . "Well, let's just say we don't appreciate his tactics," Al Harazin, the Mets vice-president, says.

Even at this stage, when virtually every player is represented in contract negotiations, Cashen still is unsettled by agents. He won't invite one home for dinner, and neither will Harazin, Cashen's disciple and the man who will negotiate all contracts.

Neader's negotiation bluster—and it is only bluster because his real first figure is closer to $700,000—further taints Cashen's view of agents. Even if $500,000 were Neader's starting point, the Mets would hardly be agreeable. Harazin says the club intends to be generous with Gooden, but for this year and this year only, the Mets hold all the cards.

Back in the bad old days before free agency, arbitration, and other signs of creeping Bolshevism, a club's salary offer came with the implied threat, "take it or leave it." The player was bound to his team forever by the all-restrictive reserve clause that gave a club the right to renew the contract for one year without the player's consent. The owners' contention, which held sway for 80 years, was that the renewed contract also contained this reserve clause, and thus could be renewed itself, and renewed again ad infinitum. The player's only available tactic was to refuse to report to spring training. But that threat could only work for so long; five-figure salaries for literal child's play were not so easy to find. Eventually, even the biggest stars would sign for salaries that are embarrassingly low by today's standards.

Free agency changed all that. After six years in the major leagues, a player can now sell his services to the highest bidder. Salaries quickly leaped into the stratosphere for free agents. And through the arbitration process, available to a player after two full years in the majors, the free-market rate becomes available to a player long before his seventh season.

In one—and only one—situation today does the game's structure grant a team the absolute power to dictate salaries. That comes when a player can't go to arbitration because he has played fewer than two full seasons. Which brings us back to Dwight Gooden.

Neader has little negotiating leverage. He can point out Gooden's record-setting performances: the most strikeouts by a rookie pitcher—276; the highest ratio ever of strikeouts per nine innings—11.39; the most strikeouts in three successive nine-inning games—43. He can point to Gooden's record—17 victories, nine defeats, and a 2.60 earned run average. He can point to attendance figures that indicate that the Mets' average attendance for home games started by Gooden was 5,423 higher than their average attendance for home games he didn't start. But the Mets only need point to the dotted line and say take it or leave it.

The Mets don't want to deal that way. But Harazin knows Gooden's contract will affect other negotiations. Richman Bry, the agent representing Darryl Strawberry, says his client should earn at least $1 more than Gooden. And Ron Darling, were he to receive only half of Gooden's 1985 salary demand, would equal the highest second-year salary ever paid, Fernando Valenzuela's $350,000, if the Mets give in.

"We'll be fair," Harazin says. "Even if [the Phillies' Juan] Samuel were to win, we'd still treat Dwight like the rookie of the year." But recognizing Gooden's stature and submitting to Neader's demands are different. "It's not going to be easy," Harazin says.

October 16

ANAHEIM—The Angels have settled on a successor to John McNamara. Their choice is Gene Mauch; he represents some unfinished business.

Mauch had succeeded Jim Fregosi as the Angels' manager in May, 1981, and remained at the helm through the 1982 season. The Angels won the division title that year, but lost the best-of-five pennant playoff to Milwaukee after winning the first two games.

Mauch was criticized by media, management, and his players for his choice of pitchers in the fourth and fifth games, and the front office took a long time before offering him the chance to return in 1983. Mauch chose to reject that offer, for reasons that remain unstated, but are widely understood.

"I never wanted to leave baseball," he has said, "but things can happen that you have no control over. I've never discussed those reasons and never will. They're very personal." This is Mauch's way of saying that he turned down the offer because of the long illness and subsequent death of his wife, Nina.

Mauch's whole career has been haunted by unfinished business.

He has long been considered one of the game's leading scientists, the thinking man's manager, an authority on the rule book, the box score, and all the strategic nuances. He ranks ninth on the all-time managerial lists in wins and games. But he also holds the dubious record of having managed the longest of any man who has never won a league championship. In addition, he has presided over two of the most notorious collapses in the game: losing the three straight to Milwaukee in 1982, and blowing a 6½ game lead with 12 to play as manager of the 1964 Phillies. His pitching selection was criticized then, too.

Mauch refuses to dwell on these events—outwardly, at least. Today, like any newly hired manager, he is only looking ahead. "For two years," he says, "I was dead certain I'd never manage again, but when the pennant race began to heat up this year, I felt those little things in my belly again and liked it. I went to look at our kids in the Instructional League when the season was over and said to myself, 'Damn, this is fun again.'

"I don't know what all the ingredients are to manage in the majors, but I do know you can't do it without enthusiasm and excitement, and I have that again. I mean, I'm not just happy about the way I feel, I'm grateful. If Mr. Autry really knew how I felt he might let me manage for nothing."

Autry says he is hopeful that Mauch's return will be for more than one year. "For the good of the club and the good of the manager," he tells the press, "I'd like to work out something longer. I'd like to see us finally keep someone around here as long as we kept (Bill) Rigney."

Mauch's return seems to be welcomed by his players. Veteran third baseman Doug DeCinces is among those who attend the press conference; he says, "He was the logical candidate. When I heard other names mentioned, I said to myself, 'Hey, what's going on? Are we going to have to go through an entire new program?' The players know and respect Gene, and he knows us. I think I can speak for others and say we're comfortable with him, we're looking forward to playing for him. To me, this was the only way to go."

DeCinces also says that Mauch's intensity and attention to detail will produce needed changes in chemistry and composition.

"I think the excitement Gene is showing can go through the entire team. We have a quiet club. A lot has been said about that recently. I think Gene's outward intensity will change that. I also anticipate our younger players will be more mentally prepared to play now, because Gene talks baseball from the time he arrives until he leaves."

ST. PETERSBURG, FLORIDA—James Neader receives a written proposal from Al Harazin, benignly identifies it as "a starting point," and acknowledges, "We're not very close." His approach is softer than it was one day earlier. The Mets have told him of their disapproval of his tactics.

October 17

ATLANTA—Bob Horner flies in from his off-season home in Dallas and takes a cab to the office of Dr. Robert Wells. The Braves' hopes for 1985 hinge largely on what Wells finds when he examines Horner's right wrist, broken on May 30. Horner, the power-hitting third baseman, missed the remainder of the season and without him in the lineup, the Braves were not a factor in the National League West race. It is difficult to imagine them contending in 1985 without Horner, either.

The purpose of this examination is to determine if a bone graft will be necessary; if so, the Braves know that Horner might miss most or all of the 1985 season.

Dr. Wells examines the wrist and rules out the bone graft. He replaces the large cast with a smaller one and tells Horner to return on December 1.

As Horner leaves the doctor's office, he insists he will be ready for spring training, and Wells concurs that Horner "can push the start button at spring training." Braves general manager John Mullen, after hearing Wells's report, says, "Now we can fully count on Bob for next year." Executive vice-president Al Thornwell adds, "We had always thought, perhaps wistfully, that he would be fine and able to play next year." Horner has missed an average of 60 games per season with injuries in his six-year career, and he still struggles with doubts about whether he'll ever play a full season. He and a lot of other people wonder what type of numbers he might compile if he did play a full season. For now, Horner says he has no reason to think next season can't consist of 162 games for him; he says he has no more reason to expect another injury than anyone else. But you wonder if he means it.

Examination and interviews complete, Horner returns to the airport for a flight to Dallas, where he says he is on a running-oriented conditioning program that has dropped his weight below the 215 pounds Horner weighed for the 1984 season. This is the same Bob Horner whose weight often has ballooned up to 230 and beyond.

October 18

ATLANTA—Joe Torre is back at the scene of his firing. Again, he is in Ted Turner's office. Again, they are talking about a job. But this time, Torre is being offered one instead of being relieved of one.

Turner offers Torre a job as a member of the Braves' broadcasting team. Yes, Turner explains, he's talking about a job traveling with the team, doing play-by-play and commentary on radio and television. Yes, Turner knows it might be awkward, especially when it comes time to comment on the strategic moves of manager Eddie Haas. But yes, Turner is serious about the offer.

Torre says no.

"Eventually, I want to get into broadcasting," says Torre, "but this situation would have been uncomfortable. If I was Eddie Haas, I wouldn't want me around."

Torre says he does not know what he'll do next year. He'd like to manage, and if that opportunity doesn't come along, maybe another broadcasting offer will develop. Anyway, he knows he's getting paid. He'll enjoy the winter.

October 19

CLEVELAND—Just because Dave LeFevre's attempt to buy the Indians has been held up in court, it doesn't mean the Tribe's baseball world stops spinning.

Tony Bernazard informs the front office that he is demanding a trade. Bernazard has been in the majors for five years. Under the basic agreement, he has the right to order a trade, but if one is made he cannot become a free agent for the next three years. Ordinarily, a player is eligible for free agency after six big-league seasons.

Gabe Paul greets the news with a yawn. Bernazard hasn't exactly been the second coming of Charlie Gehringer, or even Duane Kuiper.

"Demanding a trade is Tony's right under the rules," says Paul. "He's a nice little fellow and I have great respect for him personally."

Is Paul surprised that a .220-hitting second baseman with 20 errors has the gall to demand a trade?

"Nothing in baseball surprises me," he says.

ANAHEIM—The September appointment of Mike Port as general manager had surprised Angels observers accustomed to Gene Autry's affection for established names—on and off the field.

When Fred Haney, the club's first general manager, was replaced in 1969, it was by Dick Walsh, a former vice-president of the Dodgers who was then commissioner of the North American Soccer League.

When Walsh, whose alleged deceptions prompted the players to call him the Smiling Python, was replaced in 1971, it was by Harry Dalton, credited for being the architect of the Baltimore dynasty of the late 1960s and early 1970s.

Dalton opted to leave in late 1977 because Autry had decided to tighten the developmental purse strings and hire executive vice-president Buzzie Bavasi. Bavasi had spent more than 40 years in baseball, first as general manager of the Brooklyn and Los Angeles Dodgers and later as co-owner and president of the San Diego

Padres. This organizational instability has resulted in policies that are consistent only in their inconsistency.

The Haney expansion era was marked by the club's failure to unearth and sign the gold mine of amateur talent available in southern California. A series of lamentable trades by Walsh stripped bare an already thin farm system and led to Dalton's rebuilding efforts through a five-year plan designed to reestablish the farm system and ultimately plug holes through the new free agent reentry draft.

Dalton and the farm system seemed to be making progress when Bavasi was hired to simultaneously curtail spending and produce immediate rewards for the aging Autry. Bavasi took the obvious course. He pared the farm budget and concentrated on quick fixes via the reentry draft. He signed a parade of high-salaried, big-name free agents. He took the cream of Dalton's farm system and traded it for a number of other renowned players who were available because of their imminent free agency.

But even this policy was plagued by inconsistency. Bavasi refused to resign Nolan Ryan, but did sign a succession of sore-armed pitchers including Bruce Kison, Bill Travers, Jim Barr, and John D'Acquisto. He refused to resign the productive designated hitter and clubhouse enforcer Don Baylor, but did give a multi-year contract to Ellis Valentine.

The division titles of 1979 and 1982 were meager compensation for a seven-year tenure that ended with the 69-year-old Bavasi saying it was finally time to take a summer vacation with wife Evit. He informed Autry of his decision in spring training, before the 1984 season started. He spent the summer denying rumors, then announced it officially in September.

Friends of Bavasi say there was more to it than a desire to travel. They insist that Bavasi was apprehensive about the expanding influence of Jackie Autry and felt she was attempting to ease him out. They imply that Bavasi, through his advisory role, felt he could maintain a measure of power through his protégé, Mike Port, while escaping criticism by the media and daily scrutiny by the Autrys.

The former Jacqueline Ellam, then 39, married Autry on July

19, 1981, approximately 14 months after the death of his first wife, Ina. The new Mrs. Autry had previously handled many of Autry's Palm Springs banking accounts in her role as vice-president at Security Pacific.

This financial background helped Jackie Autry engineer a significant 1983 move by her husband in which he sold KTLA, his Los Angeles TV station, to acquire the capital that allowed him to then buy out the Signal Co., which held first option on the Angels as minority stockholder. The transaction left Jackie Autry heir to the club, and she has acknowledged a desire to run it as a legacy to her husband when he dies.

Jackie Autry also initiated a marketing study of the Angels in the wake of the 1983 season and responded to it by urging the hiring of advertising executive John Hays as vice-president of marketing. The authority given Hays significantly diminished the authority of both Bavasi and Red Patterson, assistant to the chairman of the board, and was viewed as a first step in shifting power to younger hands.

The elevation of Port, 39, was a second step. Autry named Port on the same day that he announced Bavasi's retirement. Cognizant of the post-season decisions confronting the Angels, Autry said he wanted a smooth, swift transfer and chose to avoid a long search outside the organization because of Port's familiarity and Bavasi's recommendation.

Port, who holds a business degree from San Diego's Cal Western University, says his appointment represents the chance of a lifetime, a dream come true. He had once dreamt of a long career as a major-league infielder, and had brief trials with the Dodgers and Padres, but the dream died because of a chronically sore shoulder and lack of talent.

"I was the type of player who should have paid the club for letting me have the chance to play rather than the other way around," Port says.

Released by the Padres' Key West team of the Florida State League in 1968, Port returned to his Fallbrook, California home to help out in the family clothing store. Peter Bavasi, Buzzie's son and then farm director of the Padres, called just a week later to ask Port if he would return to Key West as general manager. Port accepted.

He moved to Lodi, San Diego's affiliate in the California League a year later, and soon became the Padres' marketing and promotions director, and then an administrative assistant to Buzzie Bavasi. Bavasi brought the young executive to Anaheim as director of player personnel in 1977.

Guarded and reserved in his public posture, Port remained in the shadow of the gregarious and often controversial Bavasi. He became known as the organization's authority on rules and regulations, a tough negotiator on the contracts Bavasi didn't handle. He was also a champion of building through the farm system, and could only bide his time and watch while Autry and Bavasi lavished greenbacks on an array of famed free agents.

Port's appointment as Bavasi's successor seems to reflect the Autrys' feeling that it is time to readjust their philosophy by taking a more modest approach to free agency while finally rebuilding from within. Port, having settled the managerial question, could now test the limits of that philosophy and his authority.

October 21

CLEVELAND—Andre Thornton has learned that he is no different from any other Indian player who becomes a free agent—they all are treated with disdain by Gabe Paul and Phil Seghi.

The same rule applies to all Cleveland free agents from Dave Rosello to Sid Monge to Thornton. The Indians simply refuse to discuss a new contract until after the reentry draft. It is as if Paul and Seghi hold the players responsible for the loathsome free agent system. What the hell has happened to this game when a .220-hitting Tony Bernazard has the right to demand a trade? The guy is lucky he doesn't have to play in Buffalo.

That's what Paul and Seghi think. Of course, they don't say it. Instead, they make up their own rules, such as the Indians don't talk money with free agents until after the reentry draft.

In spring training, Thornton's agents (Alan and Randy Hendricks) sent the Indians a contract proposal for $2.5 million over three years. Thornton is on the last year of a five-year contract worth $380,000 annually. He has a no-trade clause, but no incentives or bonus clauses. The Indians barely acknowledged receiving Thornton's proposal. They said they would discuss it "later,'" which meant after the free agent reentry draft in November. Their adherence to this "rule" will cost them dearly.

October 23

ST. PETERSBURG, FLORIDA—Dwight Gooden, to the surprise of no one, places second to Rick Sutcliffe in the National League Cy Young Award balloting. James Neader, to the surprise of no one, thinks that his client's negotiating position has been greatly enhanced. "This makes our case much stronger," he says.

October 24

AUSTIN, TEXAS—The 26 general managers meet here, ostensibly to work on general matters of importance and to hear from new commissioner Peter Ueberroth, who is in his 24th day on the job. Apart from the formal caucuses and speeches are the casual conversations among the general managers that, they hope, will bear fruit.

Frank Cashen has two in mind. He seeks out Tigers' general manager Bill Lajoie and makes what he calls "my annual request" for switch-hitting third baseman Howard Johnson. Lajoie, knowing the Mets' pitching depth addresses his own team's needs, is mildly interested. Johnson had nearly been traded to the Mets the previous December. They will talk again.

Cashen also seeks out John McHale and reiterates his desire for Carter. This time, Cashen says, "I got a weak 'Maybe.' That was the first glimmer." Perhaps they will talk again.

𝒜 Making Plans

October 25

SARASOTA, FLORIDA—Eddie Haas has come here, the home of the Braves' Instructional League team, from the World Series. John Mullen, the general manager, has flown down from Atlanta. And two of Ted Turner's most trusted advisors are here too: director of scouting, Paul Snyder, and director of player development, Henry Aaron. They aren't here just to look at the young kids playing ball in the Florida sun.

It is time for them to get down to the very serious business of personnel decisions, and they have convened here for that purpose. To this point, the Braves' offseason has been hectic. But now things have settled down. They have a new manager. They have reason to believe Bob Horner will be healthy when the 1985 season opens. And they are ready to analyze where they stand, and where they want to go.

They meet, and they talk. They decide, quickly and unanimously, that the team needs no major overhaul. Although everyone here is bitterly disappointed by the team's apparent regression from its 1982 championship, they assume that a healthy Horner, a new manager, and a few relatively minor moves can reverse the slide. Haas, Mullen, Aaron, and Snyder still feel that the Braves have one of the better nucleuses of any team in the big leagues. They feel very good about their second baseman, Glenn Hubbard;

about their shortstop, Rafael Ramirez; about their third baseman, Horner; and about their center fielder, Dale Murphy. They aren't all that unhappy with their right fielder, Claudell Washington. And they aren't worried about first base, where they figure young Gerald Perry will beat out veteran Chris Chambliss in spring training, or left field, where they hope and expect that young Brad Komminsk will come into his own in 1985. They firmly believe that for the next decade or so, Horner, Murphy, Komminsk, and Perry can form one of the most potent offenses in the game.

But they aren't happy about everything. They feel they need more production—more home runs—from their catchers, and they know they need to improve their pitching staff. The Braves had trouble scoring runs in 1984, mostly because Horner was sidelined and Chambliss was suddenly unproductive; but it's also true that the pitching wasn't good enough to win anyway. And now, as the Braves look toward 1985, they must wonder if one of their starters (Len Barker) will recover from elbow surgery; and they must wonder just how good their other starters—Pascual Perez, Rick Mahler, Rick Camp, and Craig McMurtry—are. They also can't be all that confident about their bullpen. Can Donnie Moore (16 saves in 1984) repeat the best year of his life? Will Terry Forster (40 pounds overweight at the end of 1984) ever get in shape to pitch again? Will Gene Garber bounce back from back-to-back off-seasons, or is he finished? And do two straight years of late-season arm trouble mean that Steve Bedrosian lacks the arm for short relief?

Questions, questions. The Braves' brass is here to come up with some answers.

They begin to explore ways to fill their needs for a power-hitting catcher and some pitching help, preferably left-handed. Specific trade possibilities come into the discussion. The Braves have an extra infielder or two. They decide, with Horner coming back, that Ken Oberkfell should probably be traded. Might the Cardinals be interested in reacquiring Oberkfell, who was traded to the Braves for left-handed pitcher Ken Dayley and first baseman

Mike Jorgensen in June? Haas points out that he's always liked Dayley. Would the Cardinals consider trading Dayley for Oberkfell? Mullen will check on this.

Next, they discuss dealing Moore, whose marketability should be at a peak. The Phillies had made it abundantly clear at the World Series that the injury-plagued catcher Bo Diaz is available. Everyone agrees that a healthy Diaz, playing his home games in Atlanta-Fulton County Stadium, could hit up to 20 home runs. A Phillies scout at the World Series said something about liking Donnie Moore. Everyone agrees they would have no reservations about trading Moore for Diaz. Someone suggests that the Phillies might instead want Jeff Dedmon, a promising young reliever. Everyone hopes they'll take Moore. Mullen will check on this.

But if the Braves get Diaz, what do they do with their present catchers: Bruce Benedict, an all-star in two of the past three seasons, and Alex Trevino? Trade Benedict, it is agreed.

They decide to abandon a thought that had drifted through the organization for a few months—the possibility of a deal with the Boston Red Sox for Jim Rice. When the Braves and Red Sox talked about this in August, the Red Sox asked for Komminsk and Bedrosian. Ex-manager Torre hadn't thought this was such a bad idea, but new manager Haas wants no part of any deal that involves trading Komminsk or Perry, two players who produced for him in the minor leagues.

Next, they talk about the upcoming free agent reentry draft. The Braves have always loved to chase free agents, usually unsuccessfully but always flamboyantly. The four pore over the list of eligible players and quickly conclude they can forget about everyone except pitchers. They compare names to scouting reports. They compare names to specific recollections. They scratch most of the names.

They are left with four. Everyone likes Rick Sutcliffe, but they all figure he is going to re-sign with the Cubs. Everyone likes Bruce Sutter, but they all figure he is going to re-sign with the Cardinals. Everyone wants a left-handed pitcher, and they all feel Steve Trout is the best one available. A couple of people think Ed Whitson showed great progress with the Padres in 1984 and would like to make a bid for him. One person thinks that Randy Lerch might be worth a gamble, but the others disagree. Dennis Eckersley is discussed and dismissed.

And so the Braves have the list of free agents they will draft on November 8: Sutcliffe, Sutter, Trout, and Whitson. Ted Turner, Mullen reports, is ready to bid, as always.

The meeting breaks up. Mullen returns to Atlanta, where he will make phone calls to the Phillies about Diaz, to the Cardinals about Dayley, and to the agents for the four pitchers the Braves will draft. Haas returns to his home in Paducah, Kentucky, where he will remain until the winter meetings. Snyder and Aaron return to their offices in Atlanta. Everyone feels they know where the team is headed.

October 28

PHILADELPHIA—Gone are the days when the business of baseball would cease for several weeks following the World Series. The game's new contract structure has created a 12-month business climate. If there isn't someone renegotiating, another player might be becoming a free agent. Possible arbitration cases, no-trade clauses, and performance bonuses command constant attention.

The assessment of talent has no slack period, either. Baseball has developed an off-season Instructional League program in which up-and-coming prospects receive several weeks of extra playing time and veterans often refine skills or learn a new position.

So the end of the World Series didn't signal any vacation for the Phillies' executives. And their first week back home is upset by a mini-bombshell.

One of the more obscure items in the players' basic agreement concerns players traded from one team to another while serving on an existing multi-year contract. Such a player has the right to demand a trade following his season with the new club. And if the player is neither traded nor induced to drop his trade demand, the player can become a free agent on March 15.

Shane Rawley, a left-handed pitcher acquired by Philadelphia from the New York Yankees at midseason, is a player in such a position. The Phillies are aware of Rawley's rights, and had late-season meetings with the pitcher's agent, Tony Attanasio. However, Rawley on several occasions expressed happiness with being with the Phillies. He pitched consistently well after joining the club and quickly developed a close relationship with Gus Hoefling, the Phillies' strength and flexibility instructor whose tutoring had aided several Phils pitchers.

So the Phillies were jolted when Attanasio announced that he had officially filed Rawley's demand for a trade. The demand would be dropped if the Phils paid Rawley $100,000 up front and also guaranteed the final year (1987) of Rawley's contract, which was not fully guaranteed in his existing contract.

Bill Giles blew his stack in private, railing about blackmail tactics and vowing not to budge one inch on Rawley and Attanasio's demands. Giles told Tony Siegle he'd trade Rawley before bending.

However, the realities of the situation set in. Already looking for pitching, the Phillies won't help themselves by trading one of their best pitchers. And it is discovered that Rawley has a clause in the contract the Phillies inherited from New York that will pay him $100,000 if he is traded. One way or another, he is going to get that money.

So Giles decides the best course is to set up a conference call with Rawley and his agent in which he can talk directly to Rawley and appeal to the pitcher's undenied desire to stay in Philadelphia.

While that call is being set up, Siegle is in serious contract negotiations with representatives of Phils outfielder Greg Gross. Gross is eligible for the free agent draft, but the Phillies are anxious to retain him. He fills several roles as a pinch hitter, outfielder, and first baseman. And Gross is the solidest of citizens, a veteran with class and character who can be counted on to serve out a new contract with dedication and dependability.

Siegle, who is in charge of the Phillies' contract negotiations, moves quickly to keep Gross out of the draft. Aided by a cordial relationship with Gross's Houston-based agent Alan Hendricks, the negotiations go off with hardly a snag. And Gross is so close to signing with the Phillies that he passes up his chance to file for the free agent draft, scheduled for November 8.

While Rawley and Gross are the active concerns of the front office, reports are filtering back from Florida, where Owens and Felske are watching the Phillies' Instructional League contingent. They have been anxious to see the hitting progress of young short-stop Steve Jeltz, who played for the Phillies for most of September and was impressive in the field. Jeltz was sent to Florida to work on his hitting and when reports come back of his decent progress, the club's decision to shop DeJesus around is reinforced.

The club also receives good news about Darren Daulton, the organization's top catching prospect, who had been sidelined much of the 1984 season with a mysterious shoulder problem. It was eventually discovered that a nerve problem in his neck was inter-fering with his throwing. Daulton thus began an intensive off-season rehabilitation and strengthening program that has divided his time between his Kansas home and Philadelphia. And trainer Jeff Cooper lifts spirits when he sends a report to Giles saying that Daulton is making excellent early progress. With Daulton now less a question mark for 1985, trading Diaz looks less risky.

Back on the contract front, Giles and Siegle finally talk by speaker phone to Rawley and Attanasio. Giles first stresses how much the Phils want to retain Rawley, and how the trade demand seems out of line given Rawley's $700,000 salary and his happiness with the Phillies organization.

Then Siegle speaks up. A student of baseball's arcane regu-lations and contract rules, Siegle bluntly outlines for Rawley how by being traded, he could well forfeit future claims to free agency and other valuable bonuses. Siegle makes the case that by being traded Rawley might reap only a short-term satisfaction that would be dissipated in the long run.

Attanasio reminds Giles and Siegle that, despite their appeals to Rawley's emotions, the trade demand is within Rawley's rights, and is purely a business matter. Rawley interrupts. "Look, Bill," says Rawley, "I liked the Phillies a lot, I like the guys there, I like you people, and I think Gus Hoefling can do wonders for my career. I'm not blind to all that. But I'm also a professional and all this is purely a professional option I have the right to suggest. I'm not asking for anything that is out of line and I'm not asking top dollar for selling my rights either."

Rawley's cool candor sets Giles back. He says, "Well, I guess the ball is in our court," and cuts off the call. Giles resolves to remain unbending, but the conversation does set in motion some soul-searching. And thus the Rawley matter is left hanging.

October 29

ATLANTA—John Mullen telephones Bill Giles. After some preliminary fencing, Mullen works around to the subject of Diaz, whom everyone knows the Phillies are shopping. Giles in turn works around to the subject of Moore. Mullen wants to know about Diaz's knees. Giles says that, if Diaz is traded, the Phillies will guarantee his health by agreeing to take him back in spring training if he is unable to play. Everything sounds good.

Nonetheless, nothing happens. Mullen is not discouraged; he has heard through the grapevine that the Phillies may be working on some other deals. They want to trade Diaz for Moore, Mullen has heard, but they feel Diaz might be necessary to complete a different, bigger trade. Knowing the Phillies' love of wheeling and dealing in all directions at once, Mullen is hardly surprised to hear this; there will be more phone calls.

October 30

PHILADELPHIA—Each year, a major-league club must go through various bureaucratic machinations in order to legitimize its personnel through roster assignments, waiver claims, and options. One of the offseason's most significant bits of housekeeping is the November submission of the club's major-league roster.

The 40-man roster must be completed five days after the World

Series, and it can be changed until five days before the winter meetings. It will remain set until after the major-league draft held during the first official day of the meetings; it can then be changed at any time.

To the public, the list seems rather humdrum, but it is a quietly significant measure of a club's rebuilding process. Its major significance lies in which young players are included on the roster. Every player on it receives an invitation to the big-league camp for spring training; non-roster players can be invited, too, but all the players on the 40-man roster must be invited.

More importantly, players on the 40-man roster are protected from selection in the draft. Any player who has played three professional seasons but is not listed on any club's 40-man roster can be drafted by another team for $25,000. The catch is that the drafting team must keep the player on its major-league roster for the entire next season or offer him back to his original club for $12,500.

This year, the Phillies are particularly concerned about their 40-man roster because a large group of prospects have become eligible for the list. Increasingly conscious of protecting talent in a farm system that has repeatedly been raided through trades, the Phils, Jim Baumer in particular, work long and hard on putting together their major-league roster by the deadline.

Eight young players in all will be added to the club's 40-man roster, meaning they are protected from other organizations and will be at the club's spring training camp. One is a young Dominican Republic native named Ramon Caraballo, whom scouts have been watching closely since midsummer. A tall, side-arm throwing relief pitcher, Caraballo has shown enough for the Phillies to push him along quickly in hopes he could soon help.

Another of the new additions is shortstop Kenny Jackson. He hit only .240 the previous season, but played well in the Instructional League, so well that the Phils were asked about Jackson's availability by two other clubs. That served as a red flag that persuaded the Phillies to protect Jackson by putting him on the 40-man list.

To make room for the additions, people had to be dropped.

The hardest decisions involved veterans. Pitchers Renie Martin and Steve Fireovid, throw-ins in prior trades, will be released. And veteran infielder Kiko Garcia will be outrighted to Triple-A. A career reserve save for one halcyon month in 1979 when he starred for Baltimore in the playoffs, Garcia is one of those increasingly rare pros who goes about his business without making waves. He doesn't cause trouble for his manager, keeps himself ready for his bit parts, and produced for the Phillies when called upon over two seasons.

But with Jeltz around and with shortstop Ivan DeJesus still on the club despite quiet trade talks (with Montreal in particular), there isn't room for Garcia. The Phillies need his permission to send him to the minors because of his veteran status. Garcia knows the Phillies' situation, and asks only for an invitation to spring training as a non-roster player. Maybe Garcia is hoping lightning will strike twice, since he made the club in spring training in 1983 as a non-roster player. Maybe he realizes that if he is released he will have difficulty finding another club to give him a look. And perhaps it is quiet concern for his career, for Garcia and his wife had their first child just two weeks before the Phillies approached him about the move. Career decisions for Garcia have suddenly gained a whole new importance.

ST. PETERSBURG, FLORIDA—For a Kiko Garcia, these organizational decisions bring on vital career choices. But for the club executives, they represent a welcome respite from contracts and agents. To them, these meetings are "strictly baseball." Hard work, says Mets player personnel director Joe McIlvaine, "but it's work you enjoy."

McIlvaine, Frank Cashen, Al Harazin, manager Dave Johnson, minor-league director Steve Schryver, minor-league coordinator Darrell Johnson, and the scouts have gathered to discuss the minor-league personnel and establish the 40-player roster. They meet far from Shea Stadium at the Edgewater Beach, a hotel that probably would prompt complaints from players if the major-league team were to stay there. There are no distractions here, not in St. Petersburg. "Concentrated baseball," Schryver says.

There is at present only one vacancy on the roster, as injury-plagued catcher John Stearns has filed for free agency. His filing is largely a cosmetic move, as he would no doubt have been released if he didn't. Once the Mets number one catcher, Stearns has been limited by elbow miseries to four games behind the plate in the past two seasons.

The Mets believe they need six more open spots to accommodate the cream of their minor-league system so they will be protected from the December 3 draft. Dave Johnson is hoping for even more vacancies that would allow the Mets to make selections, too.

But there are a multitude of questions and few answers for the organization considered to have the most prospects in the game. What to do with Tim Leary, the phenom of spring training, 1981? What to do with Jose Oquendo, the 21-year-old shortstop, a great fielder but an incompetent hitter? Each had begun the 1984 season as a semi-regular, but each had fallen from favor with Johnson and had been optioned to Tidewater. Neither has any options remaining and, at this point, neither figures in the plans for 1985.

Cashen still considers Leary a pitcher with "plus-10" potential, one with the potential to win 10 more games than he loses in a season, as in 20–10 or 18–8. In five years with the Mets, Cashen has so classified only one other pitcher—Dwight Gooden.

But Leary, after another perplexing and mediocre season, had lost rank within the organization; so much so that when the major-league roster limit was increased to 40 on September 1, he and Jeff Bittiger were the only pitchers on the 40-man roster not brought to the major leagues. Leary understood the situation and urged his agent, Richman Bry, to speak with Cashen about a trade. But Cashen, aware of Leary's potential and wishes and Johnson's opinion, still feels compelled to keep Leary on the 40-man roster.

Oquendo retains a position in the "40" though the regular

shortstop role belongs to Hubie Brooks, and both Rafael Santana and Ron Gardenhire are better equipped to serve in reserve.

"The biggest problem we face," Cashen says, "is trying to protect our short-term future and our long-term future."

October 31

NEW YORK—A second opening is created on the 40-man roster when the Mets tell backup catcher Ron Hodges that they will not exercise their option on his contract. The club had the choice of retaining the 35-year-old Hodges and paying him $270,000 for 1985 or buying out the contract for $50,000. They chose the latter, and thereby removed the final link to the National League champion Mets of 1973.

Hodges's departure increases the chance of Clint Hurdle earning a return to the major leagues. At Johnson's urging, Hurdle, the one-time *Sports Illustrated* cover boy, had spent the entire 1984 season with Tidewater, working as a catcher and designated hitter. Hurdle had been a productive hitter for Johnson at Tidewater in 1983, and Johnson hopes to have Hurdle, still only 27, replace Hodges on two fronts—as the No. 3 catcher and as a left-handed pinch hitter.

One sticky question with no solution is what to do with Rusty Staub. Cashen knows he cannot justify retaining a one-dimensional, 40-year-old pinch hitter at the risk of losing a prospect. Yet Johnson, well aware of the club's suspect offense, is urging that Cashen protect Staub, the National League's premier bat coming off the bench.

Cashen tries to strike a compromise. He suggests that Staub accept assignment to the Tidewater roster. Such a move would expose Staub to the draft, but Cashen is confident no teams will be interested in taking Staub. Cashen had found no takers a few years earlier when Staub requested a trade.

The plan would be to have Staub remain on the Tidewater roster through the draft, and perhaps even until spring training. He would then be re-signed. But Staub, because of his veteran status, does have some options. He can decline assignment to the minors, and thereby become a free agent, eligible to sign with any club. If he does decline to be sent down, he will be under no obligation to go to a team that did select him in the draft.

This would be a perfect solution to the Mets problem. Whether Staub accepts demotion or declines it, the Mets will have opened a spot on their roster and maintained a more-than-reasonable chance of having Staub with them in spring training.

November 1

ATLANTA—There are more phone calls. One is to the Cardinals. Yes, the Cardinals may be interested in reacquiring Oberkfell, especially if second baseman Tommy Herr follows through with a threatened trade request. And yes, if the Cardinals decide they want Oberkfell back, they will be willing to consider returning Dayley to the Braves. But the Cardinals say they really want to take another look at Dayley in spring training before parting with him. Maybe the teams can talk again then. Maybe sooner.

The Oakland A's also have some interest in Oberkfell, and so do the San Francisco Giants. The Braves ask the Giants about Gary Lavelle, a veteran left-handed reliever. Oberkfell for Lavelle? Both sides agree there is something to talk about there. They'll get together at the winter meetings, perhaps.

5 *The Lottery*

CLEVELAND—On the eve of the free agent reentry draft, Gabe Paul is talking about—of all people—Rick Sutcliffe.

The reentry draft grew out of the 1975 basic agreement between the players and the owners, and represented a major concession on the part of the players. When arbitrator Peter Seitz ruled in 1975 that a player is a free agent after completing the terms of his contract (including the option year), both sides feared a wild free-for-all. They developed the reentry system to regulate this new order. In the original reentry setup, a player could be selected by just 12 teams, not counting the team he was with.

In its current structure, any player with six years of major-league service whose contract has expired is eligible for the draft. There is no longer a limit on the number of teams that can draft a player, and a team can select as many players as it pleases. All the selection means is that the team retains some ghost of a hope of signing the player.

Many in the game have favored dropping the draft altogether. Its primary purpose now is as a public relations tool for a team that can get headlines by drafting a star it can't possibly sign.

Such is the case with the Indians and Rick Sutcliffe. Sutcliffe is one of 58 players eligible for the draft and will probably be the most expensive. Sutcliffe has the Indians to thank for his unprecedented financial position.

Sutcliffe was 17–11 for the Indians in 1983 and earned $360,000. He had been in the majors for five years and had the right to demand a trade. If traded, Sutcliffe would have had to wait an additional three years before attaining free agency. The trade demand was obviously a negotiating ploy, but Sutcliffe seemed sincere about wanting to leave Cleveland's losing environment.

Sutcliffe was one of the team's most popular players, its only all-star in 1983, and its best pitcher. Trading him would have been suicide from a public relations standpoint. So the Indians made Sutcliffe an offer he couldn't refuse—a one-year contract worth $900,000, which was a 275% raise. All Sutcliffe had to do was drop his trade demand. In exchange, he became one of the highest paid pitchers in the game. He also was still able to become a free agent after 1984; the $900,000 contract meant he was in excellent position to command at least $1 million a year. In essence, the Indians paid Sutcliffe as if he had a multi-year contract, and bought themselves not one iota of added security.

The extraordinary folly of that move became quickly apparent. Sutcliffe at $900,000 a year was no happier with a losing ballclub than he had been at $360,000 a year. Certain of losing him as a free agent at the end of the year, Cleveland traded Sutcliffe to the Chicago Cubs, for whom he went 16–1, winning the Cy Young Award. So much for public relations.

"We've considered taking Sutcliffe in the reentry draft," says Paul, "but his agent (Barry Axelrod) told Pat Corrales in the spring that Rick wouldn't re-sign with Cleveland. That led to our trading him to the Cubs. That's the truth, regardless what was said in the newspapers to the contrary."

Of course. And now, having all but assured Sutcliffe of a salary anywhere from $1 to $2 million a year, the Indians can avoid pursuing him because he will be too expensive.

PHILADELPHIA—For a team that gambles more than Jimmy the Greek, the Phillies have been surprisingly reticent to jump into the free agent market. Their only notable journey into the land of the millionaires was their acquisition in 1979 of Pete Rose after a whirlwind courting of Rose that included offers of real estate, race horses, and untold riches. The Phillies won the auction by parlaying their new local television contract into an offer to Rose that, as he said, "gave me a pile of money big enough for a show dog to jump over."

Other than Rose, however, the Phillies have done very little with free agents. It isn't that they are cheap. Under both Bill Giles and former owner Ruly Carpenter, the Phils' payroll has annually been among the highest in baseball. But Carpenter was from the old school that built through trades and the farm system. He made an exception with Rose, but signing free agents has never become a Phillies habit.

This winter's free agents do not figure much in the Phillies' plans. For one thing, Tony Siegle won a philosophical interorganization battle by persuading Giles to apply for an exemption from drafting "Type A" free agents. Such an exemption prohibits clubs from drafting those players judged to be Type A through the complicated reentry draft rating system. But in exchange for not being able to draft such players, exempt teams are not required to expose any players to the pool of talent made available as compensation to those clubs losing Type A free agents.

It was the latter aspect of the rule that motivated Siegle's argument. "We have enough trouble putting together our regular 40-man roster in a way that doesn't expose any quality prospects to other organizations," argued Siegle. "The compensation pool system allows us to protect only 24 players from the entire organization. We have too many good young players who would be out there available to another club losing free agents. It isn't worth the gamble."

So the Phillies became one of 12 clubs that applied for a Type A exemption. Five were selected through a drawing and the Phils were picked, along with Boston, Oakland, Los Angeles, and Pittsburgh.

Thus as the Phils scouts and top executives meet on the eve of the draft, they don't have to consider their chances of signing the draft's two biggest jewels—Rick Sutcliffe and reliever Bruce Sutter. Since both are Type A's, the Phillies won't be allowed to join in the multimillion dollar bidding.

"I don't have any regrets about that," says Giles as he peruses the list of the remaining players. "We'd love either guy but we wouldn't be able to sign either one. And bidding wars just don't make sense any more."

Not surprisingly, the Phillies' main focus is on pitching. They put together a list of possibilities. It includes Cubs left-hander Steve Trout ("We can draft him but Dallas [Green] ain't gonna let him get away," says one scout) and Padres right-hander Ed Whitson ("I've liked him since he was in the American League," says another scout, "but, shoot, he was their only starter to get anyone out in the postseason, so how the hell can [Jack] McKeon let him go?").

The Phils also look long and hard at California reliever Don Aase. "When he's healthy, I like him, but he's healthy about two months every two years," notes one evaluator.

They consider Dennis Eckersley, a Cubs right-hander, and Chicago reliever Tim Stoddard, but Giles murmurs when their names are brought up, "I've got bad vibes about those two guys."

The Phillies spend less time on the non-pitchers. They would like to find a power-hitting first baseman, but the only power hitters on the free agent list are designated hitters who haven't played a position in years. Yet Giles queries his brain trust, "How about if we draft Bull (ex-Phillie Greg Luzinski)? That would make a lot of people in town happy, for a change." Giles' half-serious suggestion is met by blank stares from his aides. They are aware of Giles' public relations antennae and also aware that the Phillies have been taking a three-year public relations beating in Philadelphia. But Luzinski weighs around 280 pounds and is years removed from being anything but a hitter. So the Luzinski boomlet dies very quickly.

Names like Jim Wohlford, Greg Pryor, Bill Almon, Jerry Royster, and Derrel Thomas are bandied about, all bit players who would be reserves if acquired. Since there is a rule that says players drafted by fewer than five clubs can negotiate with anybody, the Phillies know there is likely little need to select any of the draft's fringe names.

While deciding whom to make bids for, the Phillies also have to decide what to do about the two players of their own who have filed for the draft: outfielder Sixto Lezcano and pitcher Tug McGraw.

Weeks ago, the consensus was reached not to retain bargaining rights to Lezcano. When they acquired him in August of 1983, the Phillies had heard the scouting reports on Lezcano: "Excellent, maybe great, ability but a pain in the ass to have on your club." Still, the Phillies hoped that maybe the Milwaukee Brewers and St. Louis Cardinals and San Diego Padres were all wrong about the thrice-traded Lezcano. A year later, the Phils had found out otherwise and would let Lezcano pass on into free agency without making any attempt to retain him.

McGraw, however, is a far different story. The decision on McGraw would go far beyond his ability to pitch in the major leagues. If this were a purely baseball decision to be made by purely baseball men, McGraw would have been gone two years ago. Phillies baseball men were almost unanimously convinced that the 40-year-old McGraw simply could not pitch well enough to remain with the club.

But decisions concerning McGraw involve marketing and public relations. There is no Phillies player more popular than McGraw. Giles marveled throughout the club's desultory, boo-filled season how an otherwise sullen crowd would perk up and erupt in delighted applause when McGraw made one of his infrequent pitching appearances. Giles and his marketing chiefs Dave Montgomery and Dennis Lehman went so far as to persuade a reluctant McGraw to submit to a stadium promotion built around his 40th birthday. Between games of a late-season double-header, McGraw performed "Casey at the Bat," and a poster commemorating McGraw's birthday was given to fans.

Giles had almost given McGraw his release late in 1983, but went against the opinions of his baseball people and renewed the pitcher's contract. And when McGraw pitched well in spring training, he made the club, only to miss several weeks later in the year with a shoulder problem.

Late in the season, McGraw approached Giles about a new contract for 1985. Giles told McGraw he preferred to wait until the winter when the Phillies would have a better idea of the makeup of their pitching staff. Giles and Paul Owens then decided to use McGraw frequently in the season's final few weeks. The Phillies weren't going anywhere, Al Holland was being booed every time he showed his face, and the rest of the bullpen wasn't exactly imposing. It was a good opportunity for the Phillies to take a look at McGraw.

The results were mixed, a string of solid performances negated by a pair of last-week disasters against the New York Mets. And so Giles was no more settled on what to do about McGraw than he was before.

Nonetheless, for the first time he tells his aides that maybe the Phillies have to bite the bullet and say farewell to McGraw. And the reentry draft could conceivably give them that opportunity. If five clubs draft McGraw, the Phils will strongly consider not retaining bargaining rights.

November 8

NEW YORK—The reentry draft held here today forces all twenty-six major league teams to face important choices about their future. It also poses an important test of the philosophical resolve of the new California front office.

The Angels had ended the season with seven players eligible for free agency: outfielder Fred Lynn; infielder Rob Wilfong; pitchers Don Aase, Bruce Kison, John Curtis, and Craig Swan; and the versatile Derrel Thomas.

In preparing for the reentry draft, Mike Port had accepted input from Gene Mauch and made the following decisions: First, the club will retain negotiating rights and attempt to re-sign Lynn, Wilfong, and Aase; but will pass on the physically suspect Kison and Swan, the ineffective Curtis, and the frequently eccentric Thomas. One factor against retaining Thomas, who had been obtained from the Montreal Expos in mid-September, was that the Angels would have been forced to send Montreal a player if they kept him for 1985.

The Angels will also select negotiating rights to pitchers Rick Sutcliffe, Bruce Sutter, Steve Trout, and Burt Hooton; and outfielders Al Bumbry, Johnny Grubb, and Lee Lacy.

Scout Al Goldis represents the club at today's draft meeting in New York. Port sits in his Anaheim Stadium office and says that he considers Sutcliffe and Sutter the premium selections, players capable of justifying big salaries through both their performance on the field and their drawing power at the gate.

He says, however, that economics might prevent the signing of more than one of the Angels' new selections, and that would also be the key in the efforts to re-sign Lynn.

Lynn, one of the game's most talented players, had been obtained from the Boston Red Sox in a four-player trade on Jan. 23, 1981. The Red Sox had made him available because of his imminent departure via free agency and their desire to get something in return. The Angels signed Lynn to a new contract, four years at $5.25 million which made Lynn the highest salaried player on one of the highest salaried teams.

Lynn's performance over the next four years was constantly measured against that contract and the high standards he had set in 1975 when he made his Boston debut and became the first player to win both Rookie of the Year and Most Valuable Player Awards. Lynn hit .300 or better in four of his six Boston seasons and twice drove in 105 or more runs. His return to the Los Angeles area, where he had been a high school (El Monte) and college (USC) star, raised great expectations, but they were never met. His four year average with the Angels was .275 and his top RBI production was 86. He was frequently hurt during that time, and his dedication came under question at times. The Angels, in evaluating Lynn's efforts, have come to the conclusion that they cannot offer him the same four-year terms.

Port cites the availability of a promising replacement, a farm product named Mike Brown, and says that Lynn, 32, will be offered a guaranteed salary significantly less than the $1.45 million he earned in 1984. The offer will feature a series of incentive proposals designed to put Lynn back in the $1.4 million neighborhood if he meets them, but will be for fewer than four years.

The concept is consistent with the club's new philosophy and restraint, but only time will tell if the Angels can resist a return to their free-spending policies of the past.

No such restraint is promised by the Braves, who take negotiation rights to four pitchers: Sutcliffe, Sutter, Trout, and Whitson.

John Mullen vows, "We will seriously pursue all of our picks. Whether we sign them or not is another question, but we are serious about this." Given the Braves' history of big bids, no one doubts this. By the end of the day, Mullen has talked to the agents for all four pitchers. "This is going to be a long, drawn-out process; nothing is going to happen quickly," he says. Mullen doubts negotiations will get serious for at least a couple of weeks but, he promises, "We're not going to let any grass grow under our feet."

The Phillies don't get the chance to make their farewell to McGraw just yet. Only the Oakland A's select McGraw; the Phillies announce they won't decide about McGraw until December.

The only minor surprise at the draft for the Phillies is their selection of California infielder Rob Wilfong along with three pitchers: Trout, Whitson, and Aase. The Phillies see Wilfong as a possibly useful reserve, but they aren't holding their breath about signing any of their selections.

The only other matter of significance is who represents the Phils at the draft. Giles, Siegle, and Baumer are not surprises. But accompanying them is Owens, who, though not in a position to make decisions anymore is still around to lend his input. It might be window dressing, but Giles is making certain that, at least publicly, Owens isn't being shoved aside.

The Indians' real interest in the draft is retaining Andre Thornton. But who will handle the contract talks?

Dave LeFevre and Tal Smith desperately want to keep Thornton, but the lawsuit keeps them from assuming control of the club.

"In the foreseeable future, the Indians are Pat O'Neill's club and only Pat O'Neill's club," says LeFevre. "Not being able to complete the sale is frustrating. It's driving me up the wall and Pat O'Neill up the wall. The current management team has been very good about keeping us informed and giving us some input."

"The O'Neill family owns the team, but there won't be any major moves made without talking to Dave LeFevre," says Paul.

Thornton wants a three-year contract worth about $2.5 million. LeFevre wonders if the delay in the sale will cost him Thornton.

"We had one meeting with Thornton over coffee at my house," says LeFevre. "We expressed an interest in keeping him, but it was clear Andy wanted to go through the draft and see what offers he'd get. We haven't talked to him since and the club hasn't made him an offer."

The Indians feel that they have to take someone in the reentry draft. They can't just say, "Hey, let's skip it. The front office is too messed up to sign any of these guys." So Tim Stoddard, Steve Trout, and Dave Rozema are selected. Since the club needs pitching, they call out the names of these three pitchers. But don't be fooled. Cleveland is worried about only one free agent—Andre Thornton.

Thornton is also picked by Baltimore, Kansas City, Minnesota, Milwaukee, Toronto, Texas, and the Yankees. The Orioles, Royals, and Twins have the most interest.

"Our priority is signing Andy Thornton," says Gabe Paul. "We want to sign him first and we're preparing a very good offer for him. We think we have a good chance of keeping Thornton because our offer will be very good. Tal Smith will deal with Andy's agents (Alan and Randy Hendricks)."

Once again, it's time to ask who is in charge here? Paul is still the Tribe's president, but Smith (a consultant) will deal with Thornton. That's unusual to say the least.

The Indians do know Thornton's value. In 1984, Thornton had one of his typical seasons—.271 with 33 homers and 99 RBI. Considering the fact that Thornton was the only established power hitter in the Cleveland lineup, his numbers are amazing. He was gunning for 100 RBI, but was walked nine times (three times intentionally) in the last six games of the season.

"It's important for the Cleveland organization to keep him," notes Reggie Jackson. "It's more important for them than it is for Andy to stay."

6 Looking to Houston

November 12

ATLANTA—John Mullen gets an interesting phone call from David Pinter, the agent for Donnie Moore, calling to talk about a new contract. Coming off the best season of his life, Moore wants a three-year contract worth upwards of $1.5 million. Mullen listens but offers nothing; he says he'll give the idea of a multi-year contract some thought and get back in touch. Moore probably has not heard that the Braves are considering trading him.

NEW YORK—The Mets formally announce that Rusty Staub has rejected assignment to Tidewater and has become a free agent. They also invite this new free agent to join them in spring training.

Staub plays his role to the hilt. "I truly felt I should have been on the roster," he says. "I felt I merited a spot on the 40-man roster. The route as a free agent is the best means open to me now. I can control my own destiny to a degree by being available to all the big-league teams. . . . I'm going to spend the winter working toward being in the major leagues in 1985. I didn't want to be in this situation. I wanted to stay with the Mets."

If his tongue is in his cheek, it never shows.

CLEVELAND—Dave LeFevre is not a man of infinite patience. He has asked a Cuyahoga County Court to rule that he doesn't need all 54 owners of the Indians to agree to the sale. Three of the minority owners have refused to sell to LeFevre. They claim they will not receive a fair cash settlement in the deal. They insist that the O'Neill family will receive a higher price per share then they will, a charge LeFevre denies. The three own less than 1% of the club, and their legal tactics seem designed to delay the sale rather than to lead to a settlement.

One of the partners, Charles Neuger, has asked the court to delay its ruling for two months. Neuger wants the judge removed from the proceedings and filed a brief asking that a new judge be appointed.

"I almost went crazy when I heard about that," says LeFevre. "That kind of delay would put us past the winter meetings. Instead of spending this crucial time building for 1985, we're bogged down with legal problems."

LeFevre obviously is unhappy with the progress of the sale.

"Is our group dissatisfied with the way things have gone? Absolutely, and with good reason. We have lost the enthusiasm of a lot of these people. It's almost the end of the year and the investors want to know where to put their money to get the greatest pay benefits. We haven't been able to spend 10 minutes on baseball because of the legal hassles. But that doesn't mean you throw up your hands and move to South America."

November 14

CLEVELAND—Dave LeFevre can't wait any longer. With LeFevre's backing, Pat O'Neill files a brief with the Ohio Supreme Court, asking the chief justice to dismiss a motion by three minor stockholders in the Indians that could delay the sale of the team to LeFevre for months. LeFevre and the O'Neill family have asked the court to rule that unanimous approval of all partners is not needed for the sale to go through. LeFevre insists that another long delay will force him to withdraw his offer and the O'Neill family would have to operate the team for another year. Daniel

Hammer, the lawyer for the O'Neill family, tells the court that the transaction must be approved by all parties by the middle of December or else it will fall apart.

LeFevre and his 12 partners originally agreed to purchase the team on June 21. Then came the lawsuit filed by the three minority stockholders—Charles Neuger, Gary Hoffman, and Harry Goodman.

In 1972, Neuger bought into the team for about $25,000. He has failed to make the cash calls over the years, and his shares are now worth less than $5,000. And yet, with so little financially at stake, he may have thrown a deadly monkey wrench into the proceedings.

November 15

CLEVELAND—Yes, it could only happen to the Cleveland Indians. This is a team that is over $10 million in the red. It hasn't been a contender since Dwight Eisenhower was president. A guy comes along with a dozen partners who are not only willing to assume the $10 million-plus in debts, but will pay another $31 million for a franchise that has no realistic chance of making a profit in the next few years. The team has 54 partners and 51 are willing to sell, including every major investor.

But the deal can't go through because three men whose combined holdings in the team is less than 1% have blocked the sale. Charles Neuger's motion has postponed the hearing for at least two months. That's two months too long for Dave LeFevre.

LeFevre has already faced one legal battle since the announcement of the sale. On June 15, a group of minority stockholders including Walter Laich, who owns about 20% of the team, sued LeFevre and the O'Neill family because LeFevre originally planned to buy only the O'Neills' 52% share of the stock. LeFevre settled that lawsuit by saying he would buy everyone's shares.

When LeFevre informs his investors of the latest legal hitch, they tell him to pull out of the sale.

"There is no way any investor would involve himself with a

situation in such a pathetic atmosphere," says Pat O'Neill, who speaks for the O'Neill family on matters of the sale.

Personally, LeFevre does not have enough money to buy the Indians, but Pat O'Neill says there are wealthy men who are part of the transaction.

"The reason for the trouble with the sale is all these damn lawsuits," says O'Neill. "The people Dave LeFevre had lined up are worth about $1 billion. But they have taken the position that they won't enter into any investment that will be dragged into court."

"My partners were looking for a place to put their money before the end of the year for tax purposes," says LeFevre. "Because of the lawsuits, they can't do it."

Put plainly, some of LeFevre's investors view the Indians as a tax shelter.

"I might try to buy the team again," says LeFevre. "But I doubt anything could be worked out for the 1985 season. The atmosphere has to be cleared before we move again."

ATLANTA—The three coaches fired with Joe Torre—Bob Gibson, Joe Pignatano, and Rube Walker—all remain without baseball jobs. They all know they will have jobs if Torre lands another managing job, but that appears unlikely for 1985. Gibson, 49, will tend to business interests around Omaha and probably not return to baseball unless it is with Torre. Pignatano, 55, a big-league coach for the past 16 years, and Walker, 58, also a big-league coach for the past 20 years, are looking for jobs in the game.

Since the day he was dismissed, Walker has been talking to Hank Aaron, the Braves' vice-president for player development, about the possibility of remaining in the organization as a minor-league pitching instructor. Aaron has asked Johnny Sain, the Braves' former minor-league instructor who will be the pitching coach in Atlanta next year, what he thinks about this. Sain disagreed radically with the pitching philosophies of Torre and Gibson, but he feels Walker is more compatible and flexible. Aaron offers Walker a job in the minor leagues; in effect, he offers him Sain's old job. Walker says yes, accepting a job in the minors after two decades in the majors.

In 1978, the Atlanta Braves' farm team at Richmond, Virginia, won the International League championship. The manager was Tommie Aaron, who was promoted the next season to a job as big-league coach. The pitching coach was Johnny Sain, who remained in the same job at Richmond six years later.

In the Braves' 1984 spring training camp, as Sain was instructing a young pitcher, he spotted Aaron.

"Hey, Tommie," he shouted, "you know I carried us at Richmond in '78, don't you? I won that pennant for you."

"I won it," Aaron shot back. "You just talked a lot."

"I won it," Sain said.

"I won it," Aaron said.

"Oh, well, maybe *we* won it," Sain said.

The two men laughed and embraced, friends who couldn't care less who was more responsible for the minor-league pennant. "We kid a lot like this," Sain said. "We kid about who was more important, me or him."

"It's all in jest," said Aaron, who died of leukemia later in 1984.

But, where Johnny Sain is concerned, such debates haven't always been in jest. That's one reason why he had been in the minor leagues for seven years when the Braves fired Bob Gibson and made Sain their major-league pitching coach after the 1984 season. And one reason why he was happy there.

"I missed certain things about the big leagues, but not the bull of coaching there," Sain said before coming back. "The politics . . . the undercurrent . . . I call it the underworld of baseball. It's in everything, a corporate climate . . . jealousies . . . people shooting at you.

"Take the year we won the pennant in Detroit, 1968. A writer from *The New York Times* spent a week with me and wrote a 12-page article in the magazine. How did that sit with the manager?

So I think that type of thing has had a bearing on my career."

This also has had a bearing: Despite the unthreatening demeanor of Sain—a grandfatherly 67-year-old with a soft voice, blue eyes, and white hair—he is extremely opinionated about pitching and pitchers. He believes that pitchers should run little, throw daily, and use lots of off-speed pitches . . . three points that have plenty of opponents in major-league baseball. Sain can be as uncompromising as he has been successful. "Maybe, at times, I pushed too hard," he says.

And this, too, has had a bearing: Major-league coaches, more often than not, are chosen for all of the wrong reasons. As Jim Bouton, a 21-game winner under Sain for the New York Yankees in 1962, put it, "The system for selecting coaches hasn't changed since Abner Doubleday. The manager picks the coaches, and managers always choose an old teammate, close friend, brother-in-law, or next-door neighbor—anybody who will be loyal to the manager. Loyalty is more important than ability. The best qualifications a coach can have is being the manager's drinking buddy. Johnny Sain drinks milk shakes and is loyal to pitchers. John got credit for winning pennants in New York, Detroit, and Minnesota. (Managers) Ralph Houk, Mayo Smith, and Sam Mele never won anywhere without him. But managers don't like it when the pitching coach gets his name in the paper more than the manager.

"I'll say this," Bouton concluded. "If I owned a baseball team, I'd hire Sain as my pitching coach and let him choose the manager."

Sain was prepared to pass on the prospect of ever returning to the majors when the Braves brought him back. He has had a full life in baseball, one so complete that he would be content to spend his final years in the bushes. Still, it seemed incongruous—Johnny Sain in the minor leagues.

This is a man who has spent 29 years in the major leagues (11 as a player, 18 as a coach), a man who has appeared in nine World Series (four as a player, five as a coach), the man who threw the first pitch to the first black in the big leagues, a man who won 21 games and hit .346 in 1947, a man with a lifetime big-league record of 139–116 who was part of the "Spahn and Sain and pray for rain" strategy that led the Boston Braves to the World Series in 1948.

And this is a man who, as a big-league pitching coach, has coached 17 20-game winners—none of whom had ever won 20 before meeting Sain—and coached on nine teams that finished first or second. He has coached under eight managers, four of whom were named manager of the year while he was their pitching coach.

But numbers cannot endorse Sain as heartily as his former students do.

Jim Kaat: "I pitched in the big leagues for 25 years, and I owe about half of those to John Sain. Until I met him, pitching was physical, not mental. He's just the best coach who ever lived."

Rick Camp: "I've said this so many times, but whatever success I've had, I owe to Johnny. I thank that man for everything."

Mickey Lolich: "He isn't so much a coach as a headshrinker. He's the best."

And, for seven years, until October 1984, he was in the minor leagues.

Sain has been in the Braves organization since 1977, when he was pitching coach under manager Dave Bristol—his seventh major-league coaching job. He coached the Kansas City A's for two seasons (1959–60), the New York Yankees for three (1961–63), the Minnesota Twins for two (1965–66), the Detroit Tigers for three (1967–69), the California Angels for one (1970), and the Chicago White Sox for five (1971–75). The Yankees appeared in three straight World Series with him as pitching coach. The Twins won their American League pennant in Sain's first year as pitching coach. The Tigers won the 1968 World Series with him as pitching coach. And the White Sox, who won only 56 games and finished last the year before Sain arrived, won 79 games and finished third in his first year and moved up to second the next year. "Johnny Sain, miracle worker" became a cliché among sportswriters.

Sain worked no miracles on the miserable Braves pitching staff in 1977, and when Bristol was fired, new manager Bobby Cox wanted to bring in his own pitching coach. Sain was offered a job in the minors.

Because Ted Turner promised to pay him as much as he paid his major-league coaches, and because Sain sincerely felt wanted and appreciated by the Braves' owner, he took the job. And there he stayed.

While the position seemed beneath his qualifications, the minor-league life style seemed to fit Sain comfortably. In Richmond, he lived in a small motor home, which he drove from his off-season home in Chicago with his 1972 Buick Skylark in tow. He parked the motor home at the same Richmond trailer park for five years and loved it there. "It was home. The first time my wife visited me there, she said, 'This is mighty small.' I said, 'Anyone can live in a big one.' I've got a comfortable bed, a microwave oven, air conditioning. What else do you need?"

Sain would go to the stadium around three o'clock every afternoon and gather his pitchers in the bullpen. They would talk pitching, which is Sain's favorite subject.

"It's the most fascinating business—fabulous—yes, it is," he says. "If anyone ever tried to make a manager of me, I'd make a jerk of myself, because it's the pitching part of the game that interests me. A pitcher and a catcher are a team within themselves. They work with the rest of the club, but they are a little separated, too.

"I've never found anything so interesting as pitching. I grew up as a mechanic; I'd work on top of the engine with my dad underneath. To me, pitching is mechanical, like working on a car. I'm not a detail person; I put things together without reading the instructions. I approach pitching the same way. It's all trial and error. I like figuring out a way to solve a problem."

His solutions can cause other problems. It was well known in the Braves organization that Sain's ideas about pitching contrasted with those of big-league manager Joe Torre and pitching coach Bob Gibson. Minutes after his firing, Torre admitted that his differences with Sain "might have had something to do with it."

The philosophical differences among Torre, Gibson, and Sain were numerous. Most pitching coaches, including Gibson, think pitchers should rest four days between starts; Sain thinks three days' rest is ample. Most coaches, including Gibson, think pitchers should do a lot of running; Sain thinks their time is better spent throwing. Most coaches, including Gibson, think power is the most important attribute in a pitcher; Sain thinks finesse can be just as effective. Most coaches, including Gibson, think it is virtually criminal to fall behind in the count on a hitter; Sain is not bothered by pitchers who open with a couple of breaking balls out of the strike zone, and he doesn't see anything wrong with throwing another breaking ball or two when behind in the count. And most pitching coaches, including Gibson, think velocity and aggressiveness are synonymous; Sain asks, "What's aggressiveness? You can be aggressive by changing speeds.

"There are as many different ideas as there are people," Sain says. "He (Gibson) was a different type pitcher than I was. He had power; I didn't. My point is, not many people have Koufax/Gibson power, but everybody can improve on their other pitches. I was released four times in Class A because I didn't have velocity. But in the end, I made it, and I did it by throwing breaking and off-speed pitches."

Before the Torre/Gibson regime became the Haas/Sain regime, Sain had no qualms about spending the rest of his career in the minor leagues. "I feel great," he said. "I like what I'm doing, and I feel appreciated. They, especially Mr. Turner, make me feel important, and this is lower pressure than being in the major leagues. I see no reason to stop. I'm not the retiring type."

At times, Sain has tried to veer his life away from his passion for pitching—always unsuccessfully. After retiring as a player in 1955, he bought a 300-acre farm, a small Chevrolet dealership, and an auto-parts store in Walnut Ridge, Arkansas. But he missed the game desperately and, after three years, welcomed an offer to join the Kansas City A's as pitching coach. Five years later, after two seasons with the A's and three with the Yankees, Sain again returned to Walnut Ridge. But a year later, he was back in baseball. "I'd started having marital problems and thought it'd be better if I got away for a while," says Sain, who joined the Twins as pitching coach and hasn't been out of baseball since. In 1972, he and his wife were divorced. "I signed everything away to my ex-wife; I came away with my baseball pension and nothing else." Sain is now remarried to a woman 18 years younger than himself. "We've recovered from the crash, and everything is beautiful.

"Everything is beautiful," Sain repeats. He is holding a baseball and looking into it, as if he is talking to the ball more than to his listener.

"I never dreamed that this little ball would take me all the way around the world," he says. And now it has taken him back to the major leagues.

November 16

CLEVELAND—Once again, the Indians are the team that can't be sold. Once again, there are rumors of people wanting to buy the team. Once again, the Indians are settled in their familiar surroundings—limbo.

Just because Dave LeFevre couldn't buy the team this time doesn't mean he'll never own the club. One rumor is that LeFevre will buy Gabe Paul's stock and assume Paul's spot on the board of directors. Eventually, LeFevre could put together another deal to buy the rest of the team, using Paul's 5% of the stock as a foundation.

This much is certain—not only are the Indians without a buyer, they need a president. Paul is sticking to his announced plan to retire on January 1, 1985.

"Gabe has tried to retire for four years," says Pat O'Neill. "But we wouldn't let him. When I took over, I asked Gabe to stay with us for a reasonable amount of time until we got the club sold. Gabe said he would so long as it wouldn't last past 1984. We're keeping our promise to him."

Gabe Paul is out. And so is Tal Smith.

"We talked to Tal about being president of the Indians," says O'Neill. "But he doesn't want to give up his consultant's business."

At least Smith doesn't want to risk his consultant's business—from which he reportedly earns $500,000 annually—to run a team in search of an owner. Being president of the Indians at this point would be like being president of a Latin American country between military coups.

"We are looking for someone to run the team," says O'Neill. "A Gabe Paul–type guy is what we need."

Qualified baseball people are not exactly lining up for the chance at what may be the toughest job in the game. Trying to win with the Indians under the best circumstances is nearly impossible because of the sad state of the franchise for the last 25 years. But attempting to do it with a lame duck ownership that is not about to spend the cash needed to make an immediate impact, well, it would be easier to transform Greenland into a industrial giant than to win big with the Indians in 1985.

Whenever the sale of the Indians falls through, there is speculation in Cleveland that the team will move. Rumors of bids from Tampa, Denver, Vancouver, and about anywhere but Greenland, surface. One sportscaster has appeared on television with a map, marking all the cities that want the Indians with little Wahoo emblems.

"We're still committed to keeping the team in Cleveland," insists O'Neill. "I'm not a baseball operator and I don't want to keep the team. If it can be sold within a reasonable time, say a year or so, it'll stay in Cleveland."

There are people who wear T-shirts saying, "CLEVELAND: YOU GOTTA BE TOUGH." In the 1980s, Northern Ohio has lost a higher percentage of its population to other areas than anywhere else in the country. Factories close, bridges are condemned, the weather is cold and wet, and about half the citizens constantly battle colds or an acute sinus condition.

Yes, Cleveland has a great orchestra. Yes, it has some lovely suburbs. But the Chamber of Commerce is off base when it says, "Cleveland is the best location in the nation." Cleveland is in trouble and the people living there know that better than anyone. That's why the thought of losing the Indians panics the community.

"If the Indians leave, this town is finished," says Pete Franklin, Cleveland's legendary sports talk show host. "The Indians may be lousy, but they make this place a big-league city. Without them, we're just another hick town."

November 17

PHILADELPHIA—Another meandering bull session is underway in Bill Giles's Veterans Stadium office.

It's a quiet day otherwise. The negotiations with Gross are stalled on some technical contract language, a time-consuming and aggravating problem but hardly threatening to what is a firm agreement. Trade talks are on hold with the winter meetings two weeks away. The Phillies have only made the most cursory contact with the free agents they drafted. So it is a time for philosophizing and plotting strategy.

Paul Owens sits in a high-backed leather chair, chain-smoking Chesterfields. Jim Baumer sits at the conference table, puffing on his omnipresent Marlboro. Giles, who on occasion smoked Tareytons or cigars, slurps on a pinch of snuff tucked in his lower lip. Jack Pastore, the portly assistant farm director who eats rather than smokes, wanders in and out of the conversation while Tony Siegle, in his ninth month of abstention from a ghastly chewing tobacco habit, sits near Giles in between phone calls.

The subject of the day is Bo Diaz and the main speaker is Owens. Reflecting his dual experience as an on-field manager and an off-field wheeler dealer, Owens weighs in with a strong argument for not trading Diaz until at least spring training.

"I just think we're taking too big a gamble by trading Diaz this quickly," Owens tells Giles. "I'm afraid we're leaving ourselves a little thin by trading him now. You and I know how hard it is to find a good catcher. And the thing is that I think his value will be more if we wait until spring."

Owens is skittish for a number of reasons. Like many in the organization, he is still not entirely convinced that Ozzie Virgil is the club's long-term answer as catcher. No one denies what a solid job Virgil did in 1984 after Diaz was injured. But it was doubt about Virgil's ability that triggered the Phillies' cataclysmic decision last spring to obtain backup catcher John Wockenfuss from Detroit; the decision led to their trading Willie Hernandez to the Tigers and Bob Dernier and Gary Matthews to the Chicago Cubs.

Now, after Virgil's solid season, doubts still persist. Owens argues there is no guarantee Virgil can repeat his 1984 success. And there is concern about depth if Diaz is traded. Though Wockenfuss chipped in with occasional offensive contributions, he proved to be a defensive liability. Trading Diaz would leave only Wockenfuss and unproven youngsters Mike Lavalliere and Darren Daulton behind Virgil. And Daulton, the organization's best catching prospect in years, is still a question mark because of his shoulder problem, despite promising early reports.

But Owens has one more reason for not trading Diaz during the winter meetings. In all talks concerning Diaz, the Phillies are being asked the same question over and over again. "What about Diaz's knees?" The Atlanta Braves, Cincinnati Reds, and others have been asking, "Can you guarantee he'll be healthy?"

Without the benefit of having clubs see Diaz play, all the Phillies can tell those clubs is that their doctors are certain Diaz is completely recovered from his operations. But until Diaz actually gets out and plays, no one will know for sure if his knees have healed. "We just won't get the same value for him now that we will in the spring when people can see he's healthy," declares Owens.

Owens's arguments are well received. Baumer believes Daulton is ready for the majors, but also believes it's wise to make sure his throwing ability has been restored before committing to his likely presence on the club.

And as Giles acknowledges, "We really don't have to be in any hurry. The winter meetings aren't what they used to be. More teams prefer to trade in the spring rather than in the winter. And like Paul says, Diaz will have better value then."

So the word will be spread that Diaz is off the trading block. The Phils will listen to interested clubs, but unless they get an overwhelming offer, they will likely wait until spring before seriously considering trading Diaz.

November 19

CLEVELAND—Pat O'Neill has done everything short of taking out a classified ad in *The Wall Street Journal's National Employment Weekly*. The Indians need a buyer. And while they are looking for a buyer, they need a president.

One candidate is Bill Virdon, former manager for Pittsburgh, the Yankees, Houston, and Montreal. Virdon is also a close friend of Tal Smith and Dave LeFevre. They may not be officially calling the shots, but Smith and LeFevre's words still carry a great deal of weight with O'Neill.

Another possibility is Danny O'Brien, the former president of the Texas Rangers and Seattle Mariners. Like Virdon, O'Brien is "between jobs." He is also a close associate of Smith and Gabe Paul.

A third candidate is Peter Bavasi, former president of the Toronto Blue Jays. After being sacked in Toronto, Bavasi went to work for a group that is trying to secure a baseball team to play in St. Petersburg. He would love the opportunity to run another team, even the Indians.

"We'll get someone," vows O'Neill. "I just don't know who."

November 20

ANAHEIM—The Angels closed their offices today for the Thanksgiving weekend. It is becoming apparent that the club is serious about avoiding long-term commitments to players of suspect age and/or ability, and are finally emphasizing the farm system.

Aase, Lynn, and Wilfong remain unsigned. There has been little effort to change that, and little effort to romance either Sutcliffe or Sutter. Agents shake their heads and say it is now almost impossible to get an answer from the Angels or a legitimate proposal that might lead to legitimate negotiations.

ATLANTA—Ted Turner loves the chase. Even more than he is a businessman, more than he is the owner of two professional sports franchises, Ted Turner is a sportsman. He loves competition; he loves winning.

Every year about this time, Turner gets a recognizable gleam in his eyes; he just loves the whole idea of selling himself, his town, his team, and his television station. He loves the thrill, the power, of outselling the other guy. And so it is that Turner annually chases free agent baseball players, determined to offer more money and more happiness than the other guy.

Turner was in on the start of this free agent madness in 1975, signing Andy Messersmith to the original free agent contract. That didn't work out particularly well for the Braves, but the experience didn't slow Turner in his aggressive pursuit of free agents.

He wanted Pete Rose when the Phillies got him. He wanted Dave Goltz when the Dodgers got him. He wanted Dave Winfield when the Yankees got him . . . and Don Sutton when the Astros got him . . . and Reggie Jackson when the Angels got him . . . and, in 1983, he wanted Goose Gossage when the Padres got him. In each chase, Turner negotiated loudly and flamboyantly, offering more money than anyone else in most cases, but he didn't sign any of the players. In the 1970s and the early 1980s, Turner was at an almost insurmountable disadvantage because his team was a non-contender, and the top free agents tend to gravitate toward teams that can win. And always, Turner was at a disadvantage with pitchers, who hate the thought of pitching half their games in cozy Atlanta-Fulton County Stadium. But every year, Turner forgets the disappointing setback of the previous fall, picks out the biggest name of the free agent crop, and sets his sights on him.

He has landed a few free agents along the way, but has missed the big catches since Messersmith (1975) and Gary Matthews (1977). When he couldn't get Rose in 1978, he settled for another free agent, Mike Lum. When he couldn't get Goltz, he settled for Al Hrabosky, an over-the-hill relief pitcher who flopped badly. When he couldn't get Reggie Jackson in 1981, he settled for Terry Forster and Pete Falcone.

This year, the prime targets are, naturally, Sutcliffe and Sutter. Either would be a marvelous addition to a team with gaps in both its starting rotation and its bullpen. But, partly because the Braves expect Sutcliffe to re-sign with the Cubs and partly because Haas has indicated he's more concerned about the bullpen, Turner has focused on Sutter. Turner began to espouse this logic: Signing Sutter would allow young, hard-throwing Steve Bedrosian to move from the bullpen to the starting rotation, in effect giving the Braves both a new relief pitcher (Sutter) and a new starter (Bedrosian). Two for the price of one, Ted figures. The price, though, will be monumental.

At this point, Turner does not know how much Sutter will cost. But he knows who the competition is, and he won't be outbid. In the past, Turner has had trouble competing with the Angels and Yankees for free agents; one reason is that the type of free agents who excite Turner also are the type of free agents who gravitate toward the mega-media markets. But Turner senses that neither the Yankees nor Angels will be negotiating for Sutter.

The competition will come principally from the Toronto Blue Jays, who would be favored to win the American League pennant in 1985 if they signed Sutter, and the Cardinals. Turner figures he has a large advantage over the Blue Jays; the Jays' salary structure is more rigid than Turner's, and the Jays face the disadvantage of Canadian tax laws and unfavorable exchange rates. That leaves the Cardinals; Turner knows he can outbid the Cardinals, but has no way of knowing if Sutter would take less money to stay in St. Louis.

Turner has learned these free agent games can't be forced. For now, he and John Mullen are staying in touch with Sutter's two agents, making it clear enough that the Braves are willing to do just about anything to get their man. But they apply no pressure, no hard sell.

They have tossed out an extravagant opening offer—five years,

$7.5 million—but both sides know it is only a starting point. With that kind of starting point, Turner figures he has Sutter's attention. The chase is on.

PHILADELPHIA—The Shane Rawley situation continues to be a concern. Giles's scouts and top aides are pressing for some sort of decision in advance of the winter meetings. If the decision is to trade him, the Phillies have to begin working on a deal, assessing what value they should place on him, and also scouting out where they could find an adequate replacement.

Throughout all this, Felske is in his Illinois home, out of direct contact with the front office. He has built a car repair business over the years, investing whatever extra money he could save from his slim salaries as a coach and minor-league manager. The business has proved successful, so much so that he is working long hours trying to put together plans for construction of a new business facility.

His contact with Giles has been only occasional. Giles has assured Felske that no moves are likely until the winter meetings, and that Felske will be consulted before any player decisions are made.

But in the meantime, Felske had heard from others about the developing crisis concerning Rawley. The new manager was not secure enough to inject himself into a contract dispute that was strictly the front office's concern, but Felske was privately aghast that the situation seemed headed for an impasse that would result in Rawley's being traded. He has developed a rapport with Rawley and an appreciation of what Felske believes to be Rawley's 20-win potential.

Felske decided to call Giles, ostensibly to be briefed on any new trade talks, but also to intimate strongly that the club try to find some common ground with Rawley that would keep the left-hander in Philadelphia.

Felske quickly learned that Giles was coming around to that position as well. Giles and Siegle, the contract expert, weren't happy about Rawley invoking his trade demand rights, but they also liked Rawley and realized it just didn't make sense for the Phillies to trade one of their key pitchers, especially when pitching was the club's major concern.

Giles then got on the phone with Attanasio. And in an effort to change the sullen atmosphere, Giles made his first offer of the entire negotiations.

Giles' proposal wasn't immediately acceptable. He offered to extend the length of Rawley's contract in exchange for Rawley's dropping his trade demand. Giles threw in a hook, saying he'd prefer to wait until negotiations for a new basic agreement between the players and owners were resolved. Once those negotiations were resolved, Giles assured Attanasio that he would go about renegotiating Rawley's contract.

Attanasio, a brassy San Diego–based agent with decades worth of experience, quickly detected Giles's change of heart. Attanasio was well aware that it would be foolish of Rawley to give up his potentially lucrative demand in exchange for a mere promise of renegotiation. But he also recognized that the atmosphere had changed and that negotiations had finally begun. So while saying it wasn't acceptable, Attanasio added he'd bounce things off Rawley and get back to Giles.

Today, Attanasio is back in touch with an alternative proposal that includes the willingness to accept a contract extension. That represents a concession since a player like Rawley, with veteran status, is giving up potential free agency when he extends his contract. Nothing is going to be resolved by phone, but both Giles and Attanasio hang up feeling confident for the first time that a trade undesired by either side will be avoided. They will have a meeting in Houston in which the negotiations will continue.

7 *Andre*

November 22

CLEVELAND—Pat O'Neill has called a press conference to give yet another "state of the sale" update. But the state of the sale is so pathetic that he doesn't want to discuss it. Instead, he goes hunting for a scapegoat for the team's current mess.

"It's all the newspaper stories," O'Neill says. "All this speculation really hurts the club. These stories have been causing distress among our players. Some of them have called the office. I thought the function of the press was to report the news and not try to guess what changes will be made in the front office. Despite all the pressure caused by the media, we intend to do things right.

"The more we speculate on problems, the more worried our personnel is becoming. It hurts the morale of the front office. I think you ought to concentrate on reporting news. What would you be reporting if you did have good management here? You wouldn't be talking about the next management. You'd be talking about what the fans want to know—like the players and how the team is progressing.

"If you guys start speculating about who is coming here and happen to get lucky and print the name of who we're talking to, you know that fellow will say, 'The heck with it, I'm not walking into that can of worms.'

"I'm not saying the Cleveland media is unique. I don't know

what they do in other cities. But I have a problem and I'm coming to you for help. If you want to solve the problem, put your money where your mouth is, buy the team and then you can make all the decisions."

O'Neill finally does say that Gabe Paul has not sold his stock or given up his seat on the board of directors to Dave LeFevre. He adds that Tal Smith will not be president of the team and Paul is sticking to his retirement plans.

"We need to get a better handle on the management of the club. We have someone in mind to run the Indians, although the emphasis will be on administrative skills, though a knowledge of talent would be nice. We won't hire a guy just to hire a guy. It is possible to run the club for a while without a president.

"But I have no intention of running the club now or in the immediate future. I have been getting irritated by reports that I'm going to be general manager of the Indians. It just won't happen."

It would seem that all this uncertainty might end any chance of Andre Thornton re-signing with Cleveland. Thornton's agents, Randy and Alan Hendricks, have held preliminary contract talks with Toronto, Baltimore, Minnesota, and Texas. The Orioles were the first to present a firm offer—three years at $2.5 million. Thornton's agents want more money, but they think Baltimore's bid is a good one, and more importantly, that the Orioles are willing to raise it. Thornton likes the idea of playing for the team that has the best record in baseball for the last 25 years. Baltimore released its designated hitter, Ken Singleton, after the season, and that seemingly cleared a roster space for Thornton. Another positive factor about Baltimore is its lineup; Thornton would be hitting before or after Eddie Murray or Cal Ripken. Their presence would guarantee Thornton some good pitches to hit; he hasn't seen too many in Cleveland.

Nonetheless, Thornton would like to return to the Indians despite the chaos of the front office and the team's unwillingness to make him a legitimate offer. But Thornton wants more than cash and a long-term contract.

"I would like to have a role with the club that extends beyond my playing days," he says. "I'd like to be a part of the organization."

Thornton has been with the Indians since 1977. He missed all 1980 and most of 1981 with various injuries. In his six healthy seasons, he's averaged 28 homers and 91 RBI. He was 35 at the end of 1984, but serving as the designated hitter enabled Thornton to play virtually every day without suffering from fatigue.

"The decision about where I play will be based primarily on business," notes Thornton. "I'll talk it over with my wife and see what is best for us. Everybody is a little apprehensive about making a change, but we'll go wherever God leads us."

From most players, the words about God would be hollow. But Thornton is not like most players.

He doesn't drink, or swear, or smoke, or party on the road. On the field, he is one of the boys. Away from it, he is his own man.

"I want to be recognized as a Christian," he has said. "But too many people think you can't be a good man and be a success. Or they think you can't be a moral man and be aggressive. You can't be a hard-nosed player and pray, too. I may not have that macho-type attitude some people think winners must have, but I run the bases well. I slide hard. I want to win badly. I am aggressive on the field. I just don't have the old Vince Lombardi stereotype."

In professional sports, players who have publicly declared themselves born-again Christians have often been viewed with disdain by other athletes. Supposedly, some use God as a cop-out, an excuse for every error and every strikeout—"It's God's will I dropped that throw." Supposedly, Christian players won't crash into a pivoting second baseman to break up a double play because someone could be injured. Supposedly, Christian players approach major-league baseball as if it were a Sunday croquet match.

But then there is Andre Thornton. He is a successful man. He is a moral man. And he plays hard. He has the reputation as a tough athlete. He is a vicious base runner, a guy willing to risk his body to prevent a double play with a roll-block slide.

Thornton believes most fans do not understand him and his faith. They don't know the anger and frustration he has experienced. They don't know how desperately he wants to win. They don't know that he passionately loves baseball.

To know Thornton, you have to go all the way back to Tuskegee, Alabama, where Thornton was born in 1949.

"My father worked at Tuskegee Institute," Thornton recalls. "I came into this world at the college itself. You see, they didn't allow black people in the hospital back then."

Harold Thornton did manual labor around Tuskegee Institute. On weekends, he was a semi-professional baseball player.

"I traveled all around Alabama with him," said Thornton. "My dad played for the black team which represented Tuskegee. On Fridays and Saturdays, they would have games with teams from other towns. I remember that there would always be big fish fries after the games. It was nice. Right after I was born, my father was asked to go to spring training in Florida and try out for a major-league team. There were no promises and even if he was signed to a minor-league contract, the money would be very bad. He had family responsibilities, so he didn't go. My mother told me that story a few years ago."

Thornton's mother worked in a Tuskegee general store. The owner also owned the team for which Harold Thornton played. But life in the deep South during the early 1950s was not promising for the Thorntons. In 1955, they moved to Phoenixville, Pennsylvania.

"I was pretty young and I don't know every reason behind our coming North," said Thornton. "I believe one of the factors was better opportunities for a black family in the Philadelphia area. Also, my older brother had just died because of water on the brain and that was a real shock. I think they hoped a change of scene would help everyone."

Phoenixville, where Thornton's father worked as a machinist, is a town of 15,000 located about 30 miles from Philadelphia, 10 minutes from Valley Forge.

"We were not well off," said Thornton. "But we never went

hungry or without the necessities of life. My father worked very hard. His only vice was a drinking problem. He is a good man, but he has been a drinker all his life. To this day, I am thankful for my parents' attention and love. I had three brothers and three sisters. My parents still live in Phoenixville and they did a great job for us."

In Phoenixville, the Thorntons did encounter some of the racial problems they thought they would leave behind in Alabama. On the street where they lived about 75% of the families were Black Muslims.

"I always knew about the white man's world and I learned about the Muslim faith," said Thornton. "I have been exposed to a lot. They tell you everything is equal, but it just isn't."

An incident when he was 11 first brought this to Thornton's attention.

"I was always a good athlete. Right after we moved to Phoenixville, I played Little League baseball. I was supposed to be nine to play, but I was actually seven. Since my birth certificate was back in Alabama, I said I was nine and they had no way to check. Baseball was all right for me as a kid. We had a manager named Samuel Griffith, a great guy. He was a close friend to me while I was growing up.

"Basketball was another story. When I was 11, I played on a team of kids that was among the top 20 in the country. We went to a tournament in Gary, Indiana. We had a white kid who was supposed to be the star, but I was the player they picked for the All-American team.

"We didn't win the tournament, and I remember the coaches wouldn't even let us stay for the banquet where I was supposed to get my award. I had to run in before, pick it up, and then we were on the bus back home. When we got home, there was an article in the paper, a real small story. At the bottom, almost like an afterthought, it said, 'and Andre Thornton was named an All-American.' I don't know why, but that really hurt me. I don't know what I expected, but it was more than that. I don't know if it was because the white kid didn't get the award or what. It was just one of those things you remember.

"As a teenager, I went through a rebellious stage. I was kicked out of school for a while for smoking. The cops picked me up a couple of times for fighting, but that was no big deal. I used to hang around the pool hall. I would play 14–16 hours a day. I made all my lunch money there. I made the money to buy my class ring from shooting pool. I made money to buy clothes. The pool hall was near an army base and the owner and I had a deal. He would let me play for nothing and I would cut him in on what I won. I did pretty well because the soldiers thought they could play. I would look for guys who thought they were sharks. You can win big against guys like that. I was a good player. I could run 80–82 balls in straight pool.

"In high school, football was the only thing which meant something to me. I felt I was a top college prospect. I had the size and the strength to do very well. I also had the determination and the attitude to be a fine player.

"Growing up in the 1960s was a tough time for me. I felt so much rage, so much hatred. In football, I took all of that out. I could really hit people. A lot of things were going on. Vietnam had heated up, and I saw friends coming back maimed and with missing limbs. The streets were angry. In my own life, I lost three close friends. When I was 12, one of them drowned. When I was 13, another was killed in a shooting. When I was 17, a very close friend named Marshall was stabbed by his new wife. I knew Marshall and his wife very well. I took all of this out on the opponents on the football field.

"I was still playing baseball. At 15, I played in the Babe Ruth World Series. An Orioles scout talked to me then and told me I had a chance to be a professional baseball player. But I thought football would be it for me."

After Thornton's senior year in high school, he was invited to a baseball tryout by the Philadelphia Phillies at Connie Mack Stadium. It was the summer of 1967.

"I batted against (Philadelphia pitching coach) Larry Shepard and hit a bunch of balls out of the park. I was not taken in the June amateur baseball draft, but the Phillies liked what they saw that day.

"The day I signed with the Philadelphia Phillies, the scout found me in the pool hall. He was a nice man, John Ogden, who was about 72 at the time. When he came to see me that day, I was in the middle of a game of nine-ball, playing for a $300 pot.

"When Mr. Ogden visited me, I knew that the Phillies wanted to sign me. He offered me a good bonus and they promised to pay for my college education. I was considering taking a college football scholarship, but the Phillies changed my mind."

At 17, Thornton ventured to Huron, South Dakota, to begin the climb up the major-league ladder in the Class A Northern League.

"Going from the Philadelphia area to South Dakota was a culture shock," said Thornton. "There weren't any blacks in Huron except on the baseball team. I lived in a house with five players. We rented it and slept in the basement."

When the 1967 baseball season ended, Thornton was sent by the Phillies to their winter Instructional League team, a squad composed of their most promising young players. At the end of that season, he entered the National Guard and was stationed at Fort Dix.

"The army is where I found Christ," said Thornton. "I had seen baseball. I had seen the streets. I was watching the result of the senseless killing going on in Vietnam. They tell you to work hard and you'll get a piece of the American Pie. They tell you things are equal. Well, I grew up knowing none of that was true. Reality was a cold place. Several times, I had been in the depths of despair. None of it made any sense.

"My mother had always been a strong Christian. I looked at her life. She handled things so well. She was at peace. I started to read the Bible just as she had been trying to get me to do. I was like a man in the desert who saw someone with a glass of water. If I didn't drink that water, I would die, and that water came from Christ. I have been often close to death. I know the problems of life, the frustrations, the hypocrisy. People tell me I am too serious. Sure, I am serious. Life is a pretty serious business."

Baseball has not been easy for Thornton. He has been traded five times in six years and on the disabled list on six occasions.

Thornton never played in the majors with Philadelphia. He was swapped from the Phillies' Class AAA Eugene team to Atlanta in 1972. The Braves then assigned him to Class AAA Richmond. The following spring, Thornton had a place on the Atlanta roster until he broke a leg in the final week of training. That was the first of several injuries which would haunt his career.

So it was back to the bushes for Thornton. He never made it to the majors with Atlanta, either. In 1973, the Braves dealt him to the Chicago Cubs for Joe Pepitone. Thornton moved from Richmond to the Cubs' Class AAA Wichita team. In September 1973 he was promoted to Chicago and hit .200 in 35 at bats.

From that point, Thornton remained in the big leagues. Staying healthy was another matter. In 1976, the Cubs swapped Thornton to the Montreal Expos for Steve Renko and Larry Biittner. Thornton was struck by a pitch and suffered a broken wrist. He played much of the season with a small cast on his left hand and batted only .194.

Cleveland Indians general manager Phil Seghi had long been a Thornton fan. In 1977, Thornton was a 6-foot-2, 205-pound first baseman. At 27, he was in his prime as a player. He needed two things, a chance to be in the lineup every day and good health. Before the 1977 season, Seghi obtained Thornton from Montreal for journeyman pitcher Jackie Brown. That stands as one of Seghi's best trades. Thornton has since become the ninth leading home run hitter in Indians' history. He was their cleanup hitter, the best player to fill that position since Rocky Colavito in the 1960s.

After the 1978 season, tragedy struck.

Two weeks after the season, the Thornton family left their suburban Cleveland home for West Chester, Pennsylvania, to attend the wedding of Andre's sister-in-law. That morning, they attended church and packed their van for the trip. Thornton checked the weather forecast. It called for rain and a chance of snow in the higher elevations. Thornton drove with his wife, Gertrude, sitting next to him holding their two-year-old daughter, and his four-year-old son in the back seat. As they hit the Pennsylvania Turnpike, the weather turned angry. Near the Somerset exit, the wind was stiff, the road icy, and it was snowing. Then a gust of wind caused Thornton to lose control of the van. Next thing he knew, the van had hit the ice and skidded off the road. Thornton fought the wheel, but the van went off the road, crashed through the guardrail and down a small hill. Thornton recalled hearing a scream, then silence, then he passed out.

Thornton regained consciousness outside the van. He had no idea how he had gotten there. He saw the van was upside down. He managed to open the door and found his son, Andy, buried under some suitcases. He was not hurt. Thornton could not see his wife or daughter. Soon, the police and an ambulance arrived. Clearly in a state of shock, Thornton was taken to a hospital. It was there he learned his son was fine, but his wife and daughter had died. Thornton's first words were to ask for a Bible and a minister.

"I won't kid you, that was a very tough time," said Thornton. "But I didn't look at this as a test of my faith. Instead, I felt the presence of God as I had never felt it before. This wasn't a time for me to reexamine my beliefs, but to become even closer to the Lord. I loved Gert. We met soon after that time in the army. We dated for a couple years and we were married for seven beautiful years. I have the greatest source of energy in the world in Christ. There are so many things that are out of my control. If I didn't have the Lord, I would be very bitter and hostile. But I don't have to be beaten down. I can go on.

"Look, people always tell you to think positive things and do your own thing and it all will work out. Well, what good does that do you when you are faced by death or faced by extreme depression? What happens when the world turns on you and you discover everything isn't how they said and things aren't what they are supposed to be? How do you deal with things that seem so unfair? Of course it is difficult to lose a loved one. But you must go on and God gives you the strength to do it. After Gert died, I prayed to the Lord to send me another wife, a good woman who would be the type of mother my son needed. I knew I couldn't find this woman. She would have to find me and she did. When one beautiful flower dies, another takes its place. That is how the Lord blessed me."

A year after his wife's death, Thornton married Gail Jones of Oberlin, the daughter of a minister.

In 1980, Thornton was confronted with another problem. During a spring training game, his knee buckled and he damaged more cartilage. He had surgery and was supposed to be sidelined for two months. Thornton pushed himself to the limit to cut his recovery period and to strengthen the knee. But he knew something was wrong. He told the Indians that his knee was not healing properly. The front office did not believe him, they placed him on the active roster and he made it as far as the on-deck circle in one game as a pinch hitter.

Thornton continued to complain about the knee. Finally, it was examined and the doctors found that the original surgery had missed some of the damaged cartilage. He had another operation and never played in 1980.

The agony over his knee is still a sore spot to Thornton. He will say little about it, but he was upset by the whispers which came from the Indians front office. Many hinted that Thornton was a malingerer who did not want to play. His attitude and integrity were attacked.

"I have given everything I have to the Indians and the city of Cleveland," said Thornton. "I'm not ashamed of anything. I always gave the Indians my full effort. It was not easy for me to forgive some of those things intimated about me. I didn't want to forgive them, but I had to or it would fester inside me."

Thornton toiled over the winter on a stringent weight program to rebuild his knee. He went to spring training in 1981 in impeccable condition. But in the first exhibition game against the Taiyo

Whales of Japan, he was hit in the right hand by a pitch that broke his thumb, and he was back on the disabled list.

In May of 1981, he was reactivated and had three hot weeks. During most of that period, the Indians were in first place. Then came the baseball strike. When baseball resumed in August, Thornton played three weeks before he suffered another injury. This time, it was stretched ligaments in his thumb and he sustained it while halting a brawl on the field between the Tribe and Angels. He was hurt pulling California slugger Don Baylor away from pitcher Rick Waits. That produced another term on the disabled list.

He was healthy once again in spring 1982, but did not homer in six weeks of games in Arizona. Manager Dave Garcia was thrilled to have Thornton back in the lineup and announced, "Thornton will bat cleanup and be our designated hitter for all 162 games this year." During Thornton's absence, Garcia had employed eight players in Thornton's number-four spot in the batting order.

On opening day, Thornton was booed before the first pitch of the season. The fans wanted Joe Charboneau in the lineup and Thornton on the bench. The hoots stung Thornton, but he did not complain.

"This is not the first time it has happened to me," said Thornton. "I know Joe Charboneau is a very popular player. On that day, it was subtle. There were innuendos. It came to Joe and me and I don't have Joe's kind of popularity. It wasn't Joe's fault. The media led the fans to believe some things, but it bothered me because I had given my all to the Indians and the community. It wasn't fair, but it is part of the business."

Thornton went 0-for-8 in Cleveland's first two games. The booing continued. In the third game of the year, he homered twice, and three weeks later he was batting .300 and was near the top of the American League in home runs and RBI.

"I have been through a lot worse than being booed," he said then. "But I do feel the Lord lifted me up and vindicated me this season."

His steel-like fundamentalist faith not only carried him through a series of trials; it has caused Thornton to speak out about issues many players avoid, whether the target is the players, the front office, or the state of baseball in Cleveland.

In 1980, a *Cleveland Plain Dealer* story about drug use in baseball quoted an unidentified baseball executive as saying, "I know this is going to sound racist, but it is a general rule that teams with a high concentration of black or Latin players run higher risks of a drug problem."

Thornton blasted the charge that minority players were often at the root of baseball's drug problems. He said that baseball wanted to ignore its drug problem, but "there are drugs on every team and they cut across all racial lines. Usually, baseball doesn't want to do anything about it until it is too late. They don't worry about what a player is doing to himself as long as he is producing. When he stops producing, they turn their backs on him."

In 1981, Thornton said the Indians and the media had built Joe Charboneau into a myth. "People in Cleveland have been waiting for a savior, a kind of big bird who will swoop down and lift up the baseball team," said Thornton. "They wanted Charboneau to be the guy. They called him Super Joe. It wasn't fair to him. It caused too much pressure for anyone to handle."

Thornton also said the Indians' front office lacked a plan. One year, the team was to be based on a strong pitching staff. The next year, it was centered around hitting. Hitters were traded for pitchers and then pitchers were traded for hitters depending upon the latest grand scheme.

"The problems of the team go back 25 years," said Thornton. "People talk about 1954 since it was the last time Cleveland won a pennant. Well, 1954 is long gone. You can't live in the past. They say wait until the Indians win again. The fans will turn out. The boos will stop. Winning cures everything. Of course winning is important, but other things can be done to help this situation. No one has worked harder to make the Indians a winner. I have taken this organization into my heart. I have pride in the Indians and I want to work here. That is not true of all players. But the team needs more stability and pride from the top.

"Maybe a player is not supposed to have a right to say something like this, but it needs to be said. This team needs a vision. It begins with the stadium.

"Something must be done to make baseball in this town an attractive package. The team itself is just part of that package. It is important, but not everything. The stadium is a dull old park. There is no music, no life. We have the worst facility in baseball to play in. I ask myself: 'If I was a fan, would I take my family to a baseball game?' Sure, I would if the team was winning or if there was a special event. But on an ordinary night with a losing team, I don't know. I have enjoyed playing for Cleveland and we have 5,000 to 7,000 of the best fans in the world. When I tip my hat after a homer, it is to them. They are great people. But the rest who come on opening day or to see the Yankees, well, they aren't your real fans.

"The ballpark and the field have made us the laughingstock of baseball. We have a poor image, an image as the worst situation in the majors. The whole organization needs a good dose of pride.

"We need one man with one vision. A team can't have 50 visions or 10 visions. We need to build pride throughout the organization. Teams like the Baltimore Orioles and Los Angeles Dodgers have it. Even the Browns have it. Correcting the externals doesn't solve everything, but it helps create a winning and positive attitude. It makes you feel good about going to the stadium, or good about playing or rooting for the Indians.

"A winner just doesn't happen overnight. You have to find players who will put the team before their own statistics. They must have character. People say you can have a team that fights like the old Oakland A's and still win. Well, the A's had the character I am talking about. They displayed it on the field. There, they had no jealousy. They didn't quit. They had the pride we need to develop here."

Re-signing Andre Thornton won't guarantee the development of that kind of pride. But failing to sign him just might make it impossible. "The Indians are in a situation where even if they improve dramatically, they are not going to be one of the top two or three contenders in the league. Yet, they are asking me to concede three or four years of my playing career with them. When they ask me to give up so much, I want to feel that the organization is truly mine. I want to be a part of it, to have the kind of job with the Indians that Sal Bando has with Milwaukee," says Thornton.

Bando is a special assistant to Milwaukee general manager Harry Dalton. Bando does some on-the-field coaching, some scouting, and takes part in organizational decisions.

"If I stay in baseball after I'm finished playing, I would look forward down the road to running a team from a general manager's standpoint," says Thornton. "So I want the opportunity to become an apprentice in that area with Cleveland. I feel I know the personnel on this club as well or better than anyone. I think I have things I can offer Cleveland even after I'm finished playing.

"As for signing with Cleveland, one of the biggest things is where the franchise is going and how soon they will get there. The ownership problem clouds things even more."

Most people are surprised by Thornton's wish to remain in baseball. Most believed he would devote full time to his Christian ministry after he retired. A few years ago, Thornton considered leaving baseball for the ministry. The hedonistic life style of many players appalled him. Cynics would claim that money kept Thornton from quitting. But Thornton said being a ballplayer gave him a forum from which he could spread Christ's word. He is interviewed on a regular basis with millions of people reading his message in newspapers and hearing it on television and on the radio.

He knows and loves the game of baseball. And he believes that he has been given little credit for his baseball knowledge. For years, he was the silent slugger, a bat in one hand and a cross in the other. But Thornton never shrugs off a question. Instead, he usually is so candid that it surprises reporters who are accustomed to players programed to say nothing in 1,000 words or more.

Thornton also has theories about how the game should be played and what a front office ought to do. He has been with the Indians since 1977 and believes they have been poorly run.

At the same time, he has no intention of giving up his ministry. Along with brother-in-law and former big-league player Pat Kelly, Thornton formed the Family Outreach Center in 1980. The Center has run summer camps for Cleveland's inner-city children ("We take 100 kids off the street and another 100 come to us from the churches," said Thornton. "We try to give them a foundation of Christian values and show them there is more to life than the street."); paid the tuition of seminary students; and helped pay for the radio broadcast of "The Hour of Freedom."

"There are people in the Indians clubhouse and everywhere else who have no idea what is going on in the world," says Thornton. "Our organization started as a dream. A lot has happened, but so much more needs to be done. I would like to have a year-round camp for problem kids, kids who have had trouble with the law. I'm worried about the family, especially the breakdown of the black family. We need to return to basic values. So many people minister to those living in the suburbs and those with money. The inner city is crying for help. And you must do more than deal with the spiritual needs of city people. They need material help and we are doing what we can."

Thornton is a dedicated and ambitious man, one who worries about the state of the Indians and the poor at the same time. Perhaps that is why most baseball people can't understand him.

The Winter Meetings

November 26

ATLANTA—Bob Horner has returned here for another examination; he hopes that the small cast on his wrist will be removed for good. But when Dr. Wells removes the cast and examines the wrist, he grows concerned. As he explains to Horner, there appears to be an "increased density" in the navicular bone. This, Horner is told, is abnormal, leads to limited flexibility, and affects the blood flow to the wrist. Since the quickness and flexibility of Horner's right wrist is essential to his productivity as a baseball player, Horner knows this is very bad news.

Wells suggests that Horner see several specialists around the country before a firm determination is made about what to do next. But the surgery that was ruled out five weeks earlier now looms in the future; the 1985 season has become very much a question mark. "I just can't believe it," Horner says.

"Obviously, if we find out we won't have Horner, we'll have to rethink our plans for the offseason," John Mullen says. But for now, the Braves can only wait and see what other doctors will tell them.

PHILADELPHIA—It is time for one last roundup of ideas before the Phillies descend upon Houston for what they hope will be an active week of dealing.

Bill Giles quickly reaffirms what everyone else knew. The club's top target will be a relief pitcher of solid caliber. They are willing to relinquish shortstop Ivan DeJesus and lower-echelon farm prospects. They'll talk about Bo Diaz, but won't get serious about trading him unless the offer is too good to refuse.

And Giles adds one other bit of instruction. He wants to get rid of Al Oliver at any cost. He'll give him away to any club interested. And Giles tells his staff half-jokingly, "Anyone who is able to swing a deal to get rid of Oliver will get a free trip to Paris."

Giles also makes it clear who will be orchestrating trade discussions. Paul Owens, back in the wheeling-dealing saddle he enjoyed more than any other role, will work with Hugh Alexander as the main negotiators.

On the surface, it represents an almost miraculous return to grace for Owens, who was deposed as manager just seven weeks ago. And Owens enjoys returning to the limelight. "I love that wheeling and dealing; it feels great to be back because I missed it the last couple of years," he says.

However, there is a somewhat cynical side to Giles's decision. For nearly three years, Giles has taken all the heat for whatever move the Phillies made. He was the eye of the storm throughout controversy after controversy, ripped to shreds by talk show zealots and questioned with intensity by ink-stained reporters.

Giles is tired of being the one to take the blame. By putting Owens on the frontline, he not only assuages Owens and takes advantage of Owens's decades worth of trade experience, but he ensures that he will not be the only person in the line of fire. Misery loves company.

November 27

ATLANTA—The Braves' original offer to Bruce Sutter of a five-year, $7.5 million contract has been on the table for more than week, and the Braves are ready to take the next step. Without changing the current dollar value of the contract, the Braves propose an elaborate scheme of deferred payments that would bring

Sutter close to $40 million, including interest, over the next 36 years. Sutter's agents have expressed interest in deferred payments, so this moves the Braves significantly closer to an accord.

"But I wouldn't say anything is close to happening; these things take time," Mullen warns. And the Braves still have the impression that Sutter truly prefers to remain in St. Louis and will sign with the Braves only if the Cardinals refuse to approach his market value—as set by Ted Turner.

Meanwhile, the Braves appear to have forgotten about the other three free agent pitchers on their shopping list. They have told agents for Trout and Whitson that there is no point in negotiating until the Sutter and Sutcliffe chases are completed. They tell Sutcliffe's agent, Barry Axelrod, to give them a call when the negotiating heats up. Their attention is focused on Sutter.

November 29

CLEVELAND—The Indians finally have a chief. Peter Bavasi is named the team's president and chief operating officer. Or, as Gabe Paul explains, "The buck will stop with Peter Bavasi."

A former president of the Toronto Blue Jays, Bavasi is a salesman first and a baseball man second. He has a quick smile, some fast jokes, and a firm handshake. He is friendly all the time, never tired, never moody, never anything but full speed ahead. He gives you the feeling that he plans to run the Indians and maybe sell a few used cars on the side.

If nothing else, the Indians went for an old-line baseball name. Peter's father is Buzzie Bavasi, who is so old-line baseball that he once worked in the Brooklyn Dodgers front office. Peter worked for his father in the farm departments of the Dodgers and Padres. Gabe Paul and Buzzie Bavasi were foxhole buddies in the baseball wars. They used to speak almost daily about trades, but seldom made one, as if they knew each other too well. Paul suggested Peter Bavasi as his replacement, and Pat O'Neill was very receptive.

But it was Dave LeFevre who put the final okay on Bavasi,

lending further credence to the theory that LeFevre will buy Paul's stock and once again make a bid to purchase the rest of the team. If LeFevre were indeed out of the picture, why would he be interviewing the team's president?

"I met with Dave LeFevre and I have the feeling I got his stamp of approval before I got the job," says Bavasi.

Bavasi, it will be revealed later, has been given a unique four-year contract that pays him $125,000 annually. Each year, it automatically renews itself. Therefore, every year Bavasi is in the first year of a four-year deal. "My contract is seldom seen in sports, but it is common in industry," Bavasi says. "If the team is sold and the new ownership doesn't want me, it will cost them plenty." All the more reason for the ownership-in-waiting to be involved in the hiring process.

At his first public appearance, Bavasi pulls out all the sentimental stops. He holds up a T-shirt that reads, "Proud to be a Cleveland Indian." He invokes the magical name of Bill Veeck, who owned the Indians in 1948 when they won the World Series and set a single season attendance record.

"I called up Bill and asked him if it could happen again in Cleveland," says Bavasi. "He told me, 'Peter, the world has changed a lot since 1948, but baseball hasn't and neither has Cleveland. The fans of Cleveland are just waiting for something good to happen.' My goal is to bring back some of that old luster, that's why I talked to the man who had made it work. Bill said, 'Go to it, boy. All your club needs is a couple of pitchers.' That's why I consider Cleveland the most exciting challenge in baseball today."

But what the Indians need isn't Veeck's advice; they need his pitchers. Veeck had Bob Feller, Bob Lemon, Mike Garcia, and Early Wynn. Bavasi has Bert Blyleven and a bunch of guys like Roy Smith and Jamie Easterly.

Actually, Bavasi says he will not be in charge of the talent end of the operation. "Phil Seghi will be in charge of player personnel," Bavasi insists.

Bavasi may come from a legendary baseball family, but he admits the need for a baseball man. He takes an almost perverse delight in telling the story of how he cost the Toronto Blue Jays a chance to deal for Ron Guidry. Blue Jay general manager Pat Gillick had worked out a trade in which Toronto would send a washed-up Bill Singer to the Yankees for a minor-league pitcher named Guidry.

Bavasi didn't like the deal for two reasons. First, he had never heard of Guidry. But more importantly, Bavasi had Singer's picture on the front of the media guide. How would it look for Toronto to trade its cover-boy Singer for a bush league lefty? Bavasi vetoed the deal and has regretted it ever since.

"It taught me to listen to my baseball people," says Bavasi.

But Pat O'Neill explains that he will be in charge of everything. "Final say on all matters rests with the board of directors," says O'Neill, who is chairman of the board. "My purpose for the board having final approval is that I don't want Peter overruling Phil Seghi about players and I don't want Phil trying to outmaneuver Peter on the business end."

According to O'Neill, Seghi and Bavasi are supposed to be on equal ground but no one believes it. Listen to this quote from Bavasi: "Our first goal is to get two starting pitchers, but that's Phil Seghi's job."

It might indeed be Phil Seghi's job, but only because Peter Bavasi—and, for now, Pat O'Neill—says so.

November 30

DALLAS—One of the foremost specialists on the surgery contemplated for Bob Horner is based in Dallas, Dr. Peter Carter. Horner and his agent, Bucky Woy, drive from their Dallas homes to Carter's office for an examination and opinion on the multi-million dollar wrist. Carter tells Horner that, in his opinion, surgery is necessary, that there is no practical alternative if Horner wants to continue a baseball career. He outlines two types of surgery: a conventional bone graft in which some bone is taken from Horner's hip and grafted in his wrist, or a more recent, more revolutionary procedure in which a screw is implanted in the bone after the graft.

The Braves and Horner want further opinions before committing to a course of action. It is decided that Horner will travel to Houston the following week for examinations by two of baseball's foremost team physicians, Dr. Frank Jobe of Los Angeles and Dr. Arthur Pappas of Boston. They are to be in Houston for a sports medicine seminar as part of the winter meetings.

December 1

HOUSTON—Owens and Alexander decided to arrive at the meetings early to get a head start on their talks. And in the course of two days and nights (especially nights, for "The Pope and Uncle Hughie Show" was a cocktail lounge production), they touched base with over a dozen different clubs.

They quickly found out that while there is the possibility of making a deal, it won't come easy. They found clubs still formulating their off-season plans, clubs uninterested in what the Phillies were offering or only interested in untouchable prospects, and clubs without pitching to spare. And they found clubs paralyzed with indecision.

But as Alexander said later, "We at least got an idea about who was compatible with us so that we wouldn't have to waste time later. Pope and I didn't come down early just to have fun."

Not surprisingly, the Phillies find out that Montreal looms as their best possibility. The Expos need a shortstop, have interest in DeJesus, and have some surplus pitching to offer. Of their available pitchers, two interest the Phillies: Bob James and Bryn Smith. It seems apparent that if the Phils swing a deal quickly, it will be with Montreal.

The Braves' thinking is in disarray. A month ago, they thought they would come here shopping Donnie Moore or Jeff Dedmon for Bo Diaz; shopping Ken Oberkfell for a left-handed relief pitcher; and maybe listening to offers for minor-league shortstop Paul Zuvella. Nothing major.

But with Horner's status now unclear and the Sutter negotiations reaching a make-or-break point, the Braves have no idea what to do at these meetings. With Horner a question mark, they can't trade Oberkfell, and it might not be such a good idea to part with Zuvella. As for Diaz, the Braves have heard that the Phillies are having serious second thoughts about trading him.

As they assemble in Mullen's hotel suite on the eve of the meetings, the Braves' brain trust agrees their first priority remains a catcher who can throw runners out and provide some offensive punch. If they aren't able to get Diaz, they agree to look elsewhere. They'll approach the A's about Mike Heath and the Yankees about Rick Cerone. And they'll reassess further priorities tomorrow, after Horner arrives and is examined by Drs. Jobe and Pappas.

December 2

HOUSTON—The lobby of the Houston Hyatt is enormous and features a bar in the middle. For five days, it will serve as a magnet for the traders at the winter meetings. Jack McKeon, Paul Owens, and other uninhibited swappers will congregate there, and the talk—and the bar—will keep them there for hours.

It repels Frank Cashen. The lobby is far too visible a setting for the Mets' type of low-key trade talk. Too much noise. Can't whisper. Too many people. Can't be discreet.

Cashen's public mood is anything but hopeful when he arrives at the meetings. He assumes his annual public posture, speaking pessimistically, noting how difficult trading has become in the era of long-term contracts and no-trade clauses. Other business, he says, preoccupies some baseball executives, and with so few of the re-entry free agents signed, general managers are uncertain of their direction.

Other general managers don't see so many obstacles. "If you want to get a player, you can always find a way to do it," Padres general manager Jack McKeon says. "If you want to trade, trade."

Cashen's pessimism is intended to mislead other clubs and the media into believing the Mets will make few or no trades. "Fanfare doesn't help make trades," he says.

Others in the organization are instructed to talk discreetly if they talk at all.

Back in December, 1981, one member of the organization allowed the startling news to escape the Mets' inner circle that they were interested in selecting pitcher Curt Kaufman from the Yankees in the minor-league draft. Cashen scolded the informant.

The password for the Mets is "Shhh."

The Braves send their men into the hotel lobby, into the coffee shop, into the bars, and into the league meetings—listening and talking. From his two-room suite on the 17th floor, Mullen directs the operation. He dispatches Paul Snyder, the director of scouting; Henry Aaron, the director of player development; Rod Gilbreath, the assistant director of scouting; Eddie Haas, the manager; and Bill Wight, a respected scout, to listen and report. At the end of each day, these men reconvene in Mullen's suite.

At the end of day one, this is the report: Indeed, Philadelphia has taken Diaz off the market. Oakland is receptive to dealing Heath, but the A's are on a major build-with-youth program and would demand a couple of the Braves' finer prospects. Snyder and Aaron resist this idea, and Haas doesn't know much about Heath, anyway.

The Yankees, Snyder has learned through New York executive Woody Woodward, are more than willing—eager was the word—to deal Cerone. Already, the Yankees have given the Braves a list of three minor leaguers whom they would take for Cerone: right-handed pitchers Dwayne Ward and Brian Fisher, and second baseman Miguel Sosa. The Braves' brass quickly and firmly tab Ward an untouchable; they think he can be the ace of the big-league staff in a few years. Sosa or Fisher? Sosa is a second baseman with power, and the Braves think he has a future in the big leagues, maybe even as an outfielder if Glenn Hubbard continues to occupy second base. Fisher?

Two years ago, the Braves were very high on him, but his standing has slipped. They'd rather keep him, but no one in Mullen's suite feels that giving him up would be catastrophic. And so, it is decided. If the Yankees are still willing the next day, and if Ted Turner gives his approval by phone from a cable-television convention in Anaheim, California, the Braves' first winter meetings trade of this decade will be consummated: Brian Fisher for Rick Cerone.

Bill Giles arrives and convenes a meeting of the Phillies brass in his 21st-floor suite. Included in the meeting are five scouts brought in for the meetings for extra input, as well as the usual suspects.

The evening's main topic is tomorrow morning's major-league selection draft. One of the winter meetings' annual events is the draft at which players either dropped from the major-league roster or eligible to be on the roster but not included are available to be selected by other clubs. There are annually no more than a dozen selections in their bargain-basement procedure, but there are often prizes culled from the endless lists of no-names.

And the Phillies have been burned in the draft before. They still wince at how they tried to sneak outfielder George Bell through the draft a few years ago, only to see Toronto select him and see Bell become one of the leading hitters in the American League.

This year, the Phillies are most concerned about losing Kiko Garcia. They have heard through the grapevine that Kansas City will almost certainly select him. Felske, for one, doesn't like the idea of losing Garcia; he saw firsthand on the Phillies bench how valuable Garcia was as an uncomplaining, versatile spare player.

The Phillies are also interested in taking a left-hander named Ed Olwine, who is the property of the New York Mets but was left exposed in the draft. Olwine is pitching for the Ponce club in Puerto Rico which is managed by Ron Clark, one of the Phillies' minor-league managers. Clark says Olwine has shown the ability to help the Phillies right away and is worth the gamble of a draft pick. The problem is that the Phillies' roster is at its 40-man limit. If they want Olwine, they have to make room.

The solution presents itself with the arrival of officials from the St. Louis Cardinals. Manager Whitey Herzog and general manager Joe McDonald had run into Alexander in the hotel lobby, and

Herzog quickly got down to business. He asked if the Phils were interested in infielder Tommy Herr, who had demanded a trade. The Phils weren't, but in the course of the conversation Herzog mentioned an interest in young Phillies catcher Mike Lavalliere. The light bulb went off in Alexander's mind and a meeting was quickly set up for later in the evening in Owens's suite.

McDonald and Herzog arrive for what, as is usual in the Phillies' suite, becomes a round of cocktails and talk. After increasingly muddled conversation ("When you deal with the Pope, you sometimes forget the next day what you decided the night before," said McDonald later), a deal is struck. Lavalliere will be sent to St. Louis for what will be announced as a player to be named later. That would drop the Phillies' roster to 39 men and enable them to select Olwine. Once the Phils are safely past the draft, they will make room on the roster for the Cardinals to send them right-handed pitcher Jeff Lahti. The Phillies believe they have made an excellent deal. Lahti is a proven middle reliever. By paying what they believe to be a small price in the unproven Lavalliere, they have obtained not only Lahti but the room with which to select Olwine.

December 3

HOUSTON—Around midmorning, Mullen reaches Turner in California. "How's it going?" Ted wants to know. "Anything new with Sutter? What about Horner's wrist?"

Horner will be examined later in the day by Drs. Jobe and Pappas, Turner is told, but it doesn't look promising. Sutter's agents are here, Mullen says, and it appears clear-cut that the battle is down to the Braves and the Cardinals. Mullen tells Turner that it might be helpful if he could free himself from the cable convention for a day and fly here for a meeting with Sutter's agents; they'll probably make a decision this week. Turner says he'll try to get away, but tells Mullen, "I'm tied up here, and I don't think I can make it. What room are Sutter's agents in? I'll call 'em."

"Good," says Mullen, and then gets to the point of the call:

Fisher for Cerone? Turner is always reluctant to trade one of his players; he grows attached to them, even those he doesn't know very well, and hates to give them up. But this year, he is committed to giving his front office more freedom, and if they want to trade Fisher ("Isn't he a bright prospect, a potential star?") to the Yankees for Cerone ("Didn't he have a pretty good season a couple of years ago?") then so be it. Mullen tells Turner the deal will probably be announced later in the day.

Mullen then gets word to the Yankees that the Braves are willing to trade Fisher for Cerone. The Yankees, through their complicated front-office structure, must get final approval from owner George Steinbrenner. The Braves don't think this will be a problem, knowing Steinbrenner has wanted to unload Cerone for a couple of years, but they've had bad experiences trying to deal with the Yankees in the past.

This time, the deal will go off without a hitch, and an announcement will be made in time for the six o'clock news shows. "I think getting away from New York and to Atlanta, Rick Cerone will benefit greatly," Mullen says.

They don't say this publicly, but privately the Braves feel Cerone has a 15-homer, 70-RBI season in him. There is a problem, though. The Braves now have three catchers earning around $600,000 per season each: Bruce Benedict, the starter for most of the last five years; Alex Trevino, who supplanted Benedict in the second half of 1984; and Cerone. The Braves project Cerone as their No. 1 catcher; they wouldn't have traded a strong, young pitcher for another backup catcher. Sometime in the days, weeks, or months ahead, the Braves will have to trade a catcher; Haas and the front-office people agree it should be Benedict.

The Mets regard other clubs' interest in their minor-league personnel as a compliment. But the fact that the other clubs select four players from the Mets organization in today's minor-league draft prompts Cashen to say he feels violated. "Bittersweet feelings," he says.

As expected, infielder Brian Giles is taken by the Brewers.

Catcher Junior Ortiz, who had come in a trade from the Pirates in June, 1983, is taken back by the Pirates. The Phillies select left-handed reliever Ed Olwine. And the Blue Jays surprise and, to some degree, annoy the Mets by selecting Louis Thornton, a 21-year-old outfielder who has never played higher than Class A.

It's not as though the Mets hadn't anticipated a raid. In a pool among club officials, one had predicted seven players would be drafted. "Four is bad enough," Cashen says. "When you've won the Organization of the Year [award] two years in a row, the predators will descend." They had descended the year before as well, with the Phillies selecting Jay Tibbs and the Athletics taking Jeff Bettendorf. But each had been returned after failing to make the 25-man regular-season roster.

"We didn't get hit quite as hard as we thought we might," minor-league director Steve Schryver says. "We expected Bambi [former Mets manager George Bamberger] would take Giles, the Pirates would take Junior, and the Phillies might take Olwine. We weren't happy to lose them, but it didn't hurt that much. But no one expected anyone to take Thornton. I don't see how Toronto can carry him all year, not when they have a chance to win it."

The Blue Jays had followed the same procedure with four other players in the past, most profitably with Willie Upshaw and George Bell. In each case, the player spent a full season with the Jays and then was optioned to the minor leagues.

"They were a growing organization then," Cashen says. "They could afford it then. Now they have a different posture. It will strain them." Wishful thinking, anyone?

By 8 A.M. the Lavalliere deal had officially been announced and the Phillies' selection of Olwine was announced at 9:45. The Phillies thus felt they had gotten their week off to a solid start.

Time once again for talking and negotiating what they hope will be their final deal to bring a proven pitcher to the club and end this phase of the club's off-season rebuilding. However, trades are easier discussed than actually done, especially at the winter meetings.

Years ago, before the days of free agents, multi-year contracts and complex salary structures, the winter meetings yielded deal after deal. But in recent years, the deals have come only in a trickle. So many players now have no-trade provisions or special clauses that trading at all times of the year has become more difficult. The free agent system serves to complicate things even more. With such pivotal players as Bruce Sutter, Rick Sutcliffe, Steve Trout, Don Aase, Andre Thornton, and others still unsigned as the week began, many teams' plans were on hold pending the resolution of those negotiations. And thus on hold were trade talks.

Also inhibiting winter meeting trades is a new trading period in the spring. Teams can trade within their own league basically year-round. However, to trade between the leagues without having waivers on players, the trade must be made during the winter meetings or, in recent years, from February 15–April 1. With this new trading period, teams can usually afford to go into spring training, look at the progress of injured players or young prospects, watch their team play for a couple of weeks, and then decide what trade moves to make. So the winter meetings, because of all these factors, tend to start slowly. The only action is usually early-week rumors.

Not surprisingly, the Phillies were instantly involved in a three-way blockbuster rumor that included (also not surprisingly) the San Diego Padres. Rumors involving the Padres and Phillies are as common as sunrises. The reasons are Alexander and McKeon, two old pals who love to make trades and love even more to talk about making trades. Even when they might not be able to deal with each other, they'll talk together and share notes, rumors, and names. And if one is having trouble trying to shake down another club, he'll go to his old pal Uncle Hughie or Trader Jack to explore the possibility of creating a three-way trade.

The rumor has surfaced that the Phils will package Ivan DeJesus and a minor-league prospect with a Padres package that would include pitcher Tim Lollar and infielder/outfielder Luis Salazar and send the collection to Montreal for third baseman Tim Wallach (who'd go to San Diego) and pitcher Bryn Smith (who'd go to Philadelphia). The trouble with that rumor was that while Alexander and McKeon loved the idea, Montreal didn't. It was shot down by midday.

Instead, Owens approached Montreal one-on-one and is hopeful on this day something can be worked out. The Phillies have touched base with a handful of clubs, but they feel confident about a deal with the Expos and do little else. The Phils will retreat to their nightly round of cocktails feeling good about the day. They got Olwine, they thought they had Lahti, they didn't end up losing Garcia (Kansas City backed off when they saw Garcia was guaranteed $200,000 for the season) and they are confident about obtaining a pitcher from Montreal.

But fortunes tend to shift hour by hour at the winter meetings, as the Phillies will ruefully discover.

The Mets initiate talks with several clubs and resume talks with others, notably the Expos. They make the first of what Cashen later estimates as 50 calls to the Expos to determine who must be included in a package for Gary Carter. "No matter what other trade possibilities I discuss, my mind is always on Carter . . . What a nice distraction," Cashen says.

But there are other possibilities to discuss. The Twins need a shortstop and a pitcher. They offer the Mets catcher Dave Engle and left-handed pitcher Brad Havens and inquire about Jose Oquendo and Tim Leary. The Brewers, aware of the Mets' lack of catching, mention the availability of Jim Sundberg and inquire about Leary and Ed Lynch. Bamberger always admired Lynch's resolve.

The Mets look to unload Danny Heep and speak with the Royals about Dane Iorg, who, like Heep, is a left-handed reserve but who is more of a contact hitter than Heep. The Royals want Ron Gardenhire, one of Dave Johnson's favorites.

At a clinic near the Houston Hyatt, Drs. Jobe and Pappas are examining Bob Horner's wrist. The Braves have heard so much bad news from doctors about Horner that they can only expect the worst again. They get it.

Both doctors say there is no question, no doubt whatsoever that Horner needs surgery. They concur with Dr. Carter's assessment of the options: the traditional bone graft or the bone graft and screw implant. The former would mean Horner would miss the whole 1985 season; the latter holds out hope he might be able to play some in 1985, but no one can say exactly when.

Horner says he will make the final decision on which type of operation to have, and indicates he'd prefer the screw implant procedure. For the moment, he is more dejected than contemplative. "What else can happen?" he asks.

The Braves' front office shares the sentiment. They meet late into the night in Mullen's suite, facing a 1985 season without Bob Horner. Haas and Aaron express tender hopes that youngsters Brad Komminsk and Gerald Perry might come into their own, filling the offensive void. But everyone, Haas and Aaron included, knows that this can't be taken for granted and that, if it failed to happen, the Braves would be a woeful offensive team. Something has to be done. Agreed. But what?

There are some power hitters being shopped around on the lobby floor. Boston, concerned that they may not be able to sign Jim Rice beyond the 1985 season, is still interested in trading him. Texas, hoping to fill several holes on its club, is willing to consider trading Larry Parrish, who just happens to be a former third baseman. Montreal, somewhat discreetly, is talking about dealing Gary Carter.

Braves' scouts have picked up on all of these things; the question is in which direction to go.

A typical winter meetings press conference. The featured speaker is Phil Seghi, general manager of the Cleveland Indians.

Q: "Phil, did you have any interesting meetings with other teams today?"

A: "You never know. You can't tell what the other guy is thinking."

Q: "How many teams did you talk to?"

A: "We always talk to a lot of teams."

Q: "Are you close to anything?"

A: "Never can tell. Sometimes you think you are and you're not. Other times, you think you don't have a chance and one word changes everything."

Q: "Who do the other teams want?"

A: "Our best players."

Q: "Who do you want?"

A: "Their best players."

Q: "Phil, did you talk to the Phillies?"

A: "We talked to a lot of teams."

At this point, Peter Bavasi jumps into the conversation. Even he can't stand listening to it any more.

"Well, Phil, did you talk to the Phillies?" asks Bavasi.

"We had a conversation," says Seghi.

"Whose name came up?" asks a writer, not expecting an answer. Whenever Seghi is asked what player he wants, Seghi says he couldn't afford to pay a $50,000 fine for tampering with another team's players. Seghi gives the tampering rule a broader interpretation than Richard Nixon gave executive privilege.

But this time, Seghi surprises everyone by saying, "Al Oliver was mentioned. If we can't retain Andre Thornton, Oliver is a possibility. But our priority is to keep Thornton."

Then Seghi sighs as if he has just sold some classified secrets to the Russians. The press conference is over.

December 4

HOUSTON—Forget Al Oliver. The Indians sign Andre Thornton. They did it the only way they could—by giving Thornton the exact contract he wanted.

It was 3:30 this afternoon when Thornton's agents, Alan and Randy Hendricks, presented the Indians and Tal Smith with their proposal. It was a last-ditch attempt by the Hendricks brothers to keep Thornton in Cleveland. They had another meeting to attend with Baltimore, and there were indications Orioles president Hank Peters would increase his three-year, $2.4 million offer for Thornton. Minnesota also wanted to talk with Thornton, and Texas had stepped out of the pack to show a sincere interest.

In other words, it was put up or kiss Andre Thornton goodbye time for the Tribe. Tal Smith said as much when he handed Thornton's proposal to Peter Bavasi.

The terms of the contract are steep: four years guaranteed with an annual salary of $400,000; a $100,000 signing bonus; and another $433,000 a year deferred money for fifteen years. Thornton will begin collecting the deferred payments in the year 2000, at which time they will be worth over $31 million because the money will be collecting 9.5% interest annually.

It is the same basic proposal the Hendricks brothers presented to Gabe Paul and Phil Seghi in the spring of 1984. But there is one difference—the original deal was $2.4 million for three years. Now, Thornton's agents have raised the ante another year and nearly $6 million. That's what it cost the Indians to wait.

"What we gave the Indians was a proposal in the form of a contract," says Randy Hendricks. "We didn't expect to hear from them so soon. But they came back and signed it. They didn't change a comma or a period."

Actually, this type of contract is a wise one for the Indians. Since the O'Neill family plans to sell the team by the end of the 1985 season, it will cost them only $500,000 for Thornton: the first year's salary and the signing bonus. The rest of the deal will be assumed by the new owners. The 15 years of deferred payments were the reason the Indians agreed to Thornton's seemingly excessive demands.

In other words, the Indians bought Andre Thornton for today while letting someone else pay for him tomorrow.

The day hasn't started out well for the Phillies. They are surprised by a report on a Philadelphia television station that John Russell, a blue-chip youngster ticketed for either first base or right field, will be undergoing knee surgery this week. A quick check of club medical personnel confirms the report. Though the surgery is a minor arthroscopic procedure for removal of a small bone spur that was the product of an old injury, the Phillies are still embarrassed they had known nothing about it.

Their mood isn't improved later when the Chicago Cubs, their bitter rival, roll in to announce a six-player trade with the Yankees that gains the Cubs a needed left-handed pitcher, Ray Fontenot. With the Phils mired in inactivity, it grates on their competitive nature to see Dallas Green, their old Philly crony, walk into Houston and engineer the meetings' first major trade.

The best the Phillies can come up with is what Owens is calling "a good feeling" that something will happen with Montreal. He says he will ready a fallback position in case things with the Expos don't work out, but that fallback won't include dealing Bo Diaz.

Montreal's executives have heard the Braves have reason to think Horner won't be available in 1985, and they are quick to pounce on the opening. Secretly, they have decided that Carter will be traded, and Carter has stipulated that he will go to only three teams: the Mets, the Braves, or the Dodgers. The Expos would like to deal with the Braves—not with the Mets because they are in the same division, not with the Dodgers because the Expos' needs seem to match better with the Braves' talent.

Murray Cook, the Expos' general manager, leaves a message for Mullen that he'd like to get together. They meet in Cook's suite. Cook tells Mullen that, if the right deal can be struck, Carter is available and has indicated he would play in Atlanta. Mullen asks, calmly, what Montreal is looking for. Cook decides to start high. You can have Carter, he tells Mullen, for Craig McMurtry, Steve Bedrosian, Bruce Benedict, and Milt Thompson. He has just mentioned two of the Braves' best pitchers, quite possibly their two most promising pitchers; a young outfielder with great promise; and a catcher who, although no longer in the Braves' plans, figures to have decent market value. Mullen does not laugh in Cook's face, but he deems the asking price far too high and decides there is no basis for further discussions.

The Braves never mention Carter again, and never inform Ted Turner of his availability.

The Braves are just as quick to dismiss the Red Sox' overtures about Rice. Months ago, the Red Sox had offered Rice to the Braves for Bedrosian and Brad Komminsk, and the Braves since have stamped "untouchable" labels on both players. They never make a counteroffer.

This leaves Parrish. Haas speaks highly and enthusiastically about Parrish, whom he remembers from Montreal. This would be a perfect fit; in losing Horner, the Braves have lost both their starting third baseman and one of their top two power hitters. In Parrish, they would be getting both commodities.

The Braves get word to the Rangers that they'd like to talk. The Rangers, also talking to several other teams about Parrish, propose a meeting the next morning.

Bill Giles gets more unsettling news. It looks impossible to deal Al Oliver. The Phillies' hopes had been heightened late the night before by interest shown in Oliver by Kansas City. But now the Royals have lost interest.

About the only apparent progress of the day comes out of a two-hour meeting between Tony Attanasio, Tony Siegle, and Phils finance overseer Jerry Clothier. The concept of extending Rawley's contract is seriously discussed amid a jovial mood. Attanasio has Siegle chortling for the rest of the night after delivering a series of jokes and stories that are largely the product of Attanasio's friendship with Dodgers manager Tommy Lasorda. But some business gets done and Attanasio feels encouraged, if for no other reason than the presence of Clothier. "You're the money man, I guess," says Attanasio. "So you guys got to be getting serious."

Both sides now believe a solution will be found that will keep Rawley in Philadelphia. Nothing is finalized, but things look good.

The same can't be said for the Phillies' trade prospects. A dinner meeting among the Phils advisors dissolves into a loud, profane argument over which minor-league prospects to offer Montreal in addition to DeJesus for Bryn Smith. There are a handful of prospects most Phillies people deem untouchable—Juan Samuel, Jeff Stone, John Russell, and Darren Daulton—but the argument starts over who else is in the group, particularly young third baseman Rick Schu. The argument gets more and more out of hand, and finally Owens lurches out of his seat and tries to act as peacemaker. But before he can say a word, Alexander thunders, "You say one wrong thing to me, Pope, and I'll take this one fist of mine and hit you with it, so help me I'll do it." Owens slumps back down as another Phillies policy meeting heads for the wee hours of the morning.

Throughout these and other sessions during the week, Felske has kept in the background. He is hardly a yes-man; he casts a strong presence, affixing an intense stare to whomever he is talking with. And Felske is under no illusions about the Phillies organization. Through his checkered career as a player, coach, and minor-league manager, Felske has worked for assorted kinds of franchises from Chicago to Milwaukee to Toronto. He is not wide-eyed about being the manager of the Philadelphia Phillies.

But he is also not stupid enough to think he would make himself heard in the loud, sometimes drunken sessions that often characterize the Phils' strategy sessions. He had privately been bothered during the season by Paul Owens's loud and profane sojourns into hotel bars. He isn't a prude, but Felske believes that when you're in public, you not only represent an organization but, more importantly in his mind, you represent yourself. And he has vowed not to make the spectacle of himself that some of the Phillies' legendary luminaries have a habit of making.

Felske also believes his advice or ideas are better offered in quiet one-on-one conversations with Giles, Baumer, or Siegle. He knows that while Owens is ostensibly running the show in Houston, the final decisions will be made, as always, by Giles. And he knows his ideas are basically in sync with Giles's.

Some people mistakenly take Felske's shadowy winter meeting presence as a sign of weakness. "I realized that I might have looked like I wasn't really part of things, that I was in the background," he later recalled. "But that was the way I wanted it. My job is manager and to manage the team given me. I'm not the guy making trades. And I wasn't going to try and give anyone the impression I was."

Felske had already shown his toughness behind the scenes in the weeks before he was officially hired. Giles discussed the possibility for several weeks before the decision was finally made. If Giles had expected Felske to blindly leap at the opportunity, he was mistaken. Felske had seen how veteran players went past Owens to Giles to express their unhappiness about the way the club was being handled. Felske had heard all the stories about how veterans had done a similar job on fired manager Pat Corrales in 1983. Felske knew he couldn't keep Giles from talking to his players. But he told Giles, when the managing job was finally offered, that the first time Giles second-guessed him, using a player's unhappiness as a reason, Felske would resign and tell the world why.

Such a stand might have cost Felske his shot at managing. But as he said, "If he couldn't hire me on those terms, then I wouldn't want the job. I love the idea of managing, I love the pressure, I love being the guy making the decisions. But I wasn't going to prostitute myself to get the job. And I wasn't going to take it knowing I'd have to wear a rear-view mirror."

So Felske will stand quietly by throughout the Phillies' week-long exercise in frustration. He watches, he listens, he laughs at the antics of Owens and Alexander. And he keeps much of his counsel to himself. He hopes a deal can be made. He hopes he won't have to open spring training with unhappy veterans like DeJesus and Oliver clouding the clubhouse atmosphere. But whatever team is presented to him, he will manage it in his own way.

More feedback from the lobby. It appears that everyone is overestimating the Mets' need for catching. The Mets are not about to deal two players for Dave Engle or Jim Sundberg. Frank Cashen surprises people with his optimism. "I'm fairly certain I'll make one trade by Friday," he says.

December 5

HOUSTON—The Yankees create the biggest splash of the week—an agreement with the Athletics to acquire Rickey Henderson. The Mets continue their quiet talks. There are brief discussions with the Expos about Carter; Cashen alerts other members of the organization to the possibility and, understandably this time, swears them to secrecy. The Expos, aware of the fuss that could develop in Montreal, have demanded the trade be handled with absolute discretion. Cashen appreciates their situation.

Speaking casually with reporters at the meetings, Pete Rose offers criticism of Carter, his teammate for four months.

" 'Kid' is the perfect name for him because he's never grown up," Rose says of the thirty-year-old catcher. "If he ever does, he'll be an awesome player."

At midmorning, John Mullen is on the phone to Ted Turner, still in California. Mullen tells Turner that he has the impression from Sutter's agents that the deal can be closed this week, that the Braves' revised contract offer is close enough to be finalized in one more session. The Braves' offer, which started at $7.5 million, has inched upward in subsequent negotiations. Sutter's agents have asked for a sixth year on the contract, and the Braves, without any reluctance, agreed. Sutter's agents proposed various ways of structuring the contract and the deferred compensation, and the Braves were agreeable to just about everything.

Turner, excited by how close the deal appears, decides to charter a plane from California to Houston. He will arrive the next morning and meet with Sutter's agents. The word begins to spread around the hotel that Sutter will sign with the Braves.

Meanwhile, the Braves talk further with the Rangers about Parrish. The Rangers mention the same name that everyone mentions in talking trade with the Braves—Steve Bedrosian. Untouchable, the Braves insist. But the Rangers have another proposal. They will consider trading Parrish to the Braves for shortstop Rafael Ramirez, catcher Bruce Benedict, and pitcher Craig McMurtry. Fine on Benedict, the Braves say. Maybe on McMurtry, the Braves concede privately later, but can they get the Rangers to take young reliever Jeff Dedmon instead? And no way on Ramirez, the Braves say, both publicly and privately. In a late afternoon meeting with the Rangers, the Braves propose a deal of Parrish for second baseman Glenn Hubbard, catcher Benedict, and reliever Dedmon. Texas, not deeming Hubbard and Dedmon adequate replacements for Ramirez and McMurtry, says no. General manager Tom Grieve tells reporters, "Unless they change their mind on who they're willing to give up, I don't see anything happening."

Privately, the Braves agree they will not deal Ramirez. But if they can make the deal by packaging Hubbard, Benedict, and McMurtry, well . . . maybe. Because the price is so high, the Braves want to wait until after Horner's surgery, scheduled for December 17, before acting.

The Phillies are still waiting for Montreal to make up its mind, and Paul Owens's patience is shot.

"I finally told them to make up their minds tonight, to let us know something tonight or so help me, I'll go out there and get a pitcher from someone else tomorrow," growls Owens.

Alexander sits nearby and adds, "And if we can't get a pitcher, we'll get our buddy Mr. McKeon to get one for us."

The Phillies are obviously sending a message to the Expos. But the Expos aren't impressed by the old-school ways of Alexander and Owens and go about their deliberate process. As it turns out, Montreal has been using the Phillies to bide their time and see what better deal they could make.

But today, the Phillies believe they're making their big push. And at midday, Owens says he expects an answer from the Expos by seven.

At seven, Expos officials John McHale and Murray Cook are munching on hors d'oeuvres at a cocktail party thrown by a group trying to bring major-league baseball to Tampa.

At eight, with the Phils' nightly round of cocktails now well underway, McHale and Cook are dining on prime rib and crab meat cocktail at a lavish dinner thrown for baseball executives by CBS Radio.

At 9:30, with Owens having left his post by the phone to wander through the hotel lobby, McHale and Cook are listening to a talk by CBS superstar Dan Rather.

Cook finally calls Owens's suite at 11:00 and asks for a meeting. But Owens is nowhere to be found. Alexander and Felske go on a secret mission to find their minister of trade. By the time Owens is found, the Expos say they'd prefer to talk tomorrow. And as somebody summed up the whole episode, "Only one name kept the Phils from swinging a trade last night. It was Jack Daniels."

December 6

HOUSTON—Turner's chartered plane arrives from California in the early morning, and he immediately meets with Sutter's agents. Turner agrees to a six-year contract worth $1.125 million a year with $5.5 million of the money funding an annuity that, at 13% interest, will pay Sutter close to $40 million over 36 years. The Cardinals have said they simply can't meet this price, and others around the meetings hear rumors of the figures and call them ludicrous. But Turner is willing and eager to sign a dotted line.

Through all of this, Sutter has been at his home outside St. Louis. But when his agents learned Turner was flying to Houston, they knew their terms would be met. They telephoned Sutter and suggested he and his wife fly to Atlanta and check out the city, and make certain they could be comfortable there.

ATLANTA—Just before noon, Mr. and Mrs. Bruce Sutter register at the plush Peachtree Plaza Hotel in downtown Atlanta. At about the same time, John Mullen arrives in Atlanta from

Houston, having closed up shop at the winter meetings to spend the day showing Sutter around Atlanta. Within hours, Turner and Sutter's agents also will fly from Houston to Atlanta. The deal is close.

Sutter spends the early afternoon driving through residential areas in Atlanta, looking at some property north of the city. He stops by the home of his friend and ex-teammate Ken Oberkfell for a chat about the team and the town. He gives Mullen the impression everything is going well.

Late in the afternoon, Mullen takes the Sutters to the Techwood Drive headquarters of the Turner Broadcasting System, a modernistic, if not futuristic, place. Turner takes great delight in giving Sutter a tour of the facilities, introducing him to employees and even arranging an exclusive interview with the Cable News Network. Still, Sutter won't commit; he'll go back to the hotel, talk things over with his wife, sleep on the matter, and meet with Turner tomorrow at 10 A.M.

When Sutter arrives back at the hotel, he is angered to see a dozen or so reporters. "There won't be a decision this week," he snaps, declining additional comment. But while Sutter's words seem firm, one of his agents advises a friendly St. Louis reporter, "You might want to come here from Houston tomorrow."

HOUSTON—With the knowledge that a Carter trade is probable and that shortstop Hubie Brooks must be part of the package, Frank Cashen must move to supplement the left side of the Mets infield. The man he wants is Howard Johnson, the Tigers' 24-year-old, switch-hitting third baseman. He has coveted Johnson "for as long as I can remember," Cashen says. Wanting becomes needing as the Carter trade moves closer.

The clubs had discussed a Johnson trade at the previous winter convention. The Mets made five offers, the last of which included Brooks, Lynch, and Heep for Johnson and Glenn Wilson. The Tigers declined their offer at that time. The Mets renewed their efforts at the October general managers meetings. It was then that Cashen realized he would have to deal one of his starting pitchers.

Walt Terrell, a right-hander who was 11–12 last season, is judged to have less potential than the others. He has also had some problems with Dave Johnson, and thus was the most likely to go. Terrell had become critical of his manager's "early hooks," and hadn't spoken with him for the second half of the season. It didn't help that Terrell's behavior on team flights had become a sore subject with the club. "A lot of my problems with the Mets weren't on the field," Terrell says. "They were 30,000 feet above the field . . . I figured I'd be the one to go."

The Tigers, worried about the durability of their third starter, Milt Wilcox, agree to swap Johnson for Terrell.

All around, bombshells are dropping. Bruce Sutter is headed for Atlanta, Rickey Henderson is headed for New York, Montreal has set in motion serious negotiations on a pair of trades, LaMarr Hoyt is on his way to San Diego, the Mets are closing in on substantial trades, and the Cubs move inexorably toward re-signing their free agent pitchers.

The Phillies' brain trust, minus some scouting personnel who were sent home, are feeling the effects of their hard day's night. They sit sullenly in Owens's suite wondering where to turn next. Even the suite reflects their depression. The once-bountiful liquor cabinet is reduced to a handful of bottles of gin, which no one drank. The once-brimming cooler of ice and beer is down to two half-open cans and warm water. The little dishes of peanuts and potato chips are filled with soggy crumbs. Room-service trays line the wall and tired Phillies executives line the couches.

"We're nowhere right now, we're not optimistic about doing anything, and I don't know where to go next," says Giles.

Owens and Alexander look for a bright side. "Well, goddamn, we know we can get value for Diaz whenever we want to move him, we've found that out, that's for sure," says Alexander. "And hell, you look at all the rosters in the whole goddamn majors and you don't find a heck of a lot of clubs who have a whole lot of pitching to give up. And we sure as hell can't give up the kids, not now."

Giles wants some action, nevertheless. Talks will be pushed

with Texas, who have been resisting entreaties all week to discuss pitcher Dave Stewart. And the Phillies will take a run at Houston, who have a large collection of relievers but are notoriously slow to trade.

But the Phillies are frustrated. Symbolic of how they wasted too much time was an earlier meeting they had with Los Angeles.

The Dodgers asked to talk and the Phillies, desperate to start something, were intrigued by the possibilities. Los Angeles did have pitching to spare, and who knows what they might want to talk about.

In strutted Al Campanis, the Dodgers general manager, and after bantering with his old employee Alexander, Campanis talked about how he was looking for the missing piece to what he termed his otherwise solid club. And then Campanis, now an hour into the meeting, asked the Phillies about the availability of Von Hayes. Owens, Alexander, and company almost fell off their chairs. Anyone looking at the Phils' roster, any baseball man with a shred of knowledge about the Phillies, knew Hayes was an untouchable. That was the tight-lipped answer the Phillies quickly gave Campanis. So out strutted the Dodgers' boss. An hour wasted.

Late last night, the Phils' moods worsened with the arrival of news that would ultimately void that lonely little trade made with St. Louis three days ago.

It seems that Mike Lavalliere had been bothered by some soreness in his knee, so he innocently visited his doctor in New Hampshire, who detected a small piece of loose cartilage. The doctor said the cartilage could be easily removed through an arthroscopic procedure and that Lavalliere would be as good as new in a matter of weeks. Young Lavalliere thought that sounded harmless, so he elected to go ahead with the surgery.

The trouble with all this was that the Phillies had no idea about the knee problem when they traded Lavalliere to the Cardinals. When they found out about it, they were embarrassed. Tony Siegle was dispatched to inform St. Louis general manager Joe McDonald.

Since there was no reason for the Phillies to hide such information in such a minor deal, McDonald knew the Phils were innocent of deception. However, he also wasn't exactly enthralled to be getting a catcher whose knee had just been sliced. So McDonald said he'd consult with his medical personnel and then get back to the Phillies about possibly voiding the trade. The whole scenario symbolized the Phillies' week. Even when they got something done, it didn't stay together.

December 7

ATLANTA—This is the day Ted Turner has long awaited. He will finally sign a free agent whom everyone wants.

At 10 a.m., a limousine pulls in front of the lobby entrance of the Turner Broadcasting System. Sutter and his two agents—all three men dressed in suits and carrying brief cases—get out of the car, nod at reporters, and enter the building. Sutter shakes hands with one reporter he knows from St. Louis and says to the group, "I'll have something to say after this meeting."

This meeting lasts six hours. Sutter has decided to sign with the Braves, and Turner has decided to commit roughly $10 million to the acquisition. The six hours are devoted to resolving contract language and structure, deciding exactly when Sutter would get various amounts of the money, deciding when Turner would put what amount of money into annuity funds, and so forth. The issue now is not where Sutter will throw his split-fingered fastball, but how to achieve the tax benefits both Turner and Sutter seek.

Around 1 p.m., Turner's secretary takes lunch into the meeting. Turner suggests that sandwiches also be ordered for the reporters downstairs. This is an unusual gesture for Turner, who charges the media for meals in the press box at Atlanta Stadium. Obviously, things are going well behind those closed doors.

At 4:00 p.m., Turner sends word to the media, "No one leave." At 4:05, he and Sutter appear live before cameras of the Turner-owned, Turner-conceived Cable News Network to announce the signing. Not only does Turner have the best relief pitcher in the league, he has a scoop.

Minutes later, Turner and Sutter meet the rest of the media. Turner, concerned that reports of the deferred income might be misinterpreted and exaggerated, announces that the contract is worth $10 million; actually, to be precise, it is $10,125,000. Sutter, wearing a Braves cap, is all smiles, and Turner cackles, "I finally got me one!"

HOUSTON—The Angels are already on their way home. They leave frustrated and empty-handed, having been unable to strengthen their woeful pitching, much to the consternation of manager Gene Mauch, who predicted the Angels would make at least one major deal. Mauch seems to forget that his club has little with which to deal, particularly since it is now determined to retain its young players.

The Angels talked to San Francisco about relief pitcher Gary Lavelle, to Oakland about starting pitchers Chris Codiroli and Bill Krueger, to St. Louis about starting pitcher Dave LaPoint, and to Pittsburgh about starting pitcher John Candelaria. It was all in vain.

Since the most celebrated of the Angels' players are protected by no-trade clauses and earn salaries that most clubs consider prohibitive, the Angels could offer only reserve first baseman Daryl Sconiers or relief pitcher Luis Sanchez. They refused to part with shortstop Dick Schofield or any of the farm system's hopefuls.

Burdened by the club's previous sins, the policies that had left him with a collection of aging superstars who could not be traded, general manager Mike Port shrugged his shoulders, packed his bags, and said there was no sense in staying.

The once-bustling hotel lobby has been reduced to lonely pockets of hangers on, trying to make one last trade.

The Phils spend most of the day trying to talk up a deal with Texas concerning Dave Stewart, whom the Rangers continue to deem untouchable. The Phils also get serious with Houston about one of their relief pitchers, but the Astros insist on young third baseman Rick Schu. The Phillies aren't desperate enough yet to deal a top prospect like him.

It has become evident that the frustrated Phillies have struck out. They'll go home empty-handed. And though they never really had to make a deal this week, their failure to swing one is still a disappointment.

Frank Cashen and his staff are also on their way out of Houston. But first he announces the acquisition of Howard Johnson for Walt Terrell. "I don't know of anything in the last several years we've pursued more," he says.

Cashen insists he is satisfied with what his organization has accomplished. The timing of the Johnson trade is perfect for Cashen, diverting attention away from anything else that might be going on. He never mentions the possible departure of Hubie Brooks as a reason for pressing his pursuit of Johnson; he merely points to Ray Knight's impending shoulder surgery. Johnson's presence will provide insurance at third.

It must be the ultimate Frank Cashen coup—he has put together the most important trade in years, and not a glimmer has leaked to the press.

December 10

SAN ANTONIO, TEXAS—John Gibbons, a 22-year-old catcher in the Mets organization, reads a report in a Texas newspaper that he had been part of a package the Texas Rangers had requested in exchange for Larry Parrish. The Mets had declined to include Gibbons, who had begun the 1984 season as the Mets starting catcher, but spent most of the year on the disabled list and in the minors. "That made me feel pretty good," Gibbons would later recall, "like they still had faith in me, and that I had a chance to win the starting job again."

Gibbons expresses those very thoughts to his brother, Bill. "Maybe you shouldn't be so happy," Bill Gibbons tells him. "The Mets just got Gary Carter."

⑨ New Homes

December 10

PALM BEACH GARDENS, FLORIDA—The deed is finally done. After a year's worth of casual suggestion, followed by a week of intense negotiation conducted with extraordinary secrecy, Frank Cashen has pulled off The Big Deal. Gary Carter is now a Met.

The deal was not without its last-minute problems, of course. The exchange of players was finalized on the last day of the winter meetings. The Mets had already agreed to give up Hubie Brooks, catcher Mike Fitzgerald, and promising young outfielder Herm Winningham; but Montreal wanted a fourth player, left-handed pitcher Randy Myers. Cashen was disturbed by the request, and began to wonder and worry about whether the deal would ever come about. Al Harazin encouraged Cashen by telling him, "We're so close to a trade that will put us over the top."

Cashen then resumed his talks with the Expos. They talked two dozen times before Montreal agreed to accept pitcher Floyd Youmans as the fourth man. "The last day was not fun," Cashen later recalled.

As with any major trade these days, the deal couldn't be finalized until Carter gave his approval. He met with John McHale on Saturday, the 8th, and said that he would have to consider the move. He consulted his family, his friends, and his advisors. "I've been a member of the Montreal Expos organization for about one-third of my life," He said. "It's difficult to think of myself as something other than that." He slept—none too well—on the decision, and on Sunday called McHale to approve the trade.

Today, Cashen and Harazin fly to Palm Beach, where Carter resides, to iron out the details. Carter picks up Cashen and Harazin at the airport, springs for lunch, and drives them in his van to his home. "All he wanted to talk about was the Mets," Cashen says later. "I don't think I've ever seen anyone so enthusiastic. His exuberance was special. In his own mind, I think he already was wearing a Mets uniform."

When they arrive at Carter's home, champagne is already on ice. This is no more presumptuous than Cashen and Harazin's bringing two first-class, round-trip tickets to New York City for Carter and his wife, Sandy.

"Guess you thought we were going to make a deal," Cashen says to Carter when he sees the champagne. "Guess *you* thought we were going to make a deal," Carter says to Cashen when he sees the tickets.

The Carters, Cashen, Harazin, player agent Richard Moss, and Carter's financial advisor Bob Engel discuss the move. Since Carter is being traded in the middle of a multi-year contract, he has the right to demand a trade at the end of the year. Carter agrees to give up this right, and the Mets extend the no-trade provision of his seven-year, $13.1 million contract through its 1989 expiration date.

The contract, fourth-highest among all major-league contracts at the time of the trade, is no problem for the Mets even though the contracts of George Foster—five years for $10.2 million—and Keith Hernandez—five years for $8.4 million—are already in place. "Bringing Gary in is not an inhibition," owner Nelson Doubleday says.

Which is not to say there aren't some snags. Carter makes one absolute demand. "One thing I have to have is No. 8," he says, prompting Cashen to wonder what is included in the No. 8 clause of Carter's contract. Then Cashen realizes Carter is talking about his uniform number.

PHILADELPHIA—Bill Giles goes home fairly early. The phone rings at around 9:30. It is Phillies public relations vice-president Larry Shenk. "Bill, the wire services just called," says Shenk. "The Expos have traded Gary Carter to the Mets for Hubie Brooks, Mike Fitzgerald, and two prospects named Winningham and Youmans."

"Oh boy," says Giles, "the Mets suddenly became the team to beat."

December 11

ATLANTA—The morning newspaper carries the story of the Gary Carter trade. Immediately, Ted Turner wonders why he didn't know Carter was available. Yes, he would like to have had a chance at obtaining Carter, Turner says. No, it would not have been a problem to pick up Carter's enormous contract. Yes, he would like to have been informed. General manager John Mullen says he did not see a need to inform Turner of Carter's availability because all their people in Houston agreed the matter should not be pursued. But, not withstanding Montreal's original demand for McMurtry, Bedrosian, Benedict, and Thompson, if the Mets got Carter for Brooks, Fitzgerald, and two minor leaguers, Turner and others wonder if the Braves could have gotten him for Ramirez, Benedict, and two minor leaguers. And with Paul Zuvella still in the organization, it was worth wondering if a chance to get a Gary Carter would have made trading Ramirez worthwhile.

PHILADELPHIA—Bill Giles's first phone call in the morning is to Murray Cook of the Expos. "I guess Brooks will play shortstop for you," says Giles. "That's right," says Cook. "And I guess it's fair to say we no longer have any interest in your shortstop (DeJesus)."

So the Phillies have spent weeks trying to make a trade that now will never be made. They will renew whatever lingering talks they still have going.

But they are suddenly possibly the third-best team in the division—or worse. And Giles will soon have to convene another of his strategy sessions to decide where to go next.

COMPTON, CALIFORNIA—Hubie Brooks learned of the trade while watching televison, and was surprised but not angry. "I guess it's a disappointment," he says. "I've come a long way with the team, and now that I'm hungry to win it all, I'm gone. The toughest part is when you've been walked on for so long. Now it was going to be our turn to walk on people. But now I've got to leave. I would have liked to stay. I did what they asked me. I had a good year. I moved to shortstop for them, and I went to the Instructional League when they asked. I didn't have to. I guess I improved myself so someone else would take me."

Then, after additional thought, Brooks recognizes the most negative aspect of his transfer. "Damn," he says, "now I gotta face Dwight."

NEW YORK—Fans at the 76ers-Knicks game at Madison Square Garden chant, "Let's Go Mets."

ANAHEIM—Mike Port is back in his Anaheim Stadium office for only a few hours when he learns that Fred Lynn has accepted a five-year, $6.8 million contract from Baltimore.

"I ended the season with an open mind," Lynn says. "I didn't know who would draft me. I didn't know what the Angels' response would be. I had hoped to stay in Anaheim, but my main goal was to be on a championship team."

The Angels offered Lynn a contract for only one year at significantly less than the $1.45 million Lynn made last year. The proposal is believed to have guaranteed Lynn a comparatively modest $800,000, with the chance to reach $1.4 million again if he achieved a series of incentives.

The Angels called it a "shared risk" concept, but Lynn wasn't interested.

"I won't say I was insulted," he says. "I hold no bitterness, no ill feelings. The Angels did what they feel they had to do. They wanted a counterproposal from us, but their offer was too unrealistic, too indicative of a lack of interest. We kept waiting for a multi-year offer we could counter, but never got it. It was disappointing, but I had other avenues, some of which were very attractive."

Port denies that he only went through the motions in his negotiations with Lynn. "We did make an offer," the general manager says. "We did try to get something going. We think we showed interest. We were looking for an exchange of ideas. You can make a counterproposal to anything."

Port says Lynn presented a difficult problem because of his high salary in 1984 and "the bottom line fact is he hadn't had a Boston-type year in his four years with us."

Lynn's departure leaves Gary Pettis, who batted .227 in his rookie season, as the center fielder, and the promising Mike Brown, who hit .284 in 148 at bats, to battle veteran Juan Beniquez in right.

"I'm surprised by the length of the Baltimore offer and I'm sorry to see Lynn go," Port says. "Anytime you lose a player when you have interest in retaining him, there's an element of concern, but we have a viable option in Brown."

Says manager Gene Mauch, "Fred Lynn has streaks during which he's as good a player as there is, but I can't go dance on Mr. Autry's desk demanding that he sign Lynn for three or four more years if it means that the club would lose money. Mike Brown has major-league ability, and he's now going to get the chance to put it to use. I'd have liked to have Fred back, but we're not naked."

December 12

ANAHEIM—Only 24 hours later, Mauch makes a similar analogy in reference to his bullpen.

It comes in response to the news that free agent relief pitcher Don Aase has followed Lynn's lead and signed with Baltimore.

The four-year package guarantees Aase $2.4 million and includes a series of incentives that could bring him even more.

Alluding to his bullpen, Mauch says, "We're not naked, but we don't have too many clothes on, either. We'll miss Don, but great things have been born out of necessity."

Asked then if it was a necessity for the Angels to acquire a quality relief pitcher, Mauch says, "Either that or Marcel (pitching coach Marcel Lachemann) is going to have to get a lot smarter than he already is."

Aase was 4–1 with eight saves and a 1.62 ERA in 23 second-half appearances after he returned from a two-year rehabilitation from elbow surgery. He pitched only once with fewer than three days rest and never in consecutive games.

The Angels responded to Aase's free agency with the same "shared risk" philosophy they exhibited with Lynn, never offering more than a one-year guarantee while continuing to question the health of Aase's arm.

Port, however, reacts angrily to Aase's departure. He says he had made two offers to Aase and his attorneys, Jerry Kapstein and Bob Teaff, and had attempted last week to make another, but wasn't given the chance. He believes Aase had a moral obligation to listen to a final Angel proposition, considering the support the club had provided during the two years of his rehabilitation.

"I'm furious at the state of affairs," Port says. "Some people are given to talking of tradition and loyalty, but it seems to me that there are only certain directions in which that exists.

"Don Aase is a local guy (he attended high school in Anaheim) who we carried through his rehabilitation and paid well while allowing him to get back on his feet, physically and financially.

"We made several offers to him dating back to October 24, but were never given the courtesy of a counterproposal other than the indication that he wanted more money and years.

"We never knew where things were or where they were headed, but we went ahead and prepared another, more significant proposal that both Don and Jerry Kapstein knew last week we wanted to present. We were never given the chance and never given an explanation."

It is difficult not to sympathize with Port's position here. The Angels have paid Aase well while he was unable to pitch because of injuries. They have overseen his rehabilitation, and now that he is healthy, he can just walk away.

The Angels' first offer, according to Teaff, was for one year at $300,000, with the club having an option on a second year at $350,000. The second offer was for one year at $300,000 and a second year at $350,000, but only half of the second-year salary was guaranteed. Aase made $272,500 in 1984.

If ever this kind of "shared risk" contract is reasonable, it is in the case of a pitcher with arm problems, a pitcher who has been limited to 91 innings of work in three seasons. But the contemporary age in baseball is hardly an age of reason.

"I was looking for a guaranteed initial offer of two or three years from which we could negotiate," Aase says of his talks with the Angels. "Instead, they made two very disappointing offers that seemed to raise questions about their confidence in my arm."

"The Angels could have signed me very easily before the re-entry draft," Aase says. "They had every opportunity to sign me during the last two months. All I can think of is that they are still skeptical about my arm, they still think there's a risk.

"In my mind, I thought I had put that behind me. In my mind, I thought I had proved the elbow was sound. If the club wasn't going to make its best offer initially, there was nothing I could do once the season ended to change its evaluation.

"I'm grateful to Dr. (Lewis) Yocum and to the Angel trainers, Rick Smith and Ned Bergert. I'm appreciative of the patience John McNamara and Marcel Lachemann showed in me and for the support of the fans and media.

"But I was hurt pitching when I probably shouldn't have been, and I don't feel I owe the Angels anything. I'm at a point where I had to place a priority on my family's security, and it simply came down to Baltimore making the best offer at a time when I had nothing on the table from the Angels and no indication they still had interest.

"I want to wish my former teammates good luck, but my future is in Baltimore."

NEW YORK—Gary Carter arrives in New York with his smile and enthusiasm and asks that the Mets start the 1985 season the following day. Ron Darling, a new teammate, greets him at the Shea Stadium press conference. "I'll be glad when the trade blows over," Darling tells Carter. "All they've shown on TV the last couple of nights is that [grand] slam you hit off me on opening day [last season]."

Carter smiles.

Of course.

Fans at the Rangers-Bruins game at Madison Square Garden chant, "Let's Go Mets."

December 13

ATLANTA—The phone in Ted Turner's office hardly ever stops ringing. He likes talking on the phone, especially on the speaker system. This afternoon, he gets a call from Barry Axelrod, Rick Sutcliffe's agent. Axelrod thanks Turner for his interest, but Sutcliffe will remain with the Cubs.

As soon as Turner finishes talking to Axelrod, he phones Mullen. Quickly, Turner tells Mullen that Sutcliffe is no longer available. "Where do we go from here?" Since Steve Trout had re-signed with the Cubs the previous week, only one of the Braves' free agent selections remains uncommitted—Ed Whitson. Ed Whitson? The Braves have scarcely given him a thought since the reentry draft, and Whitson already has had long, intense negotiating sessions with the San Diego Padres and New York Yankees. But Turner is in an active, sign-somebody-else mood, and he instructs Mullen to see if the team can enter the Whitson bidding late. Well, of course they can.

The Braves submit an opening bid of a five-year, $4.5 million contract, considerably more than either the Padres or Yankees have offered. Turner is assured that Whitson won't do anything without talking further with the Braves.

THE BRONX—George Steinbrenner grumbles in his Yankee Stadium office about how Murray Cook, the Expos general manager and former Steinbrenner subordinate, orchestrated the Carter deal to help the Mets upstage the Yankees' acquisition of Rickey Henderson.

CLEVELAND—Since Dave LeFevre's attempt to buy the Indians was smashed under a legal avalanche, everyone has been waiting for the first rumor about the franchise moving to another city.

The New York *Daily News* reports today that the New Jersey Sports and Exposition Authority met with the Indians and San Francisco Giants for "top secret talks." Supposedly, a baseball stadium will be built in the Meadowlands Athletic Complex, which contains Giants Stadium, Meadowlands Racetrack, and Brendan Byrne Arena.

"No way," says Peter Bavasi. "No one from the Indians spoke with anyone from New Jersey. Any suggestions, even the remotest hint, that the franchise will move is a figment of someone's imagination.

"Pat O'Neill has confirmed and reconfirmed his three-part commitment to the Indians. First, he regrettably has to sell the club. Second, he is committed to selling the club to local ownership that will keep it in Cleveland with the finances to make it a winner. Third, Pat O'Neill will supply the money to restore the luster of the franchise as long as he owns the team. The Indians aren't going to New Jersey or anywhere."

December 14

PHILADELPHIA—For the first time, Von Hayes feels like he is finally established as a major-league player. Unlike past off-seasons, Hayes wasn't forced to play winter baseball in order to refine his skills or massage his confidence. He wasn't forced to wonder about his future like he was after his mind-numbing 1983 experience when he was booed, benched, and saddled with the nickname "Five for One" by veteran teammates aghast that the Phillies had traded five players to obtain Hayes from Cleveland.

After his superb 1984 season, Hayes doesn't have to listen to the jeers any more. He has surfaced as a coming star and more importantly as a leader of the increasingly young Phillies. So instead of heading for Puerto Rico for winter ball like he did the previous year, Hayes is having a far different offseason.

He first spent a month in California, attending the weddings of two of his three sisters and visiting friends and relatives. After a brief visit to Philadelphia, Hayes then embarked on a hunting and fishing trip to Minnesota and Iowa. And in early December, Hayes did something that would have been unthinkable a year ago. He went to Las Vegas as the Phillies' player representative to attend a meeting of the executive committee of the Major League Baseball Players' Association.

Hayes was elected the Phils' player rep late in the season, a somewhat dubious honor since much of the job involves dreary paperwork and passing along messages. And the job is especially precarious this year because of the ongoing negotiations between players and owners for a new collective bargaining agreement. No one needs to be reminded that the last time such negotiations took place, a bitter 57-day strike ensued that gutted the 1981 season.

So the meeting in Las Vegas was hardly a junket for Hayes or any of the other players. There were long sessions in which the players were briefed on the issues expected to become crucial in the coming weeks, and on the various positions the players would likely maintain in the talks. They were also schooled on the benefits their union had gained them over the past several years.

It all was a revelation for Hayes, who like most up-and-coming players never paid attention to union matters. And he wasn't blind to how his status on the Phillies had changed over the past year. "Last year, I almost felt like I was an intruder in the clubhouse," he recalls. "I never got comfortable, some of the guys were a little tough to get close to, and I didn't help matters by losing my temper sometimes and basically having an awful year.

"Now I'm representing my teammates at the players association meetings and being called a team leader in the press. It's a heck of a change, that's for sure."

Hayes ended up bedridden in Las Vegas with a virus that caused him to miss the address to the players by commissioner Peter Ueberroth. But Hayes had gotten the gist of the week's meetings.

"I think everyone seemed in general agreement about where we are going to stand on the issues and we discussed what the owners would likely present to us. All that stuff is something I never paid much attention to. I had just a vague idea about what went on and about what was entailed in all the union stuff. So the meetings were definitely a learning experience for me.

"Things don't look like they're going to be as nasty as they were in 1981, but I guess we won't really know until we get down to the specifics. But I'm glad I'm involved. Until now, I never had a concern for anything or anybody else in baseball except myself. Now, I feel I'm representing part of the game and my teammates and future players who might benefit from what we are able to do. I feel grown up."

Hayes came back to Philadelphia from Las Vegas to begin regular workouts at Veterans Stadium. Conditioning for most professional athletes has greatly changed. Years ago, players didn't make enough money to spend their offseason in leisure. Most players needed off-season jobs, and didn't have the freedom to spend their winters working out several hours a day.

But most clubs now have most of their team working out by mid-December, and the Phillies are no exception. Hayes is among a large group of players who live locally and spend a few hours a day working out under the guidance of trainer Jeff Cooper and renowned strength and flexibility instructor Gus Hoefling.

Some players—notably Darren Daulton and outfielder Joe Le-febvre—are rehabilitating injuries. Lefebvre makes twice-weekly trips from his Connecticut home to work on his damaged right knee, and spends the rest of the week working out at nearby Yale University.

But the majority of players at the stadium just want to strengthen themselves for the coming season. "Working with Gus made me a lot stronger last year and it sure can't hurt to keep it up," says Hayes. "And it's good to be with some of the guys and start thinking baseball again. I can still remember pitches and situations from last year, and thinking them through from a distance helps a lot."

CLEVELAND— This is the winter of Bert Blyleven's content. Last season, he went 19–7 with a 2.87 ERA. He was second in the league in winning percentage (.731), third in ERA and shutouts (4), and fourth in strikeouts (170) and complete games (12). Baltimore's Mike Boddicker was the only American League pitcher to win more games.

Blyleven is a fanatic about statistics, especially his own. "There is nothing wrong with having personal goals," says Blyleven. "I'd like to have an earned run average under 3.00 and win 20 games. If I do that, wouldn't you say I'm helping the team?"

Actually, Blyleven probably would have won more than 20 games if he hadn't suffered a freak injury. It was early May and Blyleven was running laps in the outfield before a game with Toronto. He didn't see the baseball on the ground until he stepped right on it, breaking a small bone in his foot. He missed almost a month.

It was early June, while still recovering from the injury, that Blyleven went public with his wish to be traded.

"The Indians are in the middle of a youth movement and I'd like to be traded to a contender," said Blyleven. "I'm 33, and I'd like to be with a team that is going to win now, not four years from now. I'm sure the Indians could get several young players for me and that would fit in with their youth movement."

"Bert mentioned the possibility of a trade a few times," said Gabe Paul in June. "I'll tell you what, he isn't going anywhere. For two years, we paid Bert a good salary and he did nothing because he was hurt. Now, he owes us and the city of Cleveland something in return. We had two years of non-production out of him. Now that he can produce, he wants out. Forget it. This is a totally unreasonable request. It's about time he paid us back what he owes us."

Blyleven was with the Indians for only half a season in 1981 before he hurt his elbow. He missed virtually all of 1982 because of elbow surgery and half of 1983 with a variety of arm miseries.

So 1984 was billed as the year Blyleven worked off his debt to Gabe Paul and the city of Cleveland. His teammates continually reminded him of Paul's words, asking if the debt was paid yet after each of his wins. Blyleven appreciated his teammates' humor, but not Paul's comments.

"I didn't demand anything," says Blyleven. "All I did was suggest the Indians could trade me for a couple of young players. I think they could get some decent talent for me. I'm happy pitching in Cleveland, but there's not a player in Cleveland who wouldn't want to be with a contender. If the Indians could improve themselves by trading me, they should. It would work out best for all concerned.

"The Indians treated me very well while I was hurt, but I'm not a robot. I didn't plan on having an arm operation or getting a sore shoulder. I'm not Iron Mike. Even a pitching machine breaks down. I don't think I owe anyone anything because I've always given a full effort. I'm sorry I was injured for the first time in 12 years after I was traded to the Indians. I'm sorry Mr. Paul had to pay me while I was hurt, but I didn't plan it that way."

Before his first season in Cleveland, the Indians "reworked" his contract. Blyleven entered the 1981 season with a six-year pact worth $4 million. He will be receiving deferred payments from the Indians, Texas, and Pittsburgh that run to the year 2014.

As the 1984 season progressed, Blyleven continued to say he "wouldn't mind being traded to a contender." Virtually every contender except Baltimore asked the Indians about Blyleven last season. All were told he wasn't available. They're still asking, and the answer is the same.

His closest friend on the team used to be Rick Sutcliffe. Ironically, Blyleven was in Sutcliffe's room when Cubs president Dallas Green called Sutcliffe to inform him of the trade to the Cubs. Bert asked for the telephone and Sutcliffe handed it over.

"Mr. Green, this is Bert Blyleven," he said. "I was just wondering if maybe you wanted to say hello to me, too."

"Sorry, Bert," said Green. "Last I heard, you were working off your debt to the city of Cleveland."

December 17

DALLAS—Bob Horner checked into the hospital last night and struggled through a restless night. He had made it clear to his surgeon, Dr. Peter Carter, that he hoped to have the screw implant in the wrist that might speed his return to the field. Dr. Carter told Horner he wouldn't know for sure until the operation was underway whether the implant was wise. "I have complete confidence in Dr. Carter," Horner tells his wife, Chris, and his agent and best friend, Bucky Woy, just before being taken into surgery.

The operation lasts two hours. When it's over, Dr. Carter approaches Mrs. Horner and Woy.

"How'd it go?" Woy asks.

It couldn't have gone better, Carter tells him. The condition of Horner's wrist appeared perfectly compatible with a screw implant, and so it was done. The bone graft from the hip went smoothly, too. Now it will be wait-and-see.

Horner is heavily sedated the remainder of the day and remains hospitalized overnight. In Atlanta, the Braves release a surprising statement calling the operation "a complete success" and going on to speculate that Horner will be swinging a bat by spring training. Here, Dr. Carter refuses to involve himself in any prognostications about when Horner might be able to do that.

December 18

PHILADELPHIA—Christmas is only a week away but the big news is neither baseball nor Santa Claus. Rather it concerns a grinch named Leonard Tose who appeared poised to move his Philadelphia Eagles football team to Phoenix.

It seemed certain that the Eagles were gone, but midnight-hour negotiations between the city of Philadelphia and Tose stopped the move. The price was significant concessions to the Eagles concerning their Veterans Stadium lease and improvements to the city-owned stadium.

Bill Giles is a most interested observer. He has long been frustrated by the city's refusal to adjust what is the worst lease arrangement of any major-league club. The Phillies average approximately $8 million a season in various payments to the city through tickets, taxes, rentals, and concessions. As Giles often points out, the major-league average is less than $2 million a year in similar payments. Especially irritating is a 30-cent surcharge on each ticket sold that goes to the city. Giles maintains that no club in baseball has such a burden. Neither does any club have to give its city 27% of its concession sales like the Phillies do. The major-league average is only 8%.

Giles has refrained from publicly pushing for lease adjustments. With the Phillies drawing over two million fans a year and annually among the major-league leaders in salaries, it's hard to cry poverty. But when the city unlocked its vault to save the Eagles, they also opened the door for Giles.

Within a day of the announced agreement between the Eagles and the city, Giles requests a meeting with Philadelphia Mayor Wilson Goode. Giles makes no threats of a move, but armed with his statistics, he pushes for consideration of some adjustments to the Phillies' lease. "Politically and public relations-wise, I could never have done it before," says Giles later. "But this whole thing with the Eagles gave us an opening. The city appeared ready to spend $4 million on the Eagles. And while it was good to see the city's concern for them, it was also a time for us to point out that we have been working under a very unfair lease for the past 10 years.

"We're not asking for $4 million. We want to always pay our fair share. But we want to pay closer to what our competition is required to pay."

Goode is amenable to further negotiations. And what will become a time-consuming and intricate series of negotiations begins. Giles will meet several hours a day with his financial and legal aides in sessions that will be interrupted only by a week-long shutdown for the holidays. The lease issue will likely drag on for months; even if the Phillies reach a satisfactory agreement with the Goode administration, approval from the City Council is required. So the Phillies aren't holding their breath for quick relief.

December 19

DALLAS—Bob Horner, now able to talk to visitors, is optimistic. But he has been through so many injuries, so many moments of hope followed by so many moments of disappointment, that he remains somewhat subdued.

"The operation is done, and now we'll wait and see what Mother Nature does," Horner says.

His right wrist and forearm are in a cast and will remain so for approximately three weeks. Until then, he says, "I have to admit, I'll be wondering 'Why me?' "

December 20

MAUI, HAWAII—Dave Johnson upstages several Hall of Fame players in the Legends of Baseball benefit game between retired American and Japanese players. Johnson has four hits and three runs batted in, as many RBI as Ernie Banks and one more than Lou Brock and Johnson's former teammate Sadaharu Oh. The American team wins 15–9, and Johnson is voted the game's Most

Valuable Player. "We'll never hear the end of this," Mets pitching coach Mel Stottlemyre says.

HONOLULU—Johnson takes a side trip to have dinner with Sid Fernandez, the 22-year-old pitcher who is the only left-handed member of the Mets projected starting rotation. He is delighted to see that Fernandez has shed 25 of what had been 245 pounds. "I told him we're still going to count heavily on him," Johnson says.

December 21

ATLANTA—Each year, the Braves close their offices from Christmas through New Year's Day. Today, the Friday before Christmas, is the last day the Braves offices will be open until January 2. It has been a hectic, exhausting offseason for John Mullen, and he is ready for a break.

For the next 10 days, he says, he will keep his fingers crossed about Horner. He will dream of Bruce Sutter coming out of the bullpen, saving games night after night. And in one piece of unfinished business, he will wait for a call at home from Ed Whitson's agent.

December 27

CLEVELAND—One thing you have to say for Gabe Paul: He may have made bad trades, but he never made a lousy business deal. Paul officially steps out of the Indians' picture in a public announcement of his long-rumored sale of stock (about 5% of the team) to Dave LeFevre. Paul received about $1.5 million for his stock.

When Paul returned to Cleveland in 1978, team owner Steve O'Neill gave him a $250,000 interest-free loan. After selling the stock to LeFevre, Paul will repay the $250,000 to the O'Neill estate. But he had that interest-free capital for seven years; invested in bonds at 10% annual interest, that would net Paul $175,000 over and above his $180,000 a year salary, not to mention his other fringe benefits. His original investment in the team was about $500,000. Therefore, he tripled his money when he received the $1.5 million from LeFevre. Paul will also receive a three-year contract as a "team consultant" that reportedly will pay him $40,000 annually.

But there is far more to this transaction than the enrichment of Gabe Paul's retirement fund. It means Dave LeFevre finally owns the Indians—or, at least, 5% of them. It doesn't take a Wall Street investment analyst to see that LeFevre is mounting yet another attempt to purchase controlling interest in the club.

Of course, all the major parties deny this.

"This is an isolated transaction between Gabe and myself," says LeFevre.

"Dave LeFevre still wants to buy the club, but he won't buy it a little at a time," says Pat O'Neill. "This isn't a step-by-step transaction. There is no deal pending nor is there one being worked on."

But LeFevre isn't acting like a guy with only 5% of the team. He interviewed Peter Bavasi, and Bavasi was hired as the Tribe's president while he was sitting in LeFevre's office. Also, LeFevre is expected to be named to the board of directors.

"Pat O'Neill and I are sort of army buddies after all that happened (in his attempts to buy the team)," says LeFevre. "We get along fine and respect each other. He has been receptive to my ideas, but we haven't talked about my being a director."

But the Indians have been saying one thing in public and doing another behind closed doors. While the Indians were telling the press earlier this month that LeFevre had not bought Paul's stock, the deal had been cut.

ATLANTA—In the morning newspaper today, Mullen and Turner read that Whitson has reached an agreement to sign with the Yankees. The Braves' late entry into the bidding for Whitson meant that they were forced to make their best offer right up front, leaving no room for negotiation. Their offer was far ahead of what the Yankees and Padres had been willing to spend, but once it was on the table, the Yankees moved to match it. Turner had, once again, succeeded only in driving up the price someone else would have to pay a free agent.

10 *On Hold*

January 2

NEW YORK—Having created openings on their 40-man roster with the four-for-one Carter trade, the Mets finally make a move they knew they would make. Rusty Staub re-signs for another season, easing the minds of Dave Johnson, who wanted Staub as his primary pinch hitter, and Wally Backman, who was worried about losing a card player. Standing in his upper east side restaurant, Staub says, "A lot of my heart and my life are in this city."

He acknowledges that no club contacted him. That no club did is indicative of the fact that other clubs recognized the situation—that Staub had all but agreed to return to the Mets.

January 5

ANAHEIM—When the Montreal Expos filled their managing job without so much as contacting him, Joe Torre got the message that he would not be managing in 1985. And so the ex-Braves manager began looking for a job in broadcasting.

He was offered a job on the Chicago White Sox radio crew for $40,000, which would have been pocket change on top of the total of $450,000 Ted Turner is paying him not to manage the Braves in 1985 and 1986. But when Torre began dickering for more money, White Sox owner Eddie Einhorn became disenchanted and broke off the negotiations.

Today, it is announced that Torre will be a member of the California Angels' telecasting crew, working approximately 40 televised games for roughly the same $40,000 the White Sox wanted to pay him to do 162 on radio. Additionally, Torre will be free to work other assignments between games; he has received overtures from ESPN.

"I've always had interest in getting into TV," Torre says. "I didn't expect it to be now—I'd still be managing the Braves if we'd won last year—but it is something I wanted to get into. And I'm not saying I will never manage again; I suspect it's still in my blood."

Torre, whose managerial stock was very high two years earlier, has not been contacted about any managerial jobs this winter.

January 8

PHILADELPHIA—With the holidays over, preparations for a new season begin anew, albeit at a creaking pace.

A first bit of housecleaning is finished quickly; the long-stalled negotiations with Gross are finally completed. Contract language, for months the stumbling block preventing a final agreement, is finally ironed out and Gross officially signs a new three-year contract worth approximately $400,000 a year.

There is other personnel news. The Phillies' embarrassing affair involving the Cardinals and Mike Lavalliere is apparently over. The Cardinals did not offer Lavalliere a contract by December 20, so he officially became a free agent. The Phillies subsequently approached Lavalliere. With their roster at its 40-man limit, the best the Phillies could offer was a Triple-A contract at above the usual minor-league rate, plus an invitation to spring training.

Lavalliere, however, told the Phils that since he was now a free agent, he wanted to test the waters and see if he might be able to get a more attractive opportunity with another club. The Phillies had no recourse but to let Lavalliere barter his availability. Lavalliere agreed, however, to contact the Phillies by the end of January if nothing surfaced.

Meanwhile, Tony Siegle and Bill Giles have renewed their talks with Tony Attanasio, Shane Rawley's agent. The Phillies continue to narrow their offer to Rawley. In exchange for guaranteeing the last year of Rawley's current contract, the Phillies propose that Rawley agree to add a number of additional years to the contract, with those seasons at the club's option one by one. Rawley would receive $200,000 if the club chose not to exercise its option at any time. Siegle believes that the proposal is good for both sides. It gives the Phils the freedom not to retain Rawley after a certain number of years, not to mention the ongoing ability to trade him. And the proposal gives Rawley three more guaranteed years on his contract while also allowing him the opportunity to retain their option.

Attanasio and Rawley also like the possibilities, and Attanasio agrees to come to Philadelphia by mid-month for what both sides hope will be the final negotiations.

Meanwhile, Hugh Alexander reports in from his North Carolina home. He has recently spent 10 days in Puerto Rico, looking specifically at Ed Olwine, the pitcher selected from the Mets' organization. Alexander's report to Giles is mixed. "He has one hell of a slider," Alexander tells Giles. "But he was behind every hitter and I saw him get beat twice." In other words, the Phils can't count on Olwine to solve their bullpen problems.

Alexander also took a long look at Luis DeLeon, a San Diego reliever who would likely be available in a trade. But Alexander isn't exactly excited about him either. "Hell, Bill, he was getting people out down there with his slider but he wasn't throwing all that hard and just looked all right," says Alexander. "And we've got a shitload of guys already who just look all right."

Giles then suggests that a trade looked impossible. But Alexander is reassuring. "We've got plenty of time to sit back and see what develops," he says. "Right now, there isn't a whole lot of pitching available but you never know what will happen when the teams get into spring training and see what they have."

And Alexander remains convinced that, if healthy, Bo Diaz will command a lot of trade interest.

So Alexander, Owens, and Giles will maintain their contact with other clubs with an eye toward spring training, when the talking would again get serious.

ATLANTA—Rick Cerone grew up in Newark, New Jersey, and had returned home, more or less, to play for the Yankees the last five years. But today he is in Atlanta, a city he has never before visited, looking for a new home.

He had been vacationing in the Dominican Republic in December when he heard on television that he had been traded to Atlanta. Today, he has come to visit the city where he will play.

He rents a car, lines up an appointment with a real estate agent, and begins exploring. He drives several times around I-285, the highway that circles the perimeter of the city, and many times through the upper-income suburbs of north Atlanta. He and his wife decide to buy a townhouse in the Dunwoody area, an area where several Braves live among corporate executives, doctors, and lawyers.

"This is a big city," Cerone says, "bigger than I expected, somehow. And I don't know if it's just me or what, but the people seem friendly here. I think this is perfect; I think my career is really going to work out here."

ANAHEIM—The new year opens on a down note for the Angels. Rick Burleson's three-year struggle to return from a torn right rotator cuff has suffered another setback.

A former all-star shortstop, Burleson had been hopeful of competing for the Angels' second base job in spring training. He will now be unavailable until May at the earliest because of a dislocated right shoulder.

The dislocation happened on New Year's Eve, while Burleson was in a Palm Desert gym lifting weights with Fred Lynn, his former Boston and Angels teammate.

"I wouldn't hesitate doing the same exercise and lifting the same weight again," Burleson says. "I don't know how it happened, it just did. The shoulder was probably fatigued because of all the therapy I had gone through that day. I heard it pop. I knew something was wrong."

Burleson's arm will be immobilized by a sling for two weeks. He was examined by Dr. Lewis Yocum, the Angels' orthopedic specialist, and Dr. Arthur Pappas, a Boston orthopedist familiar to Burleson since his years with the Red Sox.

According to Burleson, both doctors indicated that the new injury would not affect the torn rotator cuff or prevent him from playing again. He says his concern is with a partial paralysis in his right hand.

"I either bruised or stretched a nerve and it's as if half my hand is asleep," Burleson says. "Even if my shoulder was totally in sync, I couldn't grip a ball. I can hardly write my name.

"But when I saw Dr. Pappas in Phoenix a few days ago he said there was no reason I couldn't come back. He projected that if I didn't push it, I could be ready to play in May.

"My goal was to be ready to go in spring training and ready to play every day at a new position when the season started.

"Now I'm back on hold. Now I'm back to having to shut it down for a couple of months. It looks like a fourth straight year of not being able to play a full season."

The intense Burleson was the heart and soul of the Red Sox during his seven years in Boston. He came to the Angels in a five-player trade in December of 1980, batted .293 while earning all-star recognition for the fourth time in 1981, and then tore his rotator cuff in a game against Minnesota on April 17, 1982.

Rotator tears are more common in pitchers, and are normally fatal to their careers. They're rare in infielders, and rarely career-threatening, but Burleson's greatest asset as a shortstop was his strong arm. He had surgery, and returned briefly in August of 1983, but had to go back on the disabled list in September. He suffered a new tear while competing with Dick Schofield for the starting shortstop job in the spring of 1984, was activated as a utility player in September, and then decided recently to make a new comeback at the less demanding second base spot.

"The last time I threw was New Year's Eve day," Burleson

says. "I threw as well as I ever have. I was snapping off throws from every angle, every distance. I was doing it in sets, resting in between, and it was taking me only four throws to get warm again with no stiffness.

"It was definitely devastating for this to happen, considering how far I had come from the tear. I wanted to say, 'Why me?' I'm still disappointed, but I'm not going to dwell on it. I'm encouraged by what the doctors say. I'm looking at it as one more thing to overcome. I'm anticipating having this behind me once and for all and getting back to being the player I once was."

Burleson's uncertainty further clouds an already murky infield situation. Free agent Rob Wilfong, who platooned at second base with Bobby Grich in 1984, is still unsigned. Light-hitting Rob Picciolo appears to be the only backup infielder, apart from first baseman Daryl Sconiers.

January 9

ANAHEIM—Ken Forsch learns of Burleson's latest injury via the morning newspaper. He is both saddened and puzzled.

A 14-year major-league veteran and one of the Angels' most reliable starting pitchers, Forsch dislocated his own right shoulder April 7 while making his second start of the 1984 season. He did not pitch again.

It has only been in the last month, in fact, that Forsch's own uncertainty yielded to a measure of optimism, to a feeling that he would be ready to go to spring training, ready to reclaim his berth in a rotation in desperate need of proven arms.

"I hope Burly is right when he says he'll be back by May," Forsch says, "but it's been nine months for me, and my shoulder popped right in after it had popped out. Maybe his overall damage won't be as severe as mine was."

Forsch is sitting at his locker in a nearly empty Angel clubhouse having just completed a workout at Anaheim Stadium. He is asked if there was any advice he could give Burleson.

"I don't have to offer him advice because I've never seen anyone work harder," he says. "He's got the mental toughness that few people have. This is just a shame because I had seen him throw and he was back. He was ready."

It would be a providential bonus if Forsch were to be ready, if he were to return from a career-threatening injury to join a rotation that includes only Mike Witt, Ron Romanick, and Geoff Zahn as certain starters.

"I don't want to go to spring training as a special case, as a guy still on rehabilitation," Forsch says. "I want to be part of the regular program, and right now it looks like I'll be able to do that.

"I'm really optimistic about the progress I've made in the last month. It's almost scary, particularly when I look at what happened to Burleson and consider what I've been through."

Forsch spent three weeks with his right arm tied to his side, atrophy attacking the muscles. The dislocation was compounded by a minor rotator cuff tear and the fact that a 38-year-old arm which had pitched more than 2,100 innings during a distinguished career with Houston and California does not heal as quickly as a younger one.

Now, in early January, Forsch is back throwing from a mound on Mondays and Fridays, and throwing on the side in between.

"It's hard for me to say where I'm at," he says, "but there's no pain and I'm throwing with a lot of pop. The last couple times I've had the feeling I could throw two innings, maybe three.

"It's a far cry from last summer, when I'd play catch with my daughter and she'd have better stuff than I did. It was pathetic, the pits. I've had sore arms before, but this was so bad that it would take my breath away when I tried to throw.

"The thought that my career might be finished was always there. I wouldn't see any progress for all the work I was putting in and the temptation was to say, 'What's the point?' It was like a constant whisper. I had to block it out, close my mind to it.

"Now I've reached a point where it's hard for me to sleep at night, knowing I'm going to workout the next day. I know now I have a chance. There's an excitement in being back on the mound, knowing I'm getting ready for spring training. I can feel it building again."

Forsch has come back before—from injuries to his ankle, shoulder, knee, and hand. The latest rehabilitation has reminded him of the necessity to take it only a day at a time.

"There were two low points," Forsch says, citing the discovery of the rotator cuff tear and the realization in August that he wouldn't be back to help the Angels in September. He understands that even now his optimism must be tempered.

"Physically, I feel good, but I have to go through the mental phase," he says. "I've been this route before. As much as your heart wants you to let go, something in the subconscious says, 'Whoa, careful.' There's still the uncertainty of how it will be under the pressure of a game situation when I have to cut loose.

"It's as if I'm still living on the edge. I still feel I have to push myself to continue to make progress, but I can't risk overdoing it like Burly may have done. It's a tough line for me and I tend to give the trainers fits. If I can work with 10-pound weights, I want to know why it can't be 12 or 15 pounds. If I can throw for 30 minutes, why not 35?

"This has been a period of real turmoil for me, but I feel I've given it my best shot. I haven't sat back and said, 'Hey, I've got another year on my contract, what's the difference if I make it back?' I can derive a certain peace from that."

The manner in which he suffered the injury is indicative of the competitiveness with which he has gone about his comeback. Forsch had defeated Boston, 2–1, with a six-hitter on opening night of the 1984 season. Then, in the eighth inning of his next start against Toronto, he raced off the mound to field Willie Upshaw's slow grounder to the right side. Forsch's momentum carried him toward first base, where he made a head-first dive. He landed on his right elbow, the impact jamming his shoulder out of its socket. He left immediately, his season over. The Angels, who failed to secure a quality replacement for Forsch, lost more than a game.

"I can't tell you how many times I've been asked about that

play," Forsch says in reflection. "My wife still asks me about it and my only answer is that I'd do it again the same way. If I wasn't going to be competitive, if I wasn't going to do everything I could to get that one out and win a game, I wouldn't have been around for 14 years."

Six weeks before the Angels are scheduled to report to spring training, the chances Forsch will be around for a 15th season seem to be improving.

January 10

DALLAS—The cast that has been on Bob Horner's right wrist for three weeks is removed. Dr. Peter Carter says he's pleased with the results, and outlines a program of rehabilitative therapy for Horner. But he also cautions Horner that the healing process is more natural than controllable and tells him not to try to rush anything.

It has never been Horner's nature to rush anything, anyway. And he has a level tone in his voice as he says, "I doubt I'll be in West Palm Beach for the start of spring training. Maybe, hopefully, I'll get there somewhere around the middle of camp."

The Braves have all but stopped the guessing game about when Horner might be swinging a bat. The start of spring training? The middle of spring training? Opening day? Midseason? August? The screw implant holds out promise of accelerating Horner's comeback, but there are no guarantees. "It is just too early to tell," Dr. Carter says.

NEW YORK AND ST. PETERSBURG, FLORIDA—The distance between the two cities is indicative of the distance separating the Mets and the agent representing Dwight Gooden. James Neader, waiting in his office for word from the Mets, says, "We're more than 100% apart." But he adds that "one hundred percent is not insurmountable or surprising."

Al Harazin, his annoyance with Neader more apparent, says,

"I can't say exactly what they're asking for. He changes his mind. He changes what he wants. He's given us a range of figures."

Neader has already changed one stance, denying he said his client commanded a "seven-figure" salary. Now he says, "If Dwight were on the open market, he'd get a million dollars."

Gooden remains out of the open market and, for the most part, out of the often dormant negotiations.

January 11

PHILADELPHIA—Still tucked in the background is what to do with Tug McGraw. And from Boston comes a call to Giles from McGraw's agent, Phil McLaughlin. "Let's meet in the next week or two and see where we stand," suggests McLaughlin.

Giles agrees. There is little chance that the Phillies will retain McGraw as a pitcher. But Giles is formulating a plan to somehow keep the popular McGraw connected with the Phillies, perhaps as a broadcaster or community relations representative.

However, McLaughlin and McGraw will not be pinned down on how much McGraw still wants to pitch. He has received feelers from a handful of clubs including Boston, Cincinnati, Oakland, and the New York Mets. None of the clubs have made offers and McGraw won't reveal whether he'd accept an offer to pitch elsewhere. Both McLaughlin and Giles want to meet face to face with McGraw and pin down the pitcher on his future. So a meeting for later in the month is scheduled.

ANAHEIM—The Angels finally sign one of their free agents. Second baseman Rob Wilfong agrees to a three-year contract that provides the club with an option on a fourth year.

Wilfong platooned with Bobby Grich in 1984 and hit .248 after batting much higher for most of the year. He was selected by seven teams in the reentry draft but said it was his hope to remain in southern California, where he was reared and still lives.

But it wasn't until the latest injury to Burleson that the Angels, looking for infield insurance, agreed to improve their initial, two-year offer to Wilfong.

Mike Port also announces that the club is releasing reserve infielder Rob Picciolo and that there will be no attempt to sign pitcher Ricky Steirer or infielder Steve Lubratich, two minor-league veterans who had been unimpressive in several trials with the Angels and who would now automatically become free agents.

Port says that the injury to Burleson, coupled with the release of Picciolo and Lubratich, means that the club's backup infielders will come from among the following minor-league players: shortstop Craig Gerber, 26, who hit .230 at Edmonton; shortstop Gustavo Polidor, 23, who hit .223 at Waterbury; second baseman Norm Carrasco, 22, a .285 hitter at Waterbury; and second baseman Mark McLemore, 20, who averaged .295 at Redwood.

In freeing the roster of fringe veterans and committing varsity berths to younger players, the Angels remain consistent with their new philosophy.

January 14

ANAHEIM—The Boston Red Sox will officially announce the signing of Bruce Kison to a one-year contract today. The Angels had hoped that the 35-year-old right-hander might agree to join them in spring training on a conditional basis, but Kison preferred contractual protection.

Kison joined the Angels in 1980 as a free agent after nine years with Pittsburgh. His five years with California were marred by a series of injuries. He had nerve surgery on an elbow and wrist in 1980 and back surgery in 1983. He returned to the pitching staff in the second half of 1984, but recurring back problems resulted in his being dropped from the rotation during the September pennant race.

Says Port, "I admire the courage Bruce has displayed in coming back from his injuries and I have great respect for his pitching ability when he's healthy. We wanted him in spring training but felt we couldn't make a contractual commitment until we had seen him pitch in game situations."

Those reservations are obviously not shared by John Mc-Namara, who managed Kison with the Angels in 1983 and 1984 and will now be his manager in Boston. McNamara had urged the Red Sox to sign the intensely competitive Kison.

NEW YORK—The Mets sign Ron Gardenhire, one of their seven players eligible for salary arbitration, to a one-year contract. It is a "split" contract that will pay Gardenhire at the annual rate of $100,000 for days on the major-league roster and $75,000 for days on a minor-league roster. "Ron Gardenhire can always play for one of my teams," Cashen says. The formulation of the contract shows that he's not entirely sure which one.

ATLANTA—Everywhere John Mullen turns, someone asks him why the Braves haven't traded for Larry Parrish. Mullen is very conscious of baseball's tampering rule, perhaps because Braves owner Ted Turner was once suspended from baseball for a year for violating it. So Mullen will never utter the name of any player he'd like to obtain in a trade, or address any question that includes the name of a player on another team.

Still, it's no secret in the Braves organization that the team desperately wants Parrish. It would be perfect: a power-hitting third baseman who could replace Horner both in the field and at the plate, and then move to the outfield when Horner returned. But Texas keeps mentioning two names Mullen finds unacceptable—Steve Bedrosian and Rafael Ramirez—and the talks appear to be headed nowhere.

The Braves know that Texas needs a middle infielder, a catcher, and a pitcher, and the Braves have their own way of filling in the blanks with second baseman Glenn Hubbard, catcher Bruce Benedict, and pitchers Jeff Dedmon, Donnie Moore, or (reluctantly) Craig McMurtry. This isn't a bad package, but so far Texas insists on Ramirez, Bedrosian, and Benedict.

Turner, still not nearly as fearful of the tampering rule as Mullen, is asked if he thought Parrish could be obtained. "The Rangers aren't going to trade him," he says bluntly. Well, what about going after Jim Rice? "The Red Sox are going to sign him."

"We'd like to do something, get a hitter," Turner says, "but it doesn't look to me like it's going to happen."

HAINES CITY, FLORIDA—Someone else is talking about the Larry Parrish-to-Atlanta rumors: Larry Parrish. Baseball players are very much tuned in to trade rumors that involve their name. Parrish has been hearing them for about a month now. Parrish to Pittsburgh? Parrish to Atlanta?

"For me, Atlanta would be the ideal place to play," he says. "All my family and many of my friends live in Florida. Most of them watch all the Atlanta games on cable. It would be ideal."

But will it happen? "I have no idea," Parrish says. "I'm in the dark, just waiting to see."

Money Matters

January 15

NEW YORK—Establishing a tight salary structure has not been the overriding concern for the Mets since Doubleday Sports, Inc. purchased the club from the Payson–de Roulet family in January, 1980. The Mets pay their employees, particularly their players, quite well. Since that purchase, they have given a five-year, $3.125 million contract to Craig Swan; a five-year, $3 million contract revision to Dave Kingman upon his 1981 return to the club; a five-year, $10.2 million contract to George Foster in 1982; the respective $8.4 million and $3.8 million five-year contracts for Keith Hernandez and Mookie Wilson in the winter of 1983–1984; and, of course, the club's assumption of the final five years of Gary Carter's seven-year $13.1 million contract.

"Our overall talent is not controlled by how much we have to pay to get it," owner Nelson Doubleday says. "You can call the Mets a lot of things, but you can't call us cheap. We pay what we have to pay. We're competitive in salaries. And this is New York. My guess is that costs us an extra 10% [in salaries]."

Doubleday, who owns 95% of the club, already has paid far more in players' salaries than the $21.1 million paid to purchase what he considers a "gold mine" franchise. In the first five years of his ownership, the Mets' average salary increased from the pre-Doubleday figure of $93,607 for 1979 to the $282,952 for 1984. The player payroll that had ranked 17th among major-league clubs in 1979 rose to eighth in 1982 when Foster was added, and stood 10th at $306,253 in 1983.

The average and rank fell to $282,952 and 20th in 1984 because the payroll no longer included Tom Seaver, Dave Kingman, Craig Swan, and Mike Torrez, who collectively had earned $2.635 million in 1983. In their places were young players whose earnings were around the major-league minimum of $40,000. The Mets' payroll of 28 players included 12 players earning less than $100,000 for 1984 and 22 earning less than the major-league average of $329,408.

The Major League Baseball Players' Association, which calculates players' salaries, uses only the salaries of players on the clubs' 25-player rosters and disabled lists as of August 31. So the average figures do not necessarily represent exactly how much a club paid its players. The Mets' average salary would have been higher if it had included money paid to released players such as Kingman, Swan, Torrez, Dick Tidrow, and Randy Jones, and to minor-league players with major-league contracts such as Scott Holman and Brian Giles.

CLEVELAND—Running a team stocked with young players may mean few victories, but it also means few contract problems.

Andre Thornton was the Indians' primary concern. But once they signed him at the winter meetings, that left no other Cleveland player in line for a long-term contract. In fact, the only other player on the roster with a multi-year contract was Bert Blyleven, who earns $650,000 annually through 1987.

Since Thornton was the only Indian eligible for free agency, the only negotiating ploy left for most of the Cleveland players was arbitration.

Tony Bernazard, Brett Butler, and Neal Heaton all considered that route, but found the Indians surprisingly reasonable so long as the subject was a one-year contract.

Butler will receive the biggest boost, going from $195,000 to $450,000. Butler batted .269 and led the team with 52 steals, 86 walks and 108 runs scored. He also learned how to bunt. After having only three bunt hits with Atlanta in 1983, Butler bunted 52 times for 29 hits and a .558 bunting average for Cleveland.

"I really thought the Indians would offer me a long-term contract," says Butler. "I guess with the ownership situation up in the air, they don't want to saddle the new owners with big contracts. No one said it, but that's the impression I got."

Bernazard had a deplorable year, hitting only .221, committing 20 errors in 140 games and losing his second base job to Mike Fischlin in September. He had demanded a trade, but changed his mind and signed with Cleveland for the same $365,000 he earned in 1983.

"No matter what kind of year he has, you just don't cut the salary of an established player," says Indians general manager Phil Seghi. "It probably was the middle 1970s when I last cut a name player."

Another player who ordinarily would be facing a cut is Heaton. In 1983, he was 11–7 with seven saves as a rookie. He signed a contract with a base salary of $115,000 for 1984. He would receive $25,000 for reaching each of three plateaus of 25, 30, and 35 starts.

About all Heaton can say for 1984 was that he attained all his incentives and raised his salary to $190,000. "My mind was on getting the appearance bonuses," says Heaton. "Sometimes, I pitched when I shouldn't have just to get them."

Bothered by a tender elbow early in the season, Heaton kept pitching. By the time his elbow healed, his ego was hurting and he finished with a 12–15 record and a 5.21 ERA. He can tell you all about the sophomore jinx.

Nevertheless, Heaton gets a raise—a straight salary of $220,000 with no incentives.

"I just wanted to be paid in cash," says Heaton. "I spent all of 1984 worrying about the stat sheet and that's not the right frame of mind for pitching."

"Neal did struggle," says Dick Moss, Heaton's agent. "Everyone knows it was an unimpressive year, but the Indians also realize he has a lot of talent and a great future."

Yes, $220,000 is now the going rate for a horrible year but a great future.

ATLANTA—Most of the Braves' key players, including all of their regulars except Rafael Ramirez, played 1984 under multi-year contracts and have nothing to negotiate or renegotiate this winter.

But other significant contributors to the 1984 team—players such as Ramirez and pitchers Rick Mahler, Donnie Moore, Steve Bedrosian, and Pascual Perez—are not under contract for 1985 and have the right to file for salary arbitration if they cannot reach agreement. For much of the first two weeks of the New Year, Mullen has been negotiating with these players' agents, and the talks are going smoothly in most cases.

Ramirez wants a five-year contract, and the Braves are willing to give it to him despite his .218 batting average the second half of last season. Mahler is seeking a four-year contract, and will probably get it—quite a change from a year ago when he was all but unwanted. Moore is still thinking in terms of the three-year, $2 million contract his agent had first mentioned in October, but the Braves aren't taking this too seriously. Bedrosian's agent says his client wants only a one-year contract but is not in any hurry to wrap up the negotiations. Mullen knows he is waiting to see what other players get.

PHILADELPHIA—Unlike other Phils executives, whose off-seasons are relatively relaxed and loosely scheduled, Tony Siegle is hunkered down in his office eight to ten hours a day. The reasons are contacts and salary arbitration.

Siegle is faced with signing 27 Phillies players, most of them younger players who play on one-year contracts. Among them are eight players who are eligible to go to salary arbitration. The Phillies have never gone to arbitration with a player in the 10-year history of the process, a record Siegle wants to keep intact.

However, this winter could be trouble. Among the eight players eligible for arbitration are Von Hayes and Ozzie Virgil, two of the club's 1984 mainstays and in position to make big bucks for the first time in their careers. Also eligible is reliever Larry Andersen, who had the first solid year of his career.

Veteran Jerry Koosman poses a unique potential case. He played 1984 under a one-year contract that has expired. He is not eligible for free agency because he was a free agent just last year. But he can go to arbitration, and after being the Phillies' most dependable starting pitcher for much of 1984 he is in a position to do some bargaining.

Siegle remains optimistic that he can avoid arbitration. He does his homework well, researching comparative salary figures meticulously, and maintaining an ongoing rapport with most players' agents. And he also has the security of knowing he is working for Bill Giles, a boss who is willing to spend some money on salaries and is also very cognizant of the potential negative effect arbitration cases can have.

But the presence of people like Hayes and Virgil on the potential arbitration list worries the Phillies, so they quietly decide to hire the services of Tal Smith. If the Phillies go to arbitration, they will have Smith as their hired gun. It is a weapon they hope won't be used.

But there are no guarantees what will happen when Siegle gets seriously into the various negotiations. It seems certain that most of the Phils eligibles will protect themselves by filing during the next 10 days. From then on, it will be up to Siegle to head them off before reaching the arbitrator's office, to sign the players before having to present a case.

January 16

ATLANTA—A deal is struck with Rick Mahler—four years, $2 million. "Considering where I was just a year ago, I couldn't be happier," says Mahler. "This gives me the security I've always hoped for."

January 17

ATLANTA—Today's winner is Rafael Ramirez—five years, $4.25 million. Asked to describe his contract, Ramirez says, "Perfecto." And asked about the $1 million of the contract that will be paid as deferred compensation, Ramirez says, "What do you call it? Security, right?"

CLEVELAND—One Indian who hasn't jumped at the chance to sign his contract is Ernie Camacho. Camacho thinks about holding out . . . or something. At least he wants to do it . . . whatever it is.

If all of this doesn't make much sense, don't worry. The world of Ernie Camacho is a remarkably different place from where most of us live. All relief pitchers are supposed to be slightly off their axis, but Camacho has raised eccentricity to an art form.

Ernie Camacho's fastball has been clocked between 92 and 95 mph. In one game he threw at 93 mph and then left complaining of a sore arm.

"The rest of the staff ought to have arms that are sore," said Indians manager Pat Corrales, the first man able to harness Camacho's talent. "The only problem with Ernie is between his ears."

Camacho was an afterthought in the Indians' Rick Manning–Gorman Thomas deal with Milwaukee in 1983. He came to spring training in 1984 as Corrales's special project.

"Ernie needs to do one thing—let me do his thinking for him," said Corrales. "Here is a guy who throws harder than Al Holland and all he wants to do is throw forkballs. Thinking is the reason he has been with six different organizations."

Camacho made stops with farm teams for Oakland, Pittsburgh, Baltimore, and Milwaukee, as well as a stint in Mexico City. In 1984 he was 28, but had less than a year of big-league experience.

In order to keep Camacho, Corrales convinced the Indians to cut Juan Eichelberger and swallow hard while paying off the pitcher's $300,000 contract. Camacho signed for the minimum salary of $40,000 and saved a team-record 23 games while going 5–9 with a 2.43 ERA.

He spent the year changing in front of a locker near the door.

"You never know, I could be gone any time," said Camacho. "This is the first year where my team made a deal with a player to be named later and that player wasn't me."

Corrales called Camacho "No Tricks," to remind him to throw nothing but fastballs until he got two strikes on a batter. Then, he might be allowed to throw one slider. Corrales called all the pitches from the dugout, eliminating the possibility of Camacho shaking off the catcher's signs.

Camacho's character is best revealed through his own words:

Uniforms: "I always wear No. 13," says Camacho, who signs his autograph "Ernie Camacho, 13." But Camacho opened the season with No. 42 on his back, and didn't change to 13 until May. "Doesn't matter, I'm 13 no matter what it says on my shirt."

More on uniforms: "At the start of the season I knew I could be gone at any time. Everyone else had two uniforms, but they only gave me one. No backup means they only have to take my name off one jersey to get rid of me. If I had two uniforms, I'd be like everyone else and not have to borrow someone else's pants when I get them dirty."

And more on uniforms: "I wear three pairs of sanitary socks and tie my shoelaces in three knots. It all fits in with the number three—as in three strikes and three outs."

Attention span: "Corrales would come to the mound and start hitting me in the chest to wake me up. It hurts, but it has been working. Sometimes, I just sort of drift and one of the infielders comes over and says, 'Ernie, are you with us? We're playing baseball.'"

The price of fame: "One day I had to autograph 100 pictures and my arm hurt. Sure, the other guys had to sign the pictures, but I did all mine in one day."

Geography: Camacho asked Chris Bando, "Hey, Chris, what state is Massachusetts in? New York, right?"

Motivation: "Corrales tells me that I have to keep the blood in my eyes until the game is over."

After the season, Camacho tried to be an economist. He asked the Indians for a three-year, $1 million contract. The front office wasn't amused and offered him a one-year, $125,000 deal.

"Last year, I didn't ask for anything up front," says Camacho. "The Indians traded for George Frazier and paid him $425,000 to be the stopper. He didn't do it and they traded him. Meanwhile, they got me to do the same job for $40,000. Guess what they would pay Frazier if he had the year I did? Real big money."

Camacho has virtually no contract leverage. He is almost five years from free agency and he hasn't been in the majors for the two full seasons required to qualify for the arbitration process.

"Are the Indians going to step on me?" asks Camacho. "Or will they make me happy like they did with Andre Thornton? They can have me for $1 million for three years."

The Indians know they can have Camacho for less than that, which means a contract tussle is shaping up.

PHILADELPHIA—To the casual observer, Tug McGraw has never known a serious thought. The public sees him pounding his glove against his leg, a nervous and exuberant mannerism he employs on the field. The fans see him dress in a green uniform on St. Patrick's Day or leap off the mound with arms clenched after a strikeout and see an eternal youth in a game too often played by super-cool stars jaded by big bucks.

However, McGraw is also a calculating and shrewd businessman, always cognizant of his image and with a trenchant eye on his own future.

But yesterday, on a brutally cold afternoon, he arrived at Veterans Stadium uncharacteristically beset by indecision. He had an inkling of what awaited him in his meeting with Bill Giles. From every indication, the Phillies were not going to ask him back as a player. They did seem willing to keep him in the organization in some other undefined function.

However, there were other decisions for McGraw to weigh.

He had had feelers from a handful of other clubs willing to give him a chance to pitch again. McGraw still wanted to pitch. But he also didn't want to leave Philadelphia. The area had become home for him. His children were established in schools, his garden produced an annual harvest of vegetables, his commercial endorsements and business interests abound. Like O.J. Simpson with Hertz, like Bob Uecker with Lite Beer from Miller, McGraw has become locally synonymous with First Pennsylvania Bank. It is an association that offers McGraw high visibility and a generous future. So leaving Philadelphia, if only for a year, could be an unneeded wrench this late in his career.

Meanwhile, Giles had put the tough decision-making behind him concerning McGraw. He had resigned himself to not inviting McGraw back as a player. Whatever public relations storm it might cause was probably less severe than originally believed. And by maintaining his offer of a position in the organization, Giles hoped to keep McGraw associated with the Phillies.

The meeting went easily for all concerned. Giles told McGraw what both already knew, that the Phillies would not offer McGraw a contract to continue playing. "I've sort of known that since last fall," McGraw told Giles. "Don't apologize. I understand. I understand that's the way baseball is. You have to move ahead with things."

However, McGraw could not give Giles an answer when asked to consider future employment.

"I just can't decide about that yet," responded McGraw. "Give me a few weeks to decide whether to hook on with another club. If I don't, I'll get back to you and we can talk about some specific possibilities."

Tonight McGraw is participating in an annual charity bowling tournament sponsored by Phillies outfielder Garry Maddox. He remains undecided about his future. "I'm at a point where I have to make some hard decisions that involve my family, my baseball career, and my post-career," says McGraw. "Right now, I don't know what is best for me and all the other considerations I have to keep in mind.

"But hey, I can't worry about that now. I'm in the middle of a match and I've got two strikes going. You gotta have priorities."

With that McGraw goes back to bowling, blithely kidding with spectators, and looking like a man without a care in the world.

It is breakthrough time for the Rawley negotiations. Tony Attanasio had intended to fly to Philadelphia for a final face-to-face meeting. However, after detailed phone conversations with Siegle and finance overseer Jerry Clothier, the trip isn't necessary. Aside from the legal language, the deal is all but done.

Everybody gets a little something. Rawley will get the $100,000 he wanted for dropping his trade demand, and the final year (1987) of his current contract will be guaranteed at its full $850,000 value. The Phillies get Rawley's contract extended three years, running to 1990, with none of those three years guaranteed. The Phillies will have to renew their option on Rawley in each of those three years; if they don't, Rawley will receive a $200,000 buyout. So in effect Rawley gains more than a million dollars, thanks to his now-guaranteed 1987 salary, plus the $200,000 he is guaranteed if and when the Phils don't renew his option. Even Attanasio gets something, the fee for his services being a percentage of the $100,000 Rawley receives for dropping the trade demand.

Most importantly to the Phillies, they are guaranteed Rawley's services; should he break through and become the 20-game winner they see him as being, then the Phillies have him under contract at today's market value. History suggests that today's market value should be a tremendous bargain by 1990.

January 18

NEW YORK—The career of Tim Leary has taken so many twists and turns. Today it turns away from the Mets. Leary, the phenomenon of the Mets' 1981 spring training, is dealt to the Brewers as part of a four-club trade that brings right-handed pitcher Frank Wills to the Mets.

George Bamberger gets his wish and imports Leary from the

Mets and Danny Darwin from the Rangers. Veteran catcher Jim Sundberg gets his wish and moves from the Brewers to the Royals. The Rangers get their wish and acquire catcher Don Slaught from the Royals. And Leary gets his wish—to leave the Mets organization. "I wanted out . . . to anywhere," he says. "So this is good. I have nothing against the organization, but there's no room. They have so many good young pitchers. I guess I've been passed up by some of them. So the Mets really did me a favor."

"Tim Leary is and has been a pitcher with unlimited promise," Cashen says. "With the Mets it has been a litany of promise unfulfilled."

Neither the Mets nor Royals identify the trade as a "dump" of once-promising but now unwanted players. Cashen says Wills is "on the verge of contributing on the major-league level" and that the Royals were not looking to trade him. (By the end of spring training, the Mets will deal Wills to the Mariners, and the Brewers will send Leary to the minor leagues.)

ATLANTA—Donnie Moore's agent, David Pinter, realizes he is getting nowhere in his efforts for a three-year, $2 million contract, and he realizes the Braves aren't enthusiastic about his request for a one-year contract worth around $500,000. He files for salary arbitration, asking that Moore's 16 saves of 1984 be rewarded with a $490,000 salary in 1985.

Mullen sees little hope of settling this difference before a hearing. He is thinking of submitting a $350,000 figure to the arbitrator.

ASHEVILLE, NORTH CAROLINA—Hughie and Lois Alexander are just sitting down to dinner when the phone rings. "Goddamn, Lois, tell whoever the hell it is to call back in an hour because I want to eat dinner without being interrupted," declares Alexander. Lois dutifully gives the message to the caller. "Who was that, anyway?" Hugh asks. "It was Al Campanis of the Dodgers," she replies. "I hope you just didn't screw up something by being such a stubborn SOB."

Campanis and Alexander go back five decades to when Alexander was an up-and-coming outfielder out of Oklahoma and Campanis was a Dodgers talent scout. Alexander ended up being a phenom in the Cleveland organization until he lost his hand in a drilling accident. He then became a scout. That was 51 years ago.

Campanis later hired Alexander as a scout, and they worked together with the Dodgers for 15 years before Alexander joined the Phillies in 1971. Campanis would not be surprised by Hughie telling his wife (his fifth) to hang up the phone and have dinner. Campanis has had much experience with the legendary Alexander charm.

The Dodgers general manager calls back later that evening. Usually, the two chat and exchange gossip, all the while keeping their true intentions well guarded. Both are horse traders from way back. They're always looking for an edge.

But on this evening, Campanis rambles on for over 45 minutes, reiterating how much the Dodgers need a big hitter, "one of them sons-a-bitches who can hit the damned ball over the fence," as Alexander likes to call them. Then Campanis knocks Alexander back on his heels by asking if the Phillies would be interested in Dodgers relief pitcher Tom Niedenfuer. Alexander says, "Hell yes." However, Campanis reiterates that he needs front-line, proven offensive help, something the Phillies obviously don't have to spare. So the Niedenfuer reference is taken by Alexander as a signal to spread the word to other clubs that the Dodgers are willing to relinquish Niedenfuer.

Still, Campanis wants to talk. He goes on about the Dodgers' need for a proven left-handed hitter of any kind, and Alexander quickly jumps in with the name of Al Oliver. The Phillies have been dying to get rid of Oliver all winter and when Campanis expresses interest, Alexander leaps to the attack. "Al, he's yours, I guarantee you that," says Alexander. "We've talked to some other clubs but if you really want him, we'll give you first shot. And we won't ask you for much in return, just a second-line pitcher or something like that."

Campanis counters by throwing out the name of pitcher Pat Zachry. Alexander says he'll get back to Campanis the next day.

After he gets off the phone with Campanis, Alexander calls both Owens and Giles to fill them in and gets the okay to keep talking. It is agreed Owens will call Campanis and try and sew up the deal. The Dodgers, however, will soon have other, more serious problems.

January 20

NEW YORK AND LOS ANGELES—No one expected negotiations for a new basic agreement between major-league owners and the Players' Association to be easy. The main issues—free agency, salary arbitration, and payments into the players' pension fund—are all sensitive and high-stakes items riddled with potential for impasse.

But with the antagonists of the 1981 players strike—Marvin Miller and Ray Grebey—no longer in positions of power, the atmosphere was expected to improve. A settlement would still be difficult and necessitate months of tedious bargaining and posturing, but most principals expected the climate to at least be one of mutual trust and cordiality.

However, the calm surrounding the talks is shattered today by the headstrong Dodgers. Long the most sensitive of clubs to its own image and embarrassed by a series of drug and alcohol incidents (the most notable being the Steve Howe case), the Dodgers have been advocating that mandatory, random drug testing be part of the players' contracts.

Such testing is strongly opposed by the players as an invasion of privacy. The volatile issue had apparently been sidestepped the previous summer when owners and players reached accord on a drug agreement that called for testing only by mutual consent of player and club. "It's a very tough issue and I felt it was good that we put it off until after we get through the basic agreement negotiations, which are tough enough by themselves," said Lee MacPhail, who heads the owners' negotiation team.

But both MacPhail and the Players' Association are shocked to learn that the Dodgers have taken it upon themselves to include clauses allowing random drug testing in contracts being tendered to mostly younger players who are receiving one-year offers.

The storm broke when it was revealed that such drug-testing clauses were included in contracts signed by outfielder Mike Marshall and veteran shortstop Bill Russell. The players and their agents had resisted the clauses only briefly. But Players' Association officials hit the roof.

They immediately suspend all negotiations with the owners until the drug-testing issue is confronted. Donald Fehr, the association's acting director, denounces the Dodgers' action and will fly to Los Angeles to meet with Dodgers players, whom he suspects are being pressured by Dodgers officials.

Meanwhile, MacPhail hurriedly puts together a conference of his owners' advisory panel to discuss the next step. And after a few days of charges and countercharges, the players and owners will finally reach an agreement in which the Dodgers will drop their drug-testing clauses. But the incident has soured what was an atmosphere that seemed at least professionally amicable. The players feel betrayed, and in negotiations that have not yet yielded progress, such feelings can harden positions. What the Dodgers have done sets back the negotiations indefinitely. And though no one is yet talking strike, for the first time you hear speculation about which date the players might set as a target.

ATLANTA—When the Braves signed Bruce Sutter, they bought themselves, in addition to the premier reliever in baseball, a slightly increased risk of losing a player in the procedure known as the free-agent compensation draft.

The heart of the 1981 baseball strike was the issue of compensation for free agents. The owners hoped to restrict the movement of free agents by requiring that a club signing a free agent give his former team a major-league player. The players held fast to their pool concept: Compensation would come not from that team, but from a pool to which all teams would contribute players. As noted earlier, clubs could apply for an exemption from the pool, but they were then ineligible to sign type A free agents. Ted Turner being

Ted Turner, the Braves had no interest in taking themselves out of the hunt. By signing Sutter, a type A free agent, the Braves reduced the number of players they could protect from the pool from 26 to 24.

So here they sit, trying to assemble the list of 24. "Twenty-four players from your entire organization," laments Henry Aaron. "That's 24 out of 175."

To start with, the Braves must protect all players with limited or full no-trade clauses: Bob Horner, Dale Murphy, Chris Chambliss, Claudell Washington, Len Barker, Gene Garber, Rick Camp, and Terry Forster. The proliferation of no-trade clauses, many given by Turner over the objections of his front office, is clearly a disadvantage here; if not for this restraint, the Braves would probably not have protected the expendable Garber, the overweight Forster, the erratic Camp, or the aging Chambliss. Because these four have no-trade clauses, the Braves can really only protect their 20 top players and prospects.

Next, they pencil in the names of the key members of the current team who do not have no-trade clauses: Rick Mahler, Pascual Perez, Steve Bedrosian, Craig McMurtry, Rick Cerone, Bruce Benedict, Gerald Perry, Glenn Hubbard, Rafael Ramirez, and Brad Komminsk. The list now stands at 18, and they haven't even considered the farm system yet.

Probably their greatest fear is that another club will pluck one of their top minor-league prospects. Loss of an established major leaguer can be extremely embarrassing, as the loss of Tom Seaver through this process was to the Mets last year, but loss of a top prospect can cause serious long-term damage to a club's plans. The Braves decide to protect Andrew Denson, their number-one draft pick in June 1984, and a player whom Aaron and others in the front office believe could be another Jim Rice or Leon Durham; Duane Ward and Marty Clary, two young pitchers whom Aaron says "every team in baseball wants"; Jeff Dedmon, their young reliever; Zane Smith, the young left-handed pitcher who excited the Braves in a late-1984 trial; and Paul Zuvella, a shortstop Aaron believes could start for many teams right now.

Twenty-four.

One significant absent name is Donnie Moore. The Braves rationalize leaving him off the list by reminding themselves that he was just a journeyman pitcher before last season. They hope that other clubs will still see Moore that way, and with two thousand players to choose from, they will not want to gamble that Moore can duplicate the best season of his life.

The Braves' list will be submitted to the Player Relations Committee. They can only sit back and wait until the three teams that have lost type A free agents—St. Louis, California, and Toronto—make their selections on January 24.

CLEVELAND—Pat O'Neill has said the Indians aren't moving. Peter Bavasi has said they aren't moving, squelching a Tribe-to-New Jersey rumor. Even Dave LeFevre, the majority owner in waiting, has said the club is not about to pack its bags and creep out during the dead of night.

But that isn't good enough for Ohio governor Richard Celeste, a Cleveland native who has been hearing rumors from some voters that the club is about to skip town. So Celeste travels to New York to meet with commissioner Peter Ueberroth about the plight of the Indians.

"The commissioner said he would work to keep the Indians in Cleveland," says Celeste. "But there is no way he, as the commissioner of baseball, can guarantee that the Indians will stay in Cleveland."

Celeste also asks Ueberroth how he would feel about Edward DeBartolo buying the Indians. DeBartolo lives in Youngstown, Ohio. He owns the Pittsburgh Penguins hockey team and his son owns the San Francisco 49ers.

One of the 100 richest men in the country, DeBartolo tried to buy the Chicago White Sox at the 1981 winter meetings. He was opposed by former commissioner Bowie Kuhn, who objected to DeBartolo's ownership of race tracks. Also, there were unsubstantiated rumors about possible ties to organized crime. Cleveland was the only American League team that voted to accept De-Bartolo's bid.

DeBartolo was bitter over his rejection. While a rumor of DeBartolo's buying the Indians pops up every few months, he has never made an official bid for the team.

Reportedly, Ueberroth tells Celeste that he hasn't made up his mind about DeBartolo, although Ueberroth also says he respects Kuhn's opinion on most matters.

None of this thrills LeFevre, who still insists that he isn't planning to buy majority interest in the club, but is talking otherwise.

"I heard that Celeste was pushing DeBartolo and I find that very irritating," says LeFevre.

In Ohio political circles, it is common knowledge that Celeste views DeBartolo as Santa Claus. Because of his immense wealth, DeBartolo appears capable of buying the Indians and building a much-needed domed stadium for the city.

"I don't know if DeBartolo is willing to pay what it takes to buy the Indians," says LeFevre. "I don't care how much money anyone has, one person just can't buy a team anymore. It's going to take $40 million to buy the Indians and the new owners better be ready to write a $5 million check each year to cover the losses. And if Celeste thinks that DeBartolo will build a new stadium by himself, that is really ridiculous. It just shows he is not very bright."

Celeste is obviously showboating for the cameras. He had made a similar grandstand play on the last day of the 1982 season, a miserable, rainy night in Cleveland. Fewer than 1,000 fans were there, wearing gloves and sipping hot chocolate as they braved low 40-degree temperatures.

Instead of talking to the fans, Celeste decided to address the players—with the media in attendance, of course. The governor was 30 minutes late. When the governor finally arrived, he made his way through the dressing room, smiling inanely with his hand out waiting to be shaken.

He told the players, "You guys have done a great job this year." They were in last place.

"I know you are as committed to keeping the Indians in Cleveland as I am," he said, forgetting that about half the team had publicly asked to be traded and the other half was considering it.

Celeste left to weak applause. No one was going to clap until manager Pat Corrales did and glared at the players to do the same.

The meeting with Ueberroth is being treated with equal respect.

January 21

ST. PETERSBURG, FLORIDA—James Neader says he has reduced his asking price for Gooden's 1985 salary to the "$500,000-plus range." The Mets are not impressed by what they consider "minimal movement" by Neader.

PHILADELPHIA—The long-running saga of Mike Lavalliere has finally resolved itself. After months of haggling and uncertainty, the young catcher signed with St. Louis as a free agent. And though they are not obligated to provide the Phillies with any compensation, the Cardinals decide it is only fair to send someone to Philadelphia as indirect payment for Lavalliere. The Phils end up with journeyman pitcher Ralph Citarella, who is assigned to the Triple-A roster.

And it now comes out that the Phils have not been completely forthcoming about the whole affair. Lavalliere's agent revealed that Lavalliere had in fact informed members of the Phillies' organization of his impending surgery long before the winter meeting trade with St. Louis. The embarrassed Phillies now acknowledge that Lavalliere did inform farm department assistant Jack Pastore, who neglected to tell the rest of the organization until it was too late. The Phils put up their smokescreen of blaming Lavalliere to protect Pastore.

All in all, the whole affair graphically illustrates the still-amorphous chain of command in the Phillies organization. No one holds the title of general manager, so there is no one focal point through which to funnel all information. Bill Giles of course is the titular head, but he doesn't deal with the relative minutia of injuries to lower echelon players like Lavalliere. The farm department is Jim Baumer's concern but scouting is somewhat splintered by the independent status of both Hugh Alexander and Ray Shore. Paul Owens's role is still nebulous at best, while Tony Siegle simply handles contracts and baseball regulations.

The chain of command is severely fragmented. So it was possible for the Lavalliere situation to slip between the cracks and create what ended up being an embarrassing and somewhat damaging episode. As Giles acknowledges, "We would have really liked to have Jeff Lahti, who could have helped our staff in a number of ways. Instead we wound up with someone in Citarella who the scouts think is no better than a marginal major-league possibility. The whole episode didn't help us a lot."

12 *Winners and Losers*

NEW YORK—Jesse Orosco, Doug Sisk, and Ed Lynch file for salary arbitration. Within four days, Orosco's agent, Alan Meersand, and Sisk's agent, Mike Childers, will submit figures to the Major League Baseball Players' Association, and the Mets will submit their figures to the Player Relations Committee. There is little reason to believe settlements can be reached before the cases go to hearings.

The arbitration process is an uncertain course for player and club. In general, however, even when a player loses a case, his defeat is at worst a qualified one. The Players' Association estimates that salary figures submitted for a case by a club are higher than the club's final negotiating offer in about 85% of the cases. Whether the player settles for that figure before a hearing or loses the decision, he still gains.

"There's no definite way to tell. You try to present your client in the most positive way using any means possible that the arbitrator accepts," says Peter Rose, one-time associate counsel for the Players' Association, and now an agent. "You do what you can. Sometimes you feel you've made a terrific presentation, and it fails. Sometimes you figure 'I blew it.' And you win.

"It really is up to the arbitrator. When I was working for the Players' Association we used to kid about 'getting even' decisions.

If a particular arbitrator awarded a million-dollar salary in his first case, he would be reluctant to do it again if he had another big case.

"Who knows? It might work that way. You just prepare the best case possible, present it as best you can, and hope the arbitrator agrees with you. There is no formula, unfortunately."

Among other factors, an arbitrator can take into consideration a player's performance and length of major-league service, and the salaries of players at the same position and/or with the same length of service, and a team's salary structure. He may take into consideration a player's gate appeal, or how the player is used in the club's marketing. He may weigh the statistical reports—some of which can be rather esoteric—provided by each side. But remarks reported by the media are not admissible evidence.

In the Mets' current cases involving their two top relievers, Meersand seeks $850,000 for Orosco, an increase of $325,000 over what he had earned in salary and bonuses in 1984. The Mets' offer is $650,000. Childers, whose father Jack represents Keith Hernandez, seeks an increase of more than 400% for Sisk. He wants $470,000; Sisk earned $110,000 in salary and bonuses in 1984. The Mets propose $275,000.

The Mets are stunned by Childers's proposal, but not so surprised by Meersand, the agent the Mets executives dislike most. Very little Meersand does surprises them. They don't care for his tactics. A year ago, when Meersand was trying to negotiate Orosco's 1984 contract, he took his story to the daily newspapers that cover the Mets and *The Sporting News*.

Meersand accused the Mets of being cheap, and called their offers insults to his clients. The same issue of *The Sporting News* that carried the story contained several other reports quoting Meersand as saying that clubs had "insulted" one or another of his clients with low offers.

"He's making it harder on his clients by the way he goes about his business," Lou Gorman, then a Mets vice-president, said. "We might be willing to make some provisions for a player, but not when his agent tries to play us for fools. He does that, and the next time we talk, he'll say he was misquoted. It's hard to believe he was misquoted the same way in five cities."

PHILADELPHIA—Larry Shenk, the Phillies' veteran public relations vice-president, is one of baseball's most respected public relations directors. He learned long ago to accept negative press with the positive. He has been through the vicious anti-media atmosphere which permeated the Phillies' clubhouse in the late 1970s. Back then, ugly scenes were routine in the Philadelphia press box where the cognoscenti from the area media, no less opinionated than the notorious Veterans Stadium boo-birds, are prone to voicing, loudly and arrogantly, their every opinion. To be a public relations director of a club as controversial as the Phillies one must possess the thickest of skins.

But the one thing Shenk abhors is no press at all. So with the Phillies doing precious little to attract headlines, Shenk concocted a midwinter series of events to create coverage. One was a media day at Veterans Stadium at which Felske and several players would be available for interviews. Another was Shenk's annual press caravan to outlying cities which would include a group of players, John Felske, and the club's highlight film.

Media day at the Vet didn't produce much. It happened to be one of the coldest days in Philadelphia's history and among the no-shows were several of the players and the press. Even the players who religiously work out every day didn't show up. And players who are supposed to be working out but rarely do (Al Holland was the most notable of that group) continued to stay away. "Well, at least the pizza we served wasn't bad," said Shenk.

The caravan also yielded little. Felske was obviously ill at ease talking to large groups. But he did reveal some tidbits. One was that he intended to experiment in spring training with Charles Hudson as a reliever, another sign of the Phillies' concern for their bullpen. Felske also speculated that it was not out of the realm of possibility that young Ramon Caraballo, the burly hard-throwing

Dominican reliever, might make the club if he impressed them in Florida. And Felske resurrected the near-departed Ivan DeJesus by saying that if DeJesus plays like he did in 1983 and not like he played in 1984, he would have to be seriously considered for the front-line shortstop position.

ANAHEIM—The Angels emerge from their winter's near-hibernation today to acquire needed relief pitching and left-handed hitting outfield insurance. Both events, curiously, are the result, in one way or another, of Baltimore's signing Fred Lynn.

Donnie Moore, who led the Atlanta Braves with 16 saves in 19 save opportunities, is drafted by the Angels as compensation for the loss of type A free agent Fred Lynn. And Ruppert Jones, who batted .284 and drove in 37 runs in 79 games with Detroit, is himself signed as a free agent. He receives a one-year contract that gives the Angels an option on a second year.

Lynn's departure left the Angels in need of a left-handed hitting outfielder. Jones had been selected by the Angels three days earlier in a supplementary draft for free agents who had not yet signed following last November's reentry draft. Jones was initially drafted by five teams but wasn't satisfied with the offers he received. He says his patience paid off in that he had hoped to play in California, particularly for a team close to his San Diego–area home. Jones figures to play several roles: pinch hitter, designated hitter, and perhaps some right field. He says he accepts the fact that the amount of playing time he receives will depend on his contributions.

General manager Mike Port says, "Whether he platoons with Mike Brown in right field or simply provides left-handed protection, Ruppert gives us a player who can shore up the outfield."

Remembering Jones from when he first broke in with the Mariners, Gene Mauch says, "His first year in Seattle I thought Ruppert would be a super player. I still feel he's yet to have his best year. He covers us in a lot of ways. We were short a left-handed bat and I feel fortunate to get one that's this good."

Moore could be a pivotal acquisition; the loss of free agent Don Aase left the Angels with the inconsistent Doug Corbett and Luis Sanchez as their primary stoppers out of the bullpen.

"I inquired about Donnie Moore last season," Mauch says, "and the feedback I got from National League players was that Bob Gibson had taught him how to pitch low and away. There were only three balls hit out of the Atlanta park off him and that's remarkable."

"Whether I'm the stopper or not," Moore says, "I'll get an opportunity that I wasn't going to get in Atlanta. I'm going where I'm wanted. Atlanta might be a little bitter about the arbitration but I don't care. That's now in my past."

Should Moore's arbitration case go through to a hearing, the Angels will be forced to live with the figures submitted while Moore was still with Atlanta. Port is hopeful of reaching a contract agreement before the hearing.

"This can be settled in five minutes, that's the Angels way," Moore's New York agent, David Pinter, says. "They've already opened the door for Donnie, which is what the Braves should have done."

Moore was recommended to the Angels by former Atlanta manager Joe Torre. "It probably won't be a detrimental thing that the guy who managed him last year will be doing TV for us and available to help if Donnie needs it," Port says.

The Angels selected Moore from among 2,000 players who were left unprotected by their respective clubs in the compensation draft. The Angels (Lynn), St. Louis Cardinals (Sutter), and Toronto Blue Jays (Cliff Johnson) were the only clubs to have lost a type A free agent (as determined by statistics over a two-year period), and were thus eligible to draft for compensation.

"There were some starting pitchers available, but for the most part they fit into a category of having great potential," Port says, "and we already have a few in that category. We were looking for someone who could help us immediately. Moore's relief numbers were among the best in baseball last year. I'd like to think he can be our stopper. The way he came on last year indicates he's approaching the crest of the hill, that he's on top of his game."

ATLANTA—Every few weeks, it has seemed, the front office's view of Donnie Moore's role changed. He was a journeyman pitcher when they first acquired him, but he suddenly developed into the Braves' most dependable reliever in 1984. Back in October, the Braves were considering trading him, perhaps to the Phillies for Bo Diaz. And then, as the winter progressed and Bruce Sutter was signed, the Braves began to see Moore as a possibly invaluable middle reliever, someone to set the stage for Sutter's arrival in games. And then, Moore's agent filed for salary arbitration, seeking $490,000, some $115,000 more than the normally generous Braves were offering.

But now, all of that is academic.

As it turns out, both the Angels and Blue Jays intended to pick Moore, who apparently convinced a lot of scouts last season that he had belatedly but genuinely arrived. But the Angels got the first pick because they had the poorest 1984 record of the three teams eligible.

The Braves still have Sutter, the league's best relief pitcher the year before, but they have lost their own best reliever of the previous year.

Eddie Haas, who had begun to visualize a bullpen tandem of Moore and Sutter, says he'll now be looking for veterans Gene Garber and/or Terry Forster to reestablish themselves in spring training and become the setup man for Sutter.

The significance of the Blue Jays' reported interest in Moore is not lost on his agent, Dave Pinter. He says he'll be taking out a $3-million insurance policy against injury on Moore, anticipating that his client, eligible for free agency in a year, could gain a contract worth at least that much at that time.

Indeed, a busy and bizarre winter for Donnie Moore.

January 25

PHILADELPHIA—Tony Siegle is up to his ears in contract negotiations. Today is the deadline for players to file for arbitration, and he is racing the clock to get as many of the Phillies' eight potential arbitration cases signed.

Surprisingly, one of the easiest is Von Hayes. After his strong 1984 season, it seemed that Hayes would be among the likeliest of Phils to test arbitration. However, his agent is Dick Moss, one of the most experienced participants in arbitration, and he helped to move negotiations quickly; Hayes signed a one-year contract today. "The Phillies recognize that Von is a player who will just keep getting better and their attitude toward him in these negotiations reflected that," says Moss. "We really had little trouble getting an agreement."

As it turns out, Siegle has little trouble with most of the other eight potential arbitration cases. Larry Andersen, Luis Aguayo, Tim Corcoran, and Len Matuszek all agree to terms by today's deadline. Glenn Wilson ends up filing, but that is only a precautionary gesture since he ends up signing two days later.

That leaves Ozzie Virgil and Jerry Koosman, and it has become quickly apparent that they are on the way to being the Phillies' first arbitration cases. "It doesn't look good," acknowledges Siegle when informed that both Virgil and Koosman have filed for arbitration. "We'll keep talking, but we're pretty far apart and I don't see a lot of movement happening on either side."

When the two players' arbitration figures are revealed, it is obvious why Siegle is concerned. Virgil, through his agent Arthur Rosenberg, has submitted a salary figure of $425,000, while the Phillies' figure is $275,000. Koosman, through his agent Moss, has come in with a salary figure of $865,000, while the Phillies' offer is $600,000. Negotiations will continue, but it seems evident that the Phillies will finally be indoctrinated into the high-risk world of salary arbitration.

GREENVILLE, SOUTH CAROLINA—This is the fifth of 11 stops on the Braves' own preseason promotional caravan, an annual parade made by the manager and a few players around the southeast about a month before spring training. There are interviews given, autographs signed, pictures taken—and maybe a few tickets sold. Eddie Haas, the Braves' new manager, is on his first caravan. He does it without complaint, recognizes it as part of the job he has wanted so long, but clearly this is not the part of the job that appeals to him.

The temperature is five degrees outside Haas's motel room, and President Reagan is speaking on the morning news program. Haas is watching TV with *Atlanta Journal* baseball writer Chris Mortensen. "You know, President Reagan has the gift of gab," Haas says. "I admire that in people. Things just roll off their cuff. I wish I could be like that, but I'm not. I have to think before I say anything."

Haas has had plenty to think about but little to say since he was named manager. And as he makes his way around the southeast on this promotional tour, his words are few. Questioners want to learn all they can about Eddie Haas, the consummate minor leaguer who has been thrust into the job of managing a team which dares call itself America's Team. But Haas resists answering personal questions.

"I can't be bothered that I'm not a good public relations man," he says. "Shoot, nobody is going to judge me for my public relations. The media, the fans, the front office are going to judge me for one thing: What kind of manager am I? That's all that really matters, when you get down to it. All that biographical past stuff is history, and the only time it serves any purpose is maybe in an obituary."

As Haas speaks to Rotary Clubs in the Carolinas, signs autographs at shopping malls in Tennessee, and endures press conferences in five states, he keeps trying to steer the conversation to basic baseball, nuts-and-bolts stuff.

"Baseball is a highly skilled game," he says. "But it is a simple game in that there are four things you must be able to do. You hit the ball, you run, you field the ball, you throw the ball. The idea is to refine your skills, always improve, and apply the skills it takes to play this game."

That is Eddie Haas, as he wants to be seen and heard. In the 4½ months since getting the job, he has spent some time hobnobbing at the World Series, some time working with young players in the Florida Instructional League, and some time in organizational meetings. But he also has spent much of the winter in his home in Paducah, Kentucky, driving his jeep, drinking his beer, smoking his pipe, playing cards, cutting trees with a chainsaw, helping neighbors with various projects, and spending time with his three children.

Usually, January "is our month, the family's month," says Haas's wife, Judy. But January 1985 is a month of public relations appearances for Haas.

"I think that's definitely the one area where Eddie has to adjust," his wife says. "He is not comfortable in front of a camera. He's kind of a private person. I've been going through some newspaper clips from his years in the minors, and almost every writer who has covered him says it takes about a year to get to know him. But he talks a lot more around home. He likes to have a good time with family and neighbors."

Haas will be able to return to his family and neighbors for a couple of weeks just before spring training when the promotional tour ends. It will end with the Braves Booster Club's annual banquet in Atlanta. Haas will be the featured speaker. The club bills this as his "inaugural address."

The banquet will end 45 minutes earlier than scheduled. Eddie Haas's "inaugural address" lasts 30 seconds.

ANAHEIM—Three Angels meet today's filing deadline for salary arbitration: pitcher Mike Witt, relief pitcher Luis Sanchez, and first baseman Daryl Sconiers.

Witt, who capped a 15–11 season with a perfect game, files for a 1985 salary of $600,000; the Angels offer is $450,000. Sanchez files for $425,000; the Angels' offer is $280,000. Sconiers asks for $175,000; the Angels offer $110,000. No hearing dates are set, and general manager Mike Port says he will continue negotiations with all three.

January 26

ATLANTA—Ted Turner, the Braves' owner, has been uncharacteristically quiet this winter. He yielded the spotlight to general manager John Mullen during most of the negotiations for Bruce Sutter, and he has rarely been seen around the Braves' offices at the stadium. But quietly, behind the scenes, Turner and his executives at the Turner Broadcasting System have been negotiating with the commissioner's office on an indemnity they will pay for televising Braves games into 50 states on Turner's superstation.

New commissioner Peter Ueberroth, soon after taking office, called market intrusion by superstations the biggest problem confronting baseball. And the Braves, being a contending team beamed nationally into 20 million homes, are an extreme example of the problem. Ueberroth made it clear that Turner would have to pay his fellow owners for this "intrusion" or steps would be taken to curtail Braves telecasts. Since Turner Broadcasting makes enormous profits from televising the games, Turner was willing to pay.

And pay big, it is announced today: $30 million over five years. The money will go into baseball's Central Fund, from which it will be distributed to the 26 teams—yes, 1/26 back to Turner's Braves.

"I'm glad it worked out," Turner says. "I'm trying to be a good citizen in baseball. I mean, I'd rather not pay. But you'd rather not pay alimony, too, and yet if you're in the situation of having to pay, you pay."

January 28

NEW YORK—Like Von Hayes of the Phillies, Ed Lynch is represented by Dick Moss, one of the highest profile agents in the business. Moss plays hardball, too, but doesn't use the tactics of a Meersand or Neader. The Mets' feelings toward Moss are not nearly so negative. If anything, they fear Moss and want to avoid confrontations with him.

Today, Lynch signs a 1985 contract even before Moss submits figures for an arbitration case. He receives a $90,000 increase in base salary, from $210,000 to $300,000. The contract includes the same bonus clauses that allowed Lynch to earn $30,000 in 1984. Wally Backman, another Moss client eligible for arbitration, doesn't even file for arbitration. Instead, he signs a one-year contract for $200,000.

January 30

ANAHEIM—Continuing negotiations today lead to the Angels' signing Mike Witt to a three-year contract. The arrangement is somewhat surprising in that by signing for a third year, Witt, who has four years of major-league service, sacrificed his first year of eligibility for free agency. The 24-year-old Witt says the contract security compensates for the loss of that option. He adds that he will only be 27 when the contract expires, and that he can consider free agency then.

The signing provides another intriguing example of baseball's new math. Witt had records of 8–9, 8–6 and 7–14 before blossoming with his 15–11. That adds to a 38–40 lifetime mark—and lifetime security.

The three-year contract guarantees Witt $2,150,000. He can make another $750,000 for a total of $2.9 million if he fulfills all of the incentive provisions.

This is how the contract works:

First, Witt gets a signing bonus of $100,000, and guaranteed salaries of $500,000, $700,000 and $850,000. He will get $1,667 for each inning he pitches this year between 151 and 240—or $150,000 if he pitches more. In 1986, he will get $2,222 for every inning he pitches between 151 and 240—or $200,000 if he pitches more. In 1987, he will get $2,777 for every inning he pitches between 151 and 240—or $250,000 if he pitches more. He can also make an annual bonus of $50,000 by winning the Cy Young Award.

Witt pitched 246⅔ innings in 1984 and ended the season with his perfect game. It appears that he pitched another in his contract talks.

February 1

BOSTON—As a Yale student and professional athlete, Ron Darling often has been at or near the top of a variety of lists. On this day, he is near the top of another, and is not at all pleased about it. William Weld, a U.S. attorney in Massachusetts, identifies the Mets pitcher as one of the 10 leading federal college loan debtors in Massachusetts. In his campaign to collect unpaid loans, Weld files 71 complaints in district courts in Boston and Springfield. Darling is said to owe $4,991.88.

Darling is miffed by the public announcement of his debt. "I think they could have notified me personally rather than through the media," he says. "It's not like no one knows where I work. Enough people send me letters and ask for autographs . . . I don't appreciate the fact that somebody is trying to make a name for himself at my expense.

"If they sent me letters right after I left Yale, I never got them. I had at least seven changes of address since I left. I never received it, never thought of it. I wasn't trying to duck anyone. They'll get their money."

(Five days later, Weld's office receives a check from Darling's agent covering Darling's debt. Darling will eventually speak with Weld's office to voice his displeasure with the public handling of the situation.)

February 3

SARASOTA, FLORIDA—A number of major-league players gather here to play in a benefit softball game. Darryl Strawberry, a professional hardballer and amateur eavesdropper, is standing near a group of Cubs players who have parted company with most of the others present. The Mets right fielder is struck by what he hears. "I was impressed by how close they were," Strawberry says. "They talked a lot. They talked about winning. I'd like to be talking like that soon."

ATLANTA—It would be easy to draw the wrong conclusion here. A hairline that long ago retreated from his forehead makes Chris Chambliss look older than 36. A battle against extra weight has become increasingly difficult for him. And he is spending the winter here, on the Georgia Tech campus, preparing for an antic-ipated second career in sports administration, observing the op-erations of the Georgia Tech athletic department.

Considering, too, that Chambliss in 1984 had the worst season of his major-league career, it would be natural to infer that he is acknowledging the erosion of his skills and the impending loss of his position as the Braves' first baseman by preparing for another line of work.

Wrong, Chambliss insists.

"This is by no means an act of retirement," he says. "I've seen players my age have the best years of their careers." He is confident of rebounding completely from his dismal 1984 season, when he hit .257 with nine home runs and 44 RBI, drove in only five runs after August 1, and did not hit a homer in his last 101 at-bats.

Toward that end, Chambliss has been taking batting practice during the offseason—the first time he has ever done that—and has been preparing for a spring training duel with 24-year-old Gerald Perry for the Braves' first-base job.

"Naturally, the presence of Gerald is a real thing," Chambliss says. "He is a tremendous talent. The key for me is to have a really good spring. If I don't, I won't have that much going for me. For the last several years, I haven't touched a bat until the beginning of spring training. But this year, I know I have to prove myself.

"Even if I have a good spring," Chambliss concedes, "they

may want to play Perry a lot anyway. In that case, maybe the best thing would be to talk to some other clubs."

But Chambliss, confident and comfortable with his situation, says he has talked with Eddie Haas and John Mullen, and "I've received encouragement. They tell me I will get an opportunity to play. If they had indicated I'd be a part-time player or pinch hitter, that would be different.

"You have to do what you have to do, but (being a part-time player or pinch hitter) would be hard for me. I'd really like the opportunity to play regularly. That's the way I think I will be most effective. I feel I have to win the job all over again this year. But it's been that way for 14 years. You can't live on what you did last year. Billy Martin used to tell me that all the time. He was kidding, but it's true. If you haven't done it lately, you haven't done it. I've always felt I had to prove myself."

Chambliss clearly did not like the way he was handled by former manager Joe Torre, who often benched Chambliss in favor of the now-retired Bob Watson against left-handed pitching. "Joe believed in moving things around," Chambliss says. "Despite the good things he did, he never stuck with the same team every time out. It seems like he tried to please everybody by getting everybody into the lineup.

"One of the big things for him with me was seeing that I got enough rest. But then he used Hubbard, Murphy, Benedict, and Ramirez too much. If you play every inning of every game, then you'll get tired, I don't care how young you are. It's hard to find that middle line, but if you know who the starters are, that's a beginning."

Physically, Chambliss appears in good shape, although he concedes, "I've been lighter. My weight tends to go up, but I'm working out all the time (racquetball, weightlifting). Muscles you don't use go away.

"I'd like to make the all-star team again," he says. "I've had some good seasons, but I've only made it once. And I'd like to get 100 RBI. Those are goals I think I can accomplish. They're not unrealistic. I've seen people shoot too high, get discouraged and not come close."

Chambliss is confident enough of his ability to bounce back that he talks about signing another contract after the 1986 season. "My goal," he says, "is to sign another, whether it's for one year or two years. I know I won't have the luxury of a five-year contract at my age. But if I can play into my 40s, I'll be satisfied."

And he can't visualize prolonging his career as a designated hitter in the American League. "A lot of guys my age move from another position to first base," he says. "I can do everything I've been able to do throughout my career, even better. My fielding average has always been high. I could do it (serve as a designated hitter), I suppose. There was a time when the Yankees would use two first basemen, one at first and one as a designated hitter. But the DH is for someone who can't play in the field. I can."

When his baseball career is over, Chambliss wants to be an athletic director at the major college level. That is why he is spending time this winter watching and learning from athletic director Homer Rice and others in the Georgia Tech athletic department. A graduate of Montclair (New Jersey) State College, Chambliss plans to get a masters degree in sports administration from the U.S. Sports Academy in Mobile, Alabama.

"I'd thought that being an administrator was a spinoff of what was going on down on the field," Chambliss notes. "It's not. It's business. The athletes are just one part of it."

He has no interest in a career in professional baseball after his playing days. "It's just not a very secure life. You get moved around like crazy. The Braves fired the manager, and all but one of the coaches lost their jobs, too.

"I know I can't play forever. We all know that. You never know when the last day of your career will come. But I'll play baseball until I can't play anymore. I'll be the first to know when my skills aren't there."

And will they be there in spring training? Privately, the prevailing sentiment in the Braves' organization was one of skepticism.

February 5

NEW YORK—"We're not close enough in our negotiations that a reasonable revision on our part is going to make a big difference," Mets vice-president Al Harazin says. And so the Dwight Gooden negotiations, already protracted and often dormant, remain on hold.

The club has yet to make an offer that would earn Gooden more than $265,000 in salary and incentives. James Neader's proposal is down $50,000 to $525,000. According to Harazin, Neader's proposals for incentive bonuses could earn Gooden another $200,000 over and above that. The Mets won't hear of it. Harazin indicates the club could renew Gooden's contract, as is its right under terms of the basic agreement, for $40,000. And if it does, Gooden will not be afforded any incentive clauses.

"They're not threatening me with that," Neader says from St. Petersburg. "But I'm aware of how they're thinking."

The Mets are certain that holding the line in the Gooden negotiations is vital. Foresight tells them as much. Gooden will be eligible for salary arbitration following the 1985 season. So will Darryl Strawberry and Ron Darling. The Mets recognize the potentially damaging reverberations Gooden's contract could have within the industry as well as in their own organization. "What do we give him next year," Harazin asks, "if we give him $500,000 now? If he has another great year, do we give him a million? After two years service? What do we do with Darryl if we give Dwight $500,000? What about Darling?

"There are a lot of unrealistic salary demands being made everywhere in the game. Clubs have to start holding the line. We're not doing this for anyone else. We're doing it for ourselves.We have to hold the line for our own good."

Neader continues his fight, a fight the Mets find annoying. The club is convinced Neader is in over his head, and suspects that Neader will learn to compromise when Dan Gooden, Dwight's father, tells him it's time to sign.

While Neader remains steadfast, Richman Bry, the agent representing Darryl Strawberry and someone the Mets trust, moves closer to an agreement on a one-year contract. They also discuss a multi-year contract.

February 6

TAMPA—Neader's retreat continues. He meets with Gooden and Gooden's father and is told by Dan Gooden that a spring training holdout would be unwise. "The only way he won't be there for the first day," Neader tells the Mets, "is if you don't meet with us before the first day (February 21). We've put the negotiations in a positive light. Now it's your move."

The Mets perceive Neader's latest words as an indication of a weakened position. They are not quick to respond to Neader's low-key ultimatum. They make him wait. They intend to meet with him before the start of camp as he has insisted, but they see no reason to let him know their intentions.

PHILADELPHIA—The thought of going to arbitration doesn't scare the Phillies anymore. In fact, there is some feeling within the organization—especially from hard-liner Siegle—that it will be healthy for the club to finally shed its virgin status and experience the trials and tribulations of the process. Siegle, who prides himself on his knowledge of baseball's financial structure, has long bridled at being part of the Phillies' laissez-faire image. He has listened for too long to criticisms from his fellow negotiators with other clubs that the Phillies pay their people too much and are afraid to go to arbitration.

The criticism stings Siegle because so much of it is true. Under the Carpenter regime, the Phillies were known for their easy-going approach to contracts. They always sought to avoid confrontation and things haven't markedly changed under Giles. Though Siegle doesn't necessarily relish confrontations, he believes strongly that the Phillies should at least make a stand once in a while.

Now they have the chance to do it twice with Virgil and Koosman. But making Virgil an example worries Giles. The Phils' catcher is coming off the first full season of his career. An excitable sort with little understanding of the baseball business, Virgil is almost certain to be rubbed the wrong way by the sometimes rough words of an arbitration hearing. Giles doesn't want Virgil to arrive at spring training in full sulk. He still wants to trade Diaz eventually, but if Virgil arrives mad at the club, it might affect the Phillies' ability to deal Diaz.

So Giles has sent word to Siegle to make a run at settling with Virgil before the scheduled February 12 arbitration hearing.

Arthur Rosenberg has been waiting for such a move. A local agent who has represented several past and present Phillies, Rosenberg thought the Phillies' posture with Virgil was out of character. So he was neither surprised nor unprepared when Siegle called late in the day on February 4 to reopen negotiations. They set up a meeting the next day and it was quickly apparent the Phillies were willing to meet Virgil more than halfway between the two arbitration figures.

So the breakthrough is accomplished. And with a frigid blizzard forming, Rosenberg sits in his suburban home tying up the loose ends of an agreement in a phone conversation with Siegle. Neither side gets everything it wants. Rosenberg has to come down from his $425,000 target, and the Phillies end up paying Virgil more than $75,000 more than their original cutoff figure, with incentives that could take Virgil's salary up to $400,000.

But the potential unpleasantness of arbitration is avoided. The Phillies are assured of having a happy catcher in camp when spring training opens in three weeks.

February 7

PHILADELPHIA—Paul Owens got in touch with the Dodgers' Al Campanis right after Hugh Alexander reported on the Oliver-for-Zachry possibility. The Phils and Dodgers agreed on the player-for-player swap in late January.

However, a snag developed. When the Phillies forwarded Oliver's contract to the Dodgers for their perusal, several undesirable aspects concerned the Dodgers. One was the money Oliver had deferred in his contract. The Dodgers have a longstanding policy against deferring money, and they weren't about to break precedent with a player like Oliver, who is near the end of his career.

There were other problems. Oliver still had a past salary grievance pending with the Texas Rangers from four teams ago. And he still had a clause in his contract, signed with Texas, that promised him future work with the organization after his retirement.

The Dodgers wanted no part of these complications. So until the Phillies could negotiate them away, the deal would not be official.

Negotiations between the Phillies, the Dodgers, and Oliver ended up lasting two weeks. One hangup was the effect on Oliver's tax situation if money once deferred was suddenly paid at once. Another hangup was who would buy out the other troublesome clauses, the Phillies or the Dodgers. The Phillies finally agree to pay the deferred money promised to Oliver up front with the Dodgers obligated for only his salary. The other clauses were also similarly adjusted.

So the Phils paid a hefty price for getting rid of Oliver. However, he was unwanted material they would have been happy to relinquish even if nothing came to them in return. The acquisition of a potentially helpful pitcher like Zachry is a bonus. "I would have been glad to get a minor leaguer," says Giles. "Instead we got a guy who should help our bullpen depth. To me, it was a hell of a deal."

Zachry, a down-home sort from Texas, will be a very different clubhouse personality than the cocky, outspoken Oliver. "Ah'm just happy to be going to a club that has a chance to win," says Zachry when the trade is finally official. "Ah'd like to be a starter but heck, it's all just pitchin'. And if they put me in the bullpen, Ah'll just try to be the best reliever I can for the Phillies. But y'all have to excuse me right now because I got to take care of one of the smelliest diapers in history. My little girl here just won't quit."

February 11

DALLAS—For Bob Horner, there is good news from the doctor. For a change. Dr. Peter Carter examines Horner's right wrist, says it is making good progress from the surgery, and tells Horner to begin swinging a baseball bat—lightly. Five swings, five times a day. No more. Horner smiles and says, "It's a start."

This is the best news Horner and his agent, Bucky Woy, have heard in months. "I'm not trying to play the medical expert on this thing," Woy says, "but at the rate things are going, I can't imagine Bob not being ready to play opening day. I think he'll be there."

But Horner himself is more cautious—"It's just too early to set a timetable"—and Dr. Carter will have no part of predicting when the Braves might have their team captain back in the lineup. He will thoroughly examine Horner's wrist again on March 4, and at that time will determine whether Horner can report to spring training.

"If everything's OK then, if I can leave immediately after that examination for spring training, then possibly I could get ready," Horner says.

If . . . if . . . if . . .

February 12

NEW YORK—Though morale was a major factor in the Phillies' negotiations with Ozzie Virgil, it is not a matter of concern with Jerry Koosman. The 43-year-old Koosman has been around, and he is not likely to misunderstand the necessities of arbitration. So the Phillies haven't made even a token effort to settle out of court, but instead pointed toward arbitration. Siegle prepared the case with the assistance of Tal Smith, the ubiquitous arbitration consultant. Opposing them is Dick Moss, veteran of over 50 arbitration cases and unquestionably the most able arbitration agent in the business.

The hearing begins at 9:30 A.M. in a New York office, presided over by arbitrator Robert Stutz, a University of Connecticut business professor and a professional arbitrator. Both sides think they have a strong case. The Phillies believe Koosman's age, his sub-.500 record, and the fact that they are offering to double his 1984 salary weigh heavily in their favor.

Moss is similarly confident. The Phillies' salary claims are blunted by the fact that in reality, Koosman earned $575,000 in 1984 through various bonus and incentive clauses, not just the $300,000 base salary the Phillies are claiming to be doubling with their $600,000 offer. Statistically, Koosman led the club in victories and starts and was second in innings pitched, and a start-by-start study of his season revealed several losses or no-decisions directly caused by poor offensive or defensive support.

The hearing ends up taking over four hours, with both sides making presentations that drag on with details. It is momentarily interrupted by the news that Boston's Wade Boggs has won a $1 million arbitration award. Siegle and Smith shudder.

When the hearing is completed, the consensus in the room is that Koosman has won. Says an observer from the owners' Player Relations Committee, "Well that one was a slam dunk for the player, that's for sure."

ATLANTA—Despite yesterday's encouraging news from Dallas, there are still whispers in the Braves' front office that they need a power hitter, that Horner's wrist is too precarious to bank on. But the Rangers have been unreceptive lately to talking about Larry Parrish and have obtained a catcher, Don Slaught, precluding any interest in Bruce Benedict. The Braves' not-so-secret dream of dealing Benedict, Glenn Hubbard, and Craig McMurtry or Jeff Dedmon for Parrish is obsolete. But they still hope another package might eventually woo the Rangers. Someone has told the Braves that Texas manager Doug Rader "just loves Hubbard." They cling to that morsel of information.

February 14

NEW YORK—Robert Stutz announces that he has ruled in favor of the Phillies in the Jerry Koosman case. Dick Moss is outraged. Before the hearing Moss had learned that Stutz was serving on a three-man panel with Tal Smith and former Players' Association boss Marvin Miller that would assess the value of the Boston Red Sox in a pending sale of club shares. Moss would have been within his rights to bring it up and judge whether there might be any influence on the Koosman case. But at that time he believed his case was so overwhelmingly in his favor that he decided to let the matter pass.

He is now convinced that, at least subconsciously, Stutz was influenced by his relationship with Smith. Moss does not have many avenues to pursue, however. The arbitration process does not provide for any appeal, because the arbitrator is chosen jointly by player and management.

Meanwhile, the Phillies are just pleased to have won their first arbitration case. Siegle heads back to Philadelphia late in the day, where he is jokingly greeted as a conquering hero by office staff. "At least we showed that this organization was willing to go to arbitration," says Siegle. "At least we showed we weren't afraid."

The Mets' two bullpen stalwarts, Doug Sisk and Jesse Orosco, learn in separate announcements today and tomorrow that they have lost their arbitration cases. The two will have to muddle through the 1985 season with salaries of $275,000 and $650,000, respectively.

Sisk's salary is an increase of $165,000 over his 1984 earnings. The Mets' cases were presented by Tal Smith.

In the Sisk case, Mike Childers attempted to equate Sisk's figure of $475,000 with the $425,000 award George Frazier had won against the Indians the previous year. Many baseball people say Childers was woefully unprepared for the case and that his figure was too high in the first place. Representatives of the Players' Association had to supplement his presentation.

Sisk is aware of the criticism but doesn't seem discontent. "I really didn't want to go through all this. I'm just glad it's over," he says. "I'll get by with what I'm earning."

The Orosco decision is more surprising. Alan Meersand had presented a solid case, and the Players' Association was confident Orosco would double his 1984 base salary of $425,000.

The arbitration defeat will cost Orosco in two ways. Orosco didn't win the $850,000 he had sought. Beyond that, he also forfeited an opportunity to sign a contract with lucrative incentive bonuses. If Orosco had agreed to the $650,000 base salary the Mets proposed before the arbitration case, the club would have been willing to include the same incentive bonuses that were in Orosco's 1984 contract, bonuses that enabled Orosco to earn $100,000 over his base salary. Arbitration awards cannot include incentive bonuses. "Jesse had to choose between a sure $650,000 with a chance to make another $100,000 or so," Al Harazin says, "the chance of losing and making a flat $650,000, and the chance of winning and making $850,000."

Orosco was the fifth Mets player to go through a salary arbitration case, and the fourth to lose. The Mets, of course, are delighted by winning and, in particular, by having beaten Meersand.

PHILADELPHIA—For weeks, the decisions have been taking shape for Tug McGraw. He has continued to receive inquiries from a handful of clubs, but more and more he has come to realize that he doesn't want to leave Philadelphia, that this is where he wants to remain and raise his family.

Staying in Philadelphia will mean retiring as a player, but that sacrifice seems small compared to the prospects of leaving his home. McGraw is undecided about what he will do; offers for television work have surfaced, and the Phillies still hold open their offer to be connected in some capacity with the club. But McGraw knows that his first decision has to be to announce his retirement and end the distracting inquiries from other clubs.

A Valentine's Day press conference is set up at Veterans Stadium. The news is hardly a surprise, so no one knows what kind of media treatment it will receive.

But it turns out that McGraw is even more of a local treasure than ever believed. All three major Philadelphia television stations televise McGraw's announcement live. Miles of flattering newspaper columns are written to the memory of McGraw's success and personality.

And, in keeping with his show-biz flair, McGraw comes to the press conference carrying his own personally produced highlight film of his career.

There are no tears and no regrets from anyone. McGraw is one of the lucky ones: He knew when the end had arrived and he accepted it with class and resignation. And though the Phillies will likely not miss the fading left arm, they'll never be the same after losing the man.

13 Who's Running

the Indians?

February 18

CLEVELAND—No one realized what a hole Gabe Paul created when he retired as president of the Indians. Since Paul's departure, the team has continually hired executives to handle what were once his duties.

The first was Peter Bavasi, who assumed Paul's title. Bavasi's next move was to put Phil Seghi completely in charge of major-league player personnel and make farm director Bob Quinn solely responsible for minor-league player development. Seghi and Quinn had those chores before, but Paul's heavy hand remained on their shoulders, strongly influencing their decisions.

Bavasi then hired two more people. The first was Terry Barthelmas, who was given the title of director of administration. Barthelmas was formerly the business manager of the Chicago Cubs; he has primarily the same job with the Tribe.

But the more interesting hiring was Danny O'Brien, the former general manager of the Texas Rangers (1973–78) and Seattle Mariners (1979–83). His experience and expertise is almost identical to Phil Seghi's. Does this mean O'Brien will eventually usurp Seghi?

"No way," said Bavasi when O'Brien was hired in mid-

December. "He will be my assistant and in control of revenue production. Dan has done so many things that he will be available to Phil, but Phil is in charge of the baseball end of the operation."

The hiring of Danny O'Brien naturally made Phil Seghi nervous. Cynical observers of the drift of the Indians' franchise suggest that the performance of the club rather than any front-office signings should have Seghi concerned. It isn't just that the Indians lack the talent to compete in the strong American League East. The club has suffered through a bewildering series of strategic shifts in the last few years, shifts that make fans wonder if anyone in the front office has any idea of how to build a winner.

The 1984 Indians had a surprisingly strong offense, finishing fourth in the league in runs scored. They played .500 ball over the last 112 games of the season, and did it with a group of young hitters that included Julio Franco, Mel Hall, Joe Carter, Brook Jacoby, and Pat Tabler. But their pitching was woeful; the team ERA was 4.25, third-highest in baseball, and without Bert Blyleven's terrific season it would have been an appalling 4.54. The team is going nowhere without acquiring some pitching.

Back in the early 1980s, they made a furious flurry of trades for pitchers. They traded Bobby Bonds to St. Louis for John Denny and Jerry Mumphrey. They traded Mumphrey to San Diego for Bob Owchinko. They packaged Owchinko to Pittsburgh with Gary Alexander, Victor Cruz, and Rafael Vasquez for Bert Blyleven. They sent Duane Kuiper to San Francisco for Ed Whitson; Jorge Orta, Jack Fimple, and Larry White to the Dodgers for Rick Sutcliffe and Jack Perconte; and Bo Diaz (in a three-way deal) to Philadelphia, receiving Lary Sorensen and Silvio Martinez from the Cardinals.

"Pitching is 90% of the game," said Gabe Paul at the time. "Look at the Houston Astros. For a couple of years, they could barely hit the ball out of the infield, but they won because of great pitching."

The comment ignored the difference between the Astrodome, one of the best pitcher's parks in baseball, and Cleveland Stadium, which has never been a bad park for hitters. Nonetheless, Paul had managed to assemble a pretty good crop of established pitchers. In the spring of 1982, the Tribe had in its camp no fewer than eight pitchers who had won in double figures as major-league starters: Blyleven, Sutcliffe, Denny, Whitson, and Sorensen; as well as holdovers Len Barker, Dan Spillner, and Rick Waits. Paul looked at all that pitching and declared the Indians a contender. They finished the season tied for last place.

Almost as fast as that staff was assembled, it was dispatched to points east and west. The front office lacked the patience to let some of the pitchers work through slumps and injuries, and they forgot that established players in today's game come with high price tags. In September 1982, the Tribe sent Denny to the Phillies for Roy Smith, Wil Culmer, and Jerry Reed. Two months later, Whitson went to San Diego for Broderick Perkins and Juan Eichelberger. In June 1983, Waits went to Milwaukee with Rick Manning for Gorman Thomas, Ernie Camacho, and Jamie Easterly. Len Barker was sent to Atlanta in August for Brett Butler, Brook Jacoby, and Rick Behenna. Lary Sorensen left for Oakland as a free agent at the end of the 1983 season. Spillner was dumped on the White Sox for Jim Siwy in June 1984; and, of course, Sutcliffe joined the Cubs along with George Frazier and Ron Hassey that same month for Mel Hall, Joe Carter, and Don Schulze. Only Bert Blyleven remains from that pitching crew.

Oh yes: John Denny and Rick Sutcliffe won the National League Cy Young Awards immediately after getting out of Cleveland.

The other thread running through these trades and others made by the club is fiscal. The Tribe has consistently signed its own players to expensive contracts and then sent them on to other clubs, usually for young players at or near the major-league minimum salary. In 1984 alone, Seghi and Paul reduced the Cleveland payroll by unloading the contracts of Sutcliffe ($900,000), Hassey ($500,000), Frazier ($425,000), and Spillner ($350,000). Of the four players they received in return, only Mel Hall was making more than the minimum $40,000; he made $90,000 in 1984. In addition, they sold Alan Bannister ($350,000) to Houston for $50,000. Not one notable player signed by the Indians to a long-term contract has remained with the team long enough to serve it out. This should give Andre Thornton pause.

In addition to giving Phil Seghi something to think about, the hiring of Danny O'Brien was bad news for farm director Bob Quinn. Quinn has been in charge of the Indians' farm system since 1972. Quinn has suffered as much as anyone from the disastrous swings in policy in Cleveland. He stoically accepted vicious tirades from Gabe Paul—despite his affable public face, Paul was much feared in the front office for his closed-door sessions—and Paul's orders to implement his latest policy brainstorms, always hoping that his faithful service would result in a chance at a general manager's position.

Quinn knew that he had never been given a real chance to show his talents in developing a farm system because of the constant money problems in Cleveland. Until the late 1970s, the Indians spent almost $750,000 less per year on their farm system than the average big-league team. In the mid-1970s, the club's scouting staff consisted of six men, one of them a full-time dentist. Indians farm hands were assured of getting to wear a uniform once worn by Bubba Phillips or Ken Aspromonte in the early 1960s. Each player was given four bats to last through the season; if they all broke, he had to buy his own.

Every year, Quinn would tell Paul and Seghi that the Indians needed to operate more than four minor-league teams to have any chance of competing on the major-league level. "We don't have enough prospects for four clubs," Paul would tell him, "so who needs another one?" While conditions did improve a bit in the early 1980s, the farm system's budget was still below the big-league average. This made it difficult for Quinn to enhance the big club, his reputation, or his chances of landing a general manager's job anywhere in baseball.

Even so, Quinn almost had a chance at the general manager's job in St. Louis in 1980. The Cardinals had hired Whitey Herzog as manager, and were looking for a general manager to handle the paperwork, as Herzog intended to make his own trades. Quinn was asked to interview for the position, which would at least give him the title he sought, if not all the responsibilities. Since Quinn was under contract to Cleveland, he needed permission to talk with the Cardinals, and discussed the situation with Gabe Paul.

"Herzog will be very hard to handle," said Paul. "I don't know if this is much better than what you have with us." Paul also told Quinn that the Indians were aware of his talent, and that the O'Neill family was very impressed with him. He decided to pass up the St. Louis interview, believing from what Paul had told him that he might one day take over the job with the Indians.

But now, four years later, Steve O'Neill is dead and the team is for sale. Paul has retired to Florida, and Peter Bavasi is in the president's office. And Bavasi is hiring men who will not only block any hope of Quinn's getting the general manager's job, but may well put him out of a job entirely.

The next hiring, ten days after O'Brien joined the club, was Jim Napier, who was named field director of player development for the minor leagues.

"The Indians have had their four minor-league teams sort of acting on their own," said Bavasi at the press conference to introduce Napier. "What we have to do is decide if our big-league fundamentals are the right ones. If they are, we have to pass them down to each team in the farm system. It's more than fundamentals. We have to make sure our players are playing in the right positions and that we have the right men serving as minor-league managers and coaches. We have to bring our farm system up to the level of those like Detroit, Toronto, and San Diego. When I was in Toronto, the major- and minor-league systems were completely integrated.

"There are three ways to build a roster. You can sign a free agent, which can be very expensive. You can make a trade, which is becoming increasingly difficult because of restrictive contracts. Or you can concentrate on developing your own players. We think there is a trend toward internal roster development.

"Instead of wringing your hands because you can't make a trade, you have to get involved in the next era of roster development. If you sit around and wait all year for two interleague trading periods, you're going to be spinning your wheels.

"And in many cases a club will spend the equivalent on player development as it does in paying the people on its roster. So it's important to build your team efficiently. What we have to do now is look at how to integrate the teaching and scouting of our players. Let's say a player in Double-A is good enough to bypass Triple-A and jump directly to the majors. How can we get that information? We need a system that lets us know in capsule form how every player is doing at all times.

"Jim Napier is the man who is supposed to set up that system."

Bob Quinn, who had thought he was the person who was supposed to set up that system, insisted that he didn't feel threatened by Napier's hiring. But when he heard that Joe McDonald had resigned the St. Louis general manager's spot this winter, he quickly called friends in baseball and the media, informing them of his interest in the job.

For most of the winter, the Indians operated with a virtual double bureaucracy in the front office. The muddled lines of authority between Seghi and O'Brien, both reporting to Bavasi, were sure to lead to problems. Those problems became quickly apparent in a late-January farce revolving around retired pitcher Ferguson Jenkins.

Why did Jenkins get the feeling he was going to spring training with the Indians?

"I got a call from Mr. O'Brien," Jenkins told an Associated Press reporter in Mesa, Arizona. "He left a telephone number with a Cleveland area code, but I wasn't sure it was the real thing."

"I happen to think he can still pitch and I hope he gets back to me," O'Brien was quoted as saying. "I was the guy who brought back Gaylord Perry to win his 300th (in Seattle), remember?"

Jenkins had spent the summer of 1984 pitching in a semi-pro league in Canada. He was also considering a career in politics—until O'Brien called. "I hope Fergie is not too far along in politics to come to spring training," O'Brien told the Associated Press.

Later, the story was far different. O'Brien denied ever having discussed an invitation to spring training with Jenkins. "It would be senseless. Pointless," O'Brien insisted. "I've known Ferguson for a number of years. We engaged in a brief, friendly conversation. He told me about running for some political office, and about his farm. We did talk about some baseball. I asked him if he still did any pitching and he said no. I said, 'Remember, I resurrected Gaylord Perry for his 300th.' I was just kidding."

Word around the Indians' office had it that O'Brien had indeed discussed coming back with Jenkins, but that Seghi learned about it and was upset for two reasons. First, the Indians are supposed to be on a youth movement, and the last thing they needed was a 41-year-old pitcher. Second, Seghi was angered by what he saw as O'Brien's intrusion on his turf. The Jenkins story made two things clear: one, that O'Brien and Seghi have very different ideas about what O'Brien's job is; and two, that it will be up to Bavasi to straighten out the situation—and soon.

Today is a quiet Sunday afternoon, and Cleveland Stadium is deserted, except for a couple of people in the Indians' Tower A office.

Bob Quinn is sorting through his paperwork, making sure he has packed everything for his trip to spring training. On Quinn's desk is an airline ticket he plans to use in three days. He wonders if this will be the spring training when his life finally changes. There has been no word from the Cardinals. At 48, Quinn can feel a serious midlife crisis coming on.

He has no idea how much worse it would get when he is summoned to Peter Bavasi's office. Quinn sees no special significance in the call; with spring training dawning, it is not uncommon for a team president to be in the office and to want to chat with the farm director.

Sitting behind his desk, Bavasi looks up from a piece of paper as Quinn walks in.

"Bob, we're going to make a change," says Bavasi, handing

the paper to Quinn. It is a brief press release stating that farm director Bob Quinn has resigned.

Quinn is stunned as he stares at the release.

"Of course, we plan to honor your contract," says Bavasi, as if he has a choice in the matter. Quinn is legally tied to the Indians until October of 1986, earning $50,000 annually.

"I knew better than to ask why Peter wanted my resignation," Quinn told friends later. "The deed was already done and all that. It wasn't time for conversation. Peter wanted to sweep out everyone from the Gabe Paul regime."

But Quinn does object to the wording of the release.

"I'm called farm director here," says Quinn. "But my official title is vice-president in charge of player development and scouting."

"Yeah, but in the papers you're the farm director," says Bavasi.

"I want my official title on the release," says Quinn.

Bavasi agrees, and Quinn walks out of the Indians' offices for the last time.

A little later, Phil Seghi has a meeting with Bavasi.

"When you retire, what would be your ideal job?" asks Bavasi.

Seghi says he would like to move to southern California to be near his daughter. He also wants to do some major-league scouting in that area.

"Suppose we move up the timetable on that," Bavasi says.

Like Quinn, Seghi knows this is no time for debate. He is finished, even though his contract will also run until October 1986.

"I'd like you to stay on until we get a new man," says Bavasi.

Seghi agrees. The meeting is over.

Tomorrow, Peter Bavasi will stand in front of the cameras and reporters, pulling the trigger of a baseball execution with a smile. Phil Seghi will stand by Bavasi's side, his pipe in the corner of his mouth. Bob Quinn will be represented only by the press release which called him vice-president in charge of player development and scouting.

"There was no useful purpose for us to go on as we were," Bavasi says. "You know, the players aren't dumb. They know when an organization is stagnating. These are the changes I wanted to make when I took over. We have to get this organization up to the speed of successful organizations. Things had to be done."

Seghi's new title will be "senior player personnel adviser," working from a base in southern California.

"If I were still in Toronto, I'd hire Phil in a minute," says Bavasi. "But . . ."

But the changes are necessary if Bavasi is to put his imprint firmly on the Indians. The ability of Quinn and Seghi is beside the point. In the case of the Indians, Bavasi feels change for the sake of change is necessary to purge the sins of the past.

The new front office will look like this:

President: Bavasi

Senior vice-president for baseball: To be hired. This man will replace Seghi.

Vice-president for baseball administration: Danny O'Brien, Bavasi's troubleshooting assistant.

Manager: Pat Corrales

Field director for player development: Jim Napier. He has replaced Quinn, although Napier will be in uniform and on the field.

Business administrator for farm system: Phil Thomas, who is in charge of paperwork for the farm system. He has been Quinn's assistant.

Director of scouting: To be hired.

Listening to the breakdown, Seghi says, "This is the first time I've ever heard of a general manager traded for a general manager to be named later."

In Seghi's 12 years as general manager, the Tribe's best record was 81–78 and a fourth place finish in 1978. "I have a clear conscience," Seghi insists. "As far as any regrets, it would probably be that we weren't able to put a championship team on the field. But considering the financial limits . . . well . . . you can't build a skyscraper with an erector set."

"The position of general manager is really a misnomer in baseball today," Bavasi says. "It really requires two people. One must be a baseball technician, a man totally focused on what is happening on the field. The other has to be a skillful administrator and I believe we have the best in the business in Dan O'Brien." O'Brien's main area of responsibility will be player contracts.

"I have a man in mind (to replace Seghi) but I haven't started recruiting him yet," Bavasi says. "He is presently working for another team."

And what qualities would this man have?

"He has to have a blind commitment to the Cleveland Indians. He needs complete tunnel vision. Nothing outside of baseball can matter. The Cleveland fans aren't interested in patience and that's the only way we can improve quickly . . . It also would help if the guy could walk on water. Our new guy has to be the type who likes to climb Mt. Everest just because it's there."

If nothing else, Bavasi has introduced inflation and bureaucracy to the Cleveland front office. Paul, Seghi, Quinn, and Phil Thomas held four jobs, which have become eight under Bavasi.

"You need an on-the-field technician and a front-office administrator for each of those positions," says Bavasi. "That's the way it's done in the 20th century."

14 *On to Spring Training*

February 18

ANAHEIM—General manager Mike Port avoids the often acrimonious arbitration process by reaching compromise agreements with first baseman Daryl Sconiers and pitchers Donnie Moore and Luis Sanchez. Each signs a one-year contract. Moore was hopeful of securing a multi-year contract, but accepted a 1985 salary of $375,000 rather than disrupting his new environment with a financial fight. He is eligible for free agency at the end of the year.

ST. PETERSBURG, FLORIDA—The retreat is complete. James Neader, having called for a "seven-figure" salary for his client and having promised—he said he never threatened—to keep Dwight Gooden from the Mets' spring training camp, has taken the last backward step. Gooden will not receive seven figures, or the $525,000 Neader once identified as his bottom line, or even the $350,000 that would equal the record second-year salary the Dodgers gave Fernando Valenzuela in 1982.

Gooden will work 1985 for $335,000.

On this day, Neader and Al Harazin finally reach what they identify as "an agreement in principle." The negotiations are not over; Gooden won't sign a contract for another nine days, and before he does, the Mets will find more reasons to dislike and distrust Neader. But for now, at least, there is an accord, tenuous as it might be. "You never can tell until a contract is signed . . . especially in this case," Harazin says.

The framework of the agreement calls for a salary of $275,000, which is still the second-highest ever given a second-year player. In an unusual and, so far as anyone connected with the negotiations can tell, unprecedented clause, the Mets give Gooden an additional $60,000 as an advance against future promotional or endorsement earnings. Gooden will receive the $60,000 directly from the club. Whatever money Gooden earns for promotional work up to $60,000 will go directly to the Mets. Between $60,000 and $100,000, the Mets will receive 75% of the endorsement money, though if a specific payment puts Gooden over the $100,000 mark, he and the Mets will split that surplus evenly. Any subsequent earnings are Gooden's exclusively.

Neader is willing to give the Mets a portion of money that would otherwise be Gooden's alone in order to get more money for Gooden guaranteed up front. And the Mets are willing to go along with this arrangement because it will be very difficult for anyone other than Gooden to benefit from such a clause in future negotiations or arbitration cases.

Without announcing the details of the contract, Neader says publicly that Gooden could earn as much as $575,000 under the terms of the contract. He gives no indication why he has arbitrarily selected that figure. He also says, "A half million is more realistic, though." The Mets scoff at Neader's predictions.

"This is New York, and there are a lot of opportunities for endorsements," Harazin says. "But it's not that easy to get them, and there's not that much time to make all the appearances if you're playing 162 games. How many did Darryl (Strawberry) do? He was the Rookie of the Year, too. And playing in New York, too. And Darryl's a little more extroverted than Dwight."

The Mets are pleased with the contract. They suspect their $60,000 investment may be returned. They are certain their $275,000 investment will be.

The contract provides for an additional $130,000 in possible income through incentive clauses based on awards and starts. "That's money we want him to earn," Harazin says. "If he does all that, we'll win the pennant."

February 19

WALNUT CREEK, CALIFORNIA—At 2:45 A.M. on an interstate highway a continent removed from Atlanta, another cloud positions itself over the Braves' 1985 season. Claudell Washington, the Braves' starting right fielder and projected leadoff batter, is driving his new 1985 Jaguar when officers from the Contra Costa County Police Department stop him for "weaving slightly." The officers allegedly find small amounts of marijuana and cocaine in the car, and they arrest Washington "on suspicion of possession of illegal drugs." He is released on $3,000 bond.

When word of his arrest gets back to the Braves' offices 24 hours later, general manager John Mullen can only say, "He has not been formally charged, much less convicted, so we presume he is innocent." But the Braves know all too well that the availability of their right fielder now hinges on legal developments and a sure investigation by baseball commissioner Peter Ueberroth's office, which—under precedents set by former commissioner Bowie Kuhn—could suspend Washington from baseball for one year if he is convicted of any drug-related charge.

February 20

NEW YORK—Claudell Washington remains silent immediately following his arrest. But his New York agent, Bill Kadersha, makes it clear that Washington will plead innocent if charged. "I would hope everybody is not trying to convict an innocent man," Kadersha says.

Kadersha insists Washington was not aware that any drugs were in his car. "If there was indeed a substance, which has not been officially identified, in the car, it did not belong to Claudell," Kadersha says. "He loans his car out to family and friends. A lot of people handle the car—parking attendants—besides family and friends. I'm very confident there will be no conviction."

In Walnut Creek, a police spokesman says the substances confiscated from Washington's car have been sent to a crime lab for official analysis, and the district attorney's office says it will be two weeks or so before a decision can be made on pressing the case. Meanwhile, the Braves don't know quite what to make of the situation. Publicly, they continue to speak of Washington as their right fielder. But privately, they talk of moving center fielder Dale Murphy to right, leaving youngsters Milt Thompson and Albert Hall to battle for center.

CLEVELAND—It seems Peter Bavasi never rests—at least when it comes to hiring and firing people. First, Phil Seghi and Bob Quinn.

Today, Rosemary "Posey" O'Connor and Mary Golkowski.

For 33 years, Posey O'Connor answered telephones, typed memos, and fetched coffee for her bosses in various departments of the Indians' front office. For 32 years, there were no serious complaints about her work. Furthermore, during most of that period O'Connor did not fall under a pension plan—the Indians didn't have one for its front-office employees until the commissioner's office forced them to implement one in 1982.

Despite no significant pension plan, a salary that never exceeded $20,000, and a willingness to cheerfully do the most meaningless of chores, Posey O'Connor is given the sack, along with another secretary, Mary Golkowski, who worked there for 13 years.

Both women ask if there is a problem with their work. Both are told by Indians executive director of administration Terry Barthelmas that their work is not an issue. "It's a matter of economy," says Barthelmas. By firing O'Connor and Golkowski, the Indians will save about $35,000 a year.

Is $35,000 going to put a dent in the team's $4 million deficit? It is a question the Indians don't want to address.

Bavasi's assistant, Danny O'Brien, denies that the move is a question of dollars and cents. "The work they did is being picked up by other people," says O'Brien. "I'm not even sure what they did."

When Bavasi is criticized for the firings in print by the *Cleveland Plain Dealer* reporter Russell Schneider, he promises to "do something for O'Connor." That something turns out to be a year's severance pay. This is not something Bavasi does from the heart; rather, it comes directly from his sense of public relations.

February 21

CLEVELAND—If nothing else, Peter Bavasi keeps finding ways to keep the Indians in the headlines.

"BAVASI SHUTS DOWN STADIUM BLEACHERS," proclaims the *Cleveland Plain Dealer,* in type so large that you would have thought someone murdered the mayor.

Actually, if the mayor had been rubbed out there would have been less of an outcry than there is over the death of the bleachers.

Peter Bavasi had a brainstorm that exploded in his face. He and Danny O'Brien realized that Cleveland Stadium is too large for baseball. On most nights, there are 5,000 warm bodies and 75,000 empty chairs at the stadium.

"Our research shows the average bleacher crowd was 250," says Bavasi. "Sometimes there are less than 20 people out there."

The center field bleachers are immense—room enough for 5,000 fans. They are the home of John Adams, a fan who brings a bass drum to every home game and pounds away demanding a Tribe rally. During day games, the bleachers are the one place in the park fans are assured of getting a suntan.

"We want to get people involved in the game," says O'Brien. "If this were Comiskey Park, you'd be talking about 500 seats in a 50,000-seat stadium. But when you're talking about keeping the bleachers open for three people . . . it doesn't make much sense."

The primary motivation again seems to be saving a few dollars, as they did by firing the two secretaries.

In an attempt to placate the public—and Bavasi suddenly has

to do a lot of that—the Indians decide to lower the price of the outfield reserved seats from $3.50 to $2.00, which was the charge for a bleacher ticket.

"It used to be that bleacher fans were not included in our promotions like helmet day," says O'Brien. "Now, they can pay $2.00, sit in a seat that was once $3.50, and get a helmet, too."

"Closing the bleachers will make it easier to serve the fans in the areas of concessions, ushers, and keeping the park clean," says Bavasi.

It also means the Indians will need fewer people on the payroll for most games.

"We don't plan to fire any ushers," insists Bavasi. "We will move those people where the fans are so they can get better service."

INDIAN SHORES, FLORIDA—Joe Lefebvre spent the first six weeks of the offseason hobbling with a thigh-to-ankle cast that encased his right knee. Lefebvre had undergone radical surgery in late August. His medial ligaments had been completely torn, and he elected to have reconstructive surgery in which ligaments were grafted in an attempt to rebuild the damaged parts.

The prognosis was not cheery. At best he might be able to play again within a year. At worst, the reconstruction would not take and Lefebvre's career would be over.

The first few months of the winter were difficult for him. Once he got out of the cast, he began daily workouts with a physical therapist near his home in Milbury, Connecticut. Lefebvre also drove once a week to Philadelphia to be examined by and exercise with Phillies medical personnel.

The routine and the uncertainty were difficult for both Lefebvre and his family, his wife Sandra and their year-old baby boy. "Sandy was happy to see me go to Philly some days," says Lefebvre. "I was going nuts around the house. I'm hyper to begin with and with the knee hurting and my not knowing how it would come along, I was a royal pain to live with."

In the high-glitter world of modern baseball, Lefebvre is something of a throwback. He was raised amid modest means in New Hampshire. And he acquired an appreciation for the small gifts, for being able to be paid to play ball and make a living far beyond what he would have achieved without the game.

"If I hadn't made it to the majors, I probably would be coaching or teaching phys ed for $14,000 a year and be happy to have it," says Lefebvre. "I still cannot believe I've been paid to play baseball. I see so many guys taking it all for granted. But to me it's all a little unbelievable. I mean, the money is beyond anything I ever expected to ever even come close to making.

"Maybe it comes from growing up in New England. We got to play maybe three or four months a year because of the winter and because I always had to work in high school. Guys from California play year-round and I think some of them get burned out by the time they're in college.

"All I know is that I was able to go to college only because of baseball. And I've been able to have everything materially I've ever dreamed of having because of baseball. So when things were rough this past winter, I didn't get bitter. If I never play again, I'll be thankful for what I have. But it has been frustrating. I want to will the darn knee to get better. But it just didn't come along at the beginning."

It became clear by the beginning of the new year that Lefebvre would need to have the knee reopened. Club physician Dr. Phillip Marone told Bill Giles and other club officials that Lefebvre was not achieving the range of motion he should have. Marone feared the reconstruction was not taking properly, so the decision was made to reopen the knee through use of the arthroscopic process with which the condition could be assessed.

The arthroscopic surgery brought some good news. Marone discovered that the surgery had indeed been successful. Lefebvre's continuing problem stemmed from the existence of adhesions that had built up in the knee over the years. Once those adhesions were removed, Lefebvre could feel the difference quickly. "I was able to improve my range of motion by 15 degrees in a week after the arthroscope," says Lefebvre. "For the first time, I am really making a lot of progress."

So Lefebvre celebrated. It is indicative of his values to see how he enjoys success. In 1983, he used the Phillies' losing share from the World Series to set up a florist business for himself and his wife, something his wife had always wanted. Then when Lefebvre signed the first two-year contract of his career, he splurged for the first time. "It was the first time I've ever been in a position to buy something on impulse," he says. "So I went out and got a Mercedes. I know it doesn't fit my image and it really is a little showy, I guess. But I guess we all have to splurge once in a while."

Now, in the winter of 1985, Lefebvre and his wife decided they would look for the dream house they've always wanted—a cabin in the Berkshires. "We went to a real estate guy and I told him I needed four things—privacy, some land, a big stone fireplace, and a dock nearby for a boat. Darned if he said he had two places like that, one of them already furnished. Well, we took one look and knew it was the place. All it needed was sheets for the bed and some Guinness for the refrigerator."

Lefebvre and his family spent several weekends in their new vacation home but they decided on an early trip to Florida. Lefebvre was now so encouraged by the progress of his knee that he wanted to begin daily rehabilitation under the auspices of the Phillies' medical staff. So he arrived here in Florida nearly two weeks before the reporting date to begin his intensified workouts with the early-arriving trainers.

His day is a monotonously exhausting regimen. "I get to the ballpark around 8:30 and do some strength and flexibility exercises," says Lefebvre. "Then the knee gets some whirlpool and heat treatment. Then I ride the stationary bike for several minutes. Then I try to do some easy running with the trainer. Then I do leg lifts with flexion exercises. Then I ice it for a half hour.

"The hardest part will be watching the Phillies play once the games start. I don't particularly like watching other people play. But I've had to learn some patience these past few months."

Lefebvre's daily workouts will continue indefinitely. The most optimistic prognosis has him returning to play in August. The likelihood is that he will play little if any in 1985. And with his two-year contract expiring after the season and his length of service just days short of being eligible for free agency, Lefebvre's future is in limbo.

With more pressing matters at hand, Lefebvre's situation is obviously not a burning issue with the Phillies. But Tony Siegle has already speculated that the Phils could probably retain Lefebvre cheaply. In the baseball business world, this is a rare case where management has the upper hand. From the Phillies' point of view, they will have paid Lefebvre close to $500,000 for two seasons in which he played very little. And with Lefebvre's bargaining rights virtually nil, Siegle is already pushing for renewal of Lefebvre's contract in 1986 with the maximum 20% cut in pay.

None of this gets a rise out of Lefebvre. "I might be strange, but I really don't want anything I didn't earn," he says. "I realize I have to prove my value all over again to the Phillies. I also realize I'll have no trade value because of the injury so I'm sort of at their mercy.

"But you know, Greg Gross (Lefebvre's best friend on the club) and I were talking the other night. He had just signed his new contract and he and I were sitting there marveling at the money being made. G.G will be making more in his contract than Mickey Mantle or Ted Williams or even Carl Yastrzemski made. And here G.G. is just a role player, not a front-line star. It's become a crazy business. And all I know is that if it takes a 20% pay cut to stay here, I'll take it. All I want is a chance to prove I can still play. I'm going to get this knee thing licked. It just gets better all the time. And all I want is a chance to play. If it doesn't work, I've already gotten more than I could have ever imagined."

ST. PETERSBURG, FLORIDA—He plucks a piece of litter from the clubhouse floor and deposits it in a wastepaper basket; a nice pickup by the cleanup hitter. Later, he carries a bag of baseballs from one of the fields at the Mets' Payson Complex to another. Even Barry Lyons, a non-roster rookie catcher, wouldn't stoop to such a menial task. But Gary Carter did. In those rare instances when Carter ducked from the spotlight during the Mets' first day of spring training workouts, he did so with purpose. Talk about your all-purpose catchers.

That's just what his new teammates are doing as Carter makes his in-uniform debut with the Mets. He is the focus of attention as the Mets pitchers and catchers assemble for the first time. Dwight Gooden, fresh from his unfulfilled holdout, is there; he spends 30 minutes with Harry Reasoner and a film crew from "60 Minutes." Doug Sisk and Jesse Orosco, feigning poverty because of their arbitration losses, are there, too. So, surprisingly, is Darryl Strawberry, hardly a batteryman, and not due in camp for a week.

For Carter, this is more a premiere than a debut. His personality explodes into camp. He kibitzes, cajoles, and goes out of his way to say hello. Having studied a 1984 media guide, he can identify the veteran Mets, even the young ones. And he requests a 1985 edition to see if he can learn the new faces. His is one of them, of course.

WEST PALM BEACH, FLORIDA—Today, the last of the pitchers and catchers on the Braves' major-league roster checked into the Hyatt Palm Beaches Hotel or into condominums along the Atlantic Ocean. Spring training will begin tomorrow morning.

It will be a significant spring. The Braves again will be trying to patch together a starting pitching staff, the success of which might hinge on the physical condition of Len Barker's elbow and Steve Bedrosian's shoulder. The Braves will try to find reliable set-up men for Bruce Sutter in the bullpen to replace Donnie Moore. They will see if newly acquired Rick Cerone is any improvement over holdover catchers Bruce Benedict and Alex Trevino. They will anxiously await early-March medical reports from Dallas, and then hopefully have Bob Horner and his new wrist in camp. They will stage an intriguing competition at first base between veteran Chris Chambliss and young Gerald Perry. They will look at a number of candidates—Brad Komminsk, Milt Thompson, Terry Harper, and Albert Hall—in left field, and perhaps in right, pending legal developments from California regarding Claudell Washington. They will keep channels of communication open regarding possible trades; they are still interested in Larry Parrish.

And it will be the first spring training as a major-league manager for Eddie Haas.

NEW YORK—In the last of the arbitration decisions to be handed down, Tim Raines wins his case against the Expos and gets the highest salary ever awarded in arbitration, $1.2 million.

The clubs win seven of 13 cases, but the players are nonetheless hardly losers; the seven will see their salaries increase an average of $120,643. The complete scorecard for 1985:

PLAYER	TEAM	1984 EARN- INGS*	PLAYER'S FIGURE	TEAM'S FIGURE	WINNER
Wade Boggs	**Boston Red Sox	$525,000	$1,000,000	$675,000	Boggs
Tom Brunansky	**Minnesota Twins	215,000	600,000	425,000	Twins
Carlos Diaz	Los Angeles Dodgers	93,500	170,000	120,000	Dodgers
Leon Durham	Chicago Cubs	500,000	1,100,000	800,000	Cubs
Jerry Koosman	**Philadelphia Phillies	584,000	865,000	600,000	Phillies
Jesse Orosco	**New York Mets	525,000	850,000	650,000	Mets
David Palmer	**Montreal Expos	162,500	375,000	235,000	Palmer
Tim Raines	**Montreal Expos	800,000	1,200,000	1,000,000	Raines
Bobby Ramos	**Montreal Expos	113,000	150,000	115,000	Expos
Bert Roberge	**Montreal Expos	51,000	95,000	60,000	Roberge
Dave Schmidt	Texas Rangers	115,000	344,000	230,000	Schmidt
Mike Scioscia	Los Angeles Dodgers	165,000	435,000	350,000	Scioscia
Doug Sisk	**New York Mets	110,000	470,000	275,000	Mets

*Includes salary and incentive bonuses.

**Clubs represented by Tal Smith at the hearings.

February 22

CLEVELAND—People who never spent an inning in the bleachers have been making calls and writing letters to the Indians and to newspapers. They want the bleachers to stay open. And John Adams, the 250-pounder who has been pounding away on a bass drum for 11 years at Indians games, has become a hero giving interviews.

"I'm not turning my back on the Indians because of this," says Adams. "This is the fans' team. Guys like Bavasi come and go, but the fans are the real owners.

"I thought Bavasi's job was putting a winning team on the field, not counting the fans in the bleachers. If this is a money move, it's pinching pennies, especially after they fired those two secretaries. What is Bavasi going to do the next time there is a small crowd, shut the doors and tell everyone to go home because there's not enough people?"

Fans say they prefer the long-bench seats in the bleachers. A few say that if the Indians are too boring, the benches give them the option of stretching out and taking a nap until they are awakened by some cheers.

Newspapers are running letters from people recalling the glory days of the Indians when you couldn't get a seat anywhere—in the grandstand or the bleachers. Others maintain that the bleachers are as much a part of Cleveland baseball lore as fireworks after every Indians home run at the stadium.

Bavasi is being chastised in print as "bush . . . carrying a big stick as he knocks off heads and walks over people."

On and on it goes.

"You have to understand that the enormity of the stadium detracts from, not adds to, its character," says Bavasi. "Character comes from intimacy—like Wrigley Field—and we want to make the stadium more intimate. What would give character to the stadium would be us having enough fans so we have to open the bleachers."

February 23

ST. PETERSBURG, FLORIDA—Two years ago, his talent impressed anyone who ventured into the Mets camp. One year ago, his words impressed those who heard him speak—some favorably, some not so favorably. As Darryl Strawberry prepares for his third major-league season, his mere presence impresses people quite favorably. The fact that Strawberry has already begun his preparation, days before he is even due to report to camp, is as significant a development as the acquisition of Carter. Strawberry himself notes as much, saying, "We might have two new players in the lineup this year . . . I'm going to be a different player than I was last year. I'm going to be better. I'm going to be the player I should have been last year."

Such pledges are made annually throughout Florida and Arizona, but few have the potential impact of Strawberry's. Few players have the potential of the Mets right fielder. His is such that he innocently pluralizes the word—"I'm not aware of what my potentials are," he says—as if the singular would not convey the thought. His potential is such that even his best work is almost taken for granted. "What he did early last year (batting .363 with five home runs and 13 RBI in his first 22 games) was awesome," Ed Lynch says. "But he wasn't playing over his head. That's what he can do. He's got more ability than any player I've ever seen. And I think most of the guys think that way."

They do, and consequently, Strawberry's talent is a blessing and a curse. "I expect a lot from myself," he says. "Sometimes I think others expect more. I don't know what to expect. What would be a good year for me? I'm waiting to know. I know I let the team down at times. I think of those months (May and August) when I didn't hit a home run and didn't even drive in 10 runs. How good could I have been if I didn't have those down periods? How could they happen? I asked myself that a lot after the season."

Several teammates, notably Keith Hernandez and Rusty Staub, accused Strawberry of giving up on himself and not fighting the adversity that every player experiences. "It's something I had to live with over the winter," Strawberry says. "I didn't like hearing it, but I guess it was true. I got down on myself and didn't know how to get back up. I always got by on my natural talent. I didn't know what good work habits meant. I didn't know what it took to be a good player."

Now he says he knows, and his actions support his words. Hernandez has already noticed a difference. "He's taking batting practice with a purpose now," Hernandez says. Strawberry works on his throwing and other outfield skills. He seldom arrives early for practice, but he never arrives late either. He had experienced trouble with promptness the preceding season. He stays late after practice, working with exercise and strength machines, something he never did before.

"I think I've learned it takes more to succeed in this game than talent," Strawberry says. "Jimmy Frey (the Cubs manager and former Mets coach) told me I had to work to be good. When he left, I just forgot what he said. Now, I'm dedicated again. There are some big things I want to do."

WEST PALM BEACH, FLORIDA—Len Barker, who underwent surgery last August to have the ulnar nerve rerouted and a bone spur removed from his right elbow, takes the mound for the first time this spring. In the Braves' efforts to patch together a starting pitching staff Barker figures prominently. If his arm proves sound, he will be a key member of the rotation.

He stands on the mound and glares at his catcher. His first pitch bounces five feet in front of the plate. Eddie Haas, standing beside the batting cage, looks at the ground. A few coaches wince. Barker laughs.

"Just kidding, guys," he says. And then he pops a fastball, and another, and another. It will be a month or more before the Braves will know if Barker is sound, but the process has begun.

February 24

INDIAN SHORES, FLORIDA—The Phillies have quietly knocked on wood for years that they were fortunate enough to escape any stain from the ongoing string of drug and alcohol problems that dot the baseball landscape. Aside from a mini-scandal several years ago involving players who allegedly obtained illegal prescriptions for amphetamines, the Phillies have been one of the clean teams.

So when Bill Giles got an early-morning call from Von Hayes and Hayes said the word "arrest," Giles was scared stiff. He sat for hours on the porch of his rented condo that sits on a strip of the Gulf of Mexico and feared the worst. His first instinct was to think of some kind of drug connection, but Giles couldn't believe the level-headed, clean-living Hayes could be involved in something like that.

Later in the day, Giles is able to breathe a sigh of relief. When all the facts are forwarded to him, the arrest, albeit serious, does not involve drugs.

Hayes had arrived in Florida 10 days ago, and palled around with fellow bachelor Larry Christenson, a former Phillies pitcher whose career was ended by arm problems. Christenson was in town to sell his beachfront condominium, and while he was wheeling and dealing also engage in some fun in the sun.

Hayes and Christenson spent a long day wind-surfing, romancing beach lovelies, and sipping beer. Neither are big drinkers. "I can go about three or four beers and that's it for me," says Hayes.

After dinner, Hayes and Christenson decided to visit Phillies outfielder Joe Lefebvre. They got directions and headed for a nearby condo complex. However, they got mixed up in the driveway and, somewhat fuzzy from their beer, rang the wrong doorbell. Then they pounded on the door, and the tenant immediately called the police.

When the police arrived, one thing led to another. Hayes was told to move his Porsche, and when he had trouble negotiating it into a proper space, the police yanked him out of the car, threw beer cans Hayes and Christenson had been holding onto the car's upholstery, and started a search. Hayes lost his temper, and by the time everything settled down he had been arrested for drunken intoxication, criminal mischief, and resisting arrest with violence— the last charge a felony. Hayes was locked up in an Indian Shores cell, where he punched a hole in a wall in his frustration while bail was raised by Christenson.

The whole incident will take weeks to unravel. The Phillies connect Hayes with a local attorney and publicly back his side of the story. They weren't enamored with the whole affair, but all Giles could keep thinking was, "It's serious, but when you hear the things players are getting arrested for over the past few years, charges of drunk and disorderly almost sound nice by comparison."

With that lovely episode, the Phillies open spring training.

15 *Working Out*

February 25

DALLAS—Bob Horner's progress continues. He has a doctor's appointment on March 4, at which time he hopes to get permission to report to spring training and resume his career. "I've got my bags packed," he says. "All indications are that everything is going much better than we ever anticipated."

While awaiting his appointment with Dr. Peter Carter, Horner is rehabilitating under the guidance of occupational therapist Georgiann Laseter. She says Horner has 78% return of motion with the up-and-down movement in his wrist and 90% with the side-to-side movement.

"In his line of work," she notes, "the side-to-side movement is more critical. As far as grip strength goes, his right hand is now 10% stronger than his left hand. That's very good."

Horner is swinging a bat that has been hooked up to a resistance device called the BTE Work Simulator. This is a machine built by Baltimore Therapeutic Equipment that has several attachments to test one's ability to perform specific occupational skills. But the simulator had no attachment for a baseball player until two weeks ago.

Laseter contacted John Vermette of BTE and told him about Horner's case. Vermette contacted the Braves and asked for two bats. He connected one to a rope pulley for resistance on the machine.

Horner has used the simulator every day for about a week, and the exercises are building his muscle strength as measured by a computer. "He's got blisters from swinging," Laseter says. "It's not the total answer, but it's more scientific data for us to use. Every day, we get more hopeful."

"I really, really can hardly wait any longer," Horner says.

CLEVELAND AND TUCSON—After closing the bleachers, firing the secretaries, and leaving footprints all over Bob Quinn, the best thing for Peter Bavasi and the Indians is to get out of town.

For that reason, spring training could not come at a better time.

In Tucson, there will be no talk of the bleachers or loyal employees being kicked out the door. Instead, the subjects will be sun, baseball, and a new beginning—at least, that is what Bavasi hopes.

And as camp officially opens in Tucson, the news could not be better for Bavasi. That's because phenom Cory Snyder is there to do interviews and take the spotlight off the front office.

Snyder was the Tribe's first-round pick in the June 1984 draft out of Brigham Young University. In college last spring, he hit .450 with 27 homers and 85 RBIs. Snyder was recruited by BYU as a pitcher. But he hit the ball an awfully long way in batting practice. And in his first collegiate start, he saw three pitches: a fastball, a curve, and a changeup. He took three swings and each pitch sailed out of the park. Such is the stuff of legends.

To get his bat in the lineup, he was converted to shortstop, and his throws to first base were clocked at 90 mph.

The Indians signed Snyder for a $135,000 bonus. Instead of spending the summer in the minors, Snyder played for the U.S. Olympic team, where he was second on the club with 10 homers and 32 RBIs.

Cleveland sent Snyder to its Florida Instructional League team, and this is where the story got very interesting. Through 36 games,

Snyder was hitting .456 with 12 homers and 43 RBIs. He was also playing second base, a spot the Indians are trying to fill.

"I spent a week watching Snyder," says Indians manager Pat Corrales. "In Florida, he was like a man playing against boys. They say that Manny Trillo has a great arm for a second baseman. Well, Snyder has twice the arm of Trillo."

Corrales has high hopes for Snyder. The right-handed hitter is only 22 and has never appeared in a minor-league game, but he was invited to spring training with the big club.

"Cory could make the team," says Corrales. "As a hitter, he isn't very far away. I mean that Snyder looks better now than Dave Winfield did when he came out of the University of Minnesota. Winfield and I were teammates in San Diego during Dave's rookie year, so I can make the comparison. That's also why I know Snyder is the best-looking hitter to come along in a long, long time."

As for Snyder's play at second base, well, he isn't exactly the reincarnation of Bill Mazeroski. So the Indians have brought in Brian Doyle, a former Yankee second baseman who had a brief moment in the headlines during the 1978 World Series, to teach Snyder how to catch a ground ball.

As a shortstop at Brigham Young, Snyder made 33 errors in 56 games and most scouts felt third base would be his best position because of Snyder's strong arm. But the Tribe's biggest hole is at second, and that's where Snyder is working out—at least for now.

At 6-foot-3, Snyder towers over fellow second baseman Tony Bernazard (5-foot-10), Junior Noboa (5-foot-8), and Mike Fischlin (6-foot).

"I don't feel like a giant," says Snyder. "Being tall means I have to work on my feet, making them quicker on the double-play pivot. I'd rather play short or third base, but I don't get to pick my position."

"What Snyder does on the field won't surprise me," says Corrales. "The big thing is the pressure. You have to watch for clues. The way he goes after his first ground ball could determine the tone of his entire spring.

"So far, it seems nothing bothers him. He's cocky, but not with his mouth. It's like he is thinking, 'I'll show you I belong.' I don't think he is the type of kid who says, 'Wow, what am I doing here?' He thinks like Julio Franco used to, like, 'Why are they wasting my time in Class AAA?' Cory won't say that, but that's what he's thinking."

Corrales does have one concern about Snyder: his father. A former Class AA player for the Braves, Jim Snyder came with his son to spring training.

"What we have here is a little-league father," Corrales tells a few of his coaches. "I don't like it."

"My dad is an extension of me," says Snyder. "I like him to watch me. If I do something wrong, he'll spot it. It's like having an extra pair of eyes or a videotape of myself."

"When Cory was eight, I knew he'd be a great player," says Jim Snyder.

When told of Jim Snyder's remark by a reporter, Corrales screams, "Damn it, the kid ain't a great player. He ain't even a big leaguer. Hell, he ain't even played a pro game yet. And I don't want this in the damn paper, either."

"I always put Cory in leagues with older kids," Jim Snyder recalls. "It started when he was eight. I had him playing with 11–12 year olds. I suppose all fathers think their sons will be great players, but I knew."

Jim Snyder spends his son's first day in a big-league camp running around the field taking pictures. But he hits a roadblock when he tries to enter the clubhouse.

"I'm sorry, Mr. Snyder, no relatives in the clubhouse. It's club policy," Corrales says sincerely.

As Jim Snyder departs, all Corrales can do is shake his head.

February 27

WEST PALM BEACH, FLORIDA—The Braves hold their first full-squad workout of spring training, and Paul Zuvella makes an immediate impression.

In batting practice, he sprays line drives all over the field.

In infield practice, he is smooth and confident at shortstop, second base, and third base. And in general, he just looks like a player.

"He is a very good player and a very intelligent one, too," says Eddie Haas, who has managed Zuvella at Richmond for the past three years.

Through three years of watching Zuvella, a 26-year-old Stanford graduate, Haas has come to be his biggest fan. Several times during the offseason, the Braves were approached by other clubs regarding Zuvella, but Haas convinced the front office to ignore these overtures. And when it was time to choose the 24 players the Braves would protect from the compensation pool, Haas insisted that Zuvella be among the protected players.

"Paul Zuvella can play shortstop for a lot of big-league teams right now," John Mullen says during the team's first full workout. But on this team, Rafael Ramirez is entrenched as the starting shortstop and Glenn Hubbard as the starting second baseman. Ramirez has just signed a five-year, $3.375 million contract, and Hubbard is entering the third year of his own five-year megabucks contract. Zuvella's immediate future appears to be as a utility infielder on the Braves. "For now, I can be happy with that," he says. And he probably has heard some of the whispers in the front office that, ultimately, the team will be in a good position to trade Ramirez or Hubbard for a pitcher because of Zuvella's presence.

A side note from the Braves' first workout: Claudell Washington, who had assured the club he would be here for the start of spring training, is nowhere to be seen.

MESA, ARIZONA—After less than a week of spring drills with his pitchers and catchers, Gene Mauch says the Angels have the most impressive array of young arms he has ever seen.

"I don't know how I'll feel two weeks from now, but after five days I don't have a care in the world," he says.

Spring hyperbole?

"Well I'll tell you what I told my coaches. I told them that never in my 24 years as a major-league manager have I been in a camp with this much young (pitching) talent.

"It's not difficult to recognize real good stuff."

He alludes to the early efforts of rotation candidates Kirk McCaskill, 24, Urbano Lugo, 22, and Bob Kipper, 20. He also mentions bullpen candidate Pat Clements, 23, who would be making a jump from Double A Waterbury of the Eastern League.

February 28

MESA, ARIZONA—The first spring surprise comes when Mauch says he wants Reggie Jackson, a designated hitter for most of 1983 and 1984, to return to right field. Mauch thinks Jackson will be more productive with more involvement.

"I saw him have one great year as our right fielder," Mauch says, referring to 1982, when the Angels won a division title and Jackson tied for the American League lead with 39 homers. "And I saw him have two below average years as a DH. We won 93 games with Reggie in right, so he obviously didn't hurt us."

Jackson, 37, is excited about the move, despite having played only three games in the outfield in 1984 and 47 in 1983.

"Gene recognizes that I'm a people person, that I'm more effective when I'm in the mainstream, because I feed off the reaction of fans and other players," Jackson says. "The only way I'll ever have a Gold Glove is by going to Standard Brands to buy the paint, but I can be OK out there. It's like riding a bike. You never really forget."

ST. PETERSBURG, FLORIDA—Darryl Strawberry is nearly late for practice. His 9:59 A.M. appearance—one minute early— on the field prompts mock applause from his teammates, who have assembled earlier than usual for calisthenics. "I just gave him a look," Dave Johnson says, "to let him know that I knew."

Later, Gooden offers a semi-serious challenge to Strawberry as he throws batting practice for the first time. "You duckin' me, Straw?" he says. "You ready for me?"

Strawberry replies, "You're lucky I'm not in this group. You know I'd smoke you."

WEST PALM BEACH, FLORIDA—Claudell Washington arrives in time for the Braves' second full-squad workout. The Contra Costa County district attorney's office still has not decided whether to file felony charges against him, but a California judge ruled that Washington could leave the state.

"I have absolutely nothing to do with drugs," says Washington. "I'm innocent of all the accusations against me. No charges have been filed, and I don't know if there will be. I'm here to play baseball, and that's about the size of it."

The size of it, according to Eddie Haas, is this: "He's just another player, and he'll be treated like just another player." The Braves have decided to presume the best: that Washington will not be convicted of anything, that he will not be suspended by the commissioner, and that he will be their opening-night right fielder. The commissioner's office has said it will not comment on Washington's situation until legal proceedings in California have run their course.

March 1

CLEARWATER, FLORIDA—With a new manager and a large collection of unknowns to be analyzed, the Phillies opened spring training vowing not to jump feet-first into the trade market or to stir up rumors unnecessarily. An order was discreetly issued throughout the organization to be more closed-mouth than usual, to downplay any rumor that surfaced, and to emphasize that the club wants to see what talent it had on hand before opening talks with other clubs.

It is a good plan in theory. But veteran players know better, having experienced countless other Phillies spring training camps in which similar claims were made, only to have the apparent serenity shattered by a rush of personnel moves. They need not go any further back in history than last year when, after cruising through a smooth four weeks, the Phillies were rocked by a pair of blockbuster trades within 72 hours of each other.

However, for a few days anyway, the Phils have focused on who is in camp. As pitchers and catchers arrived for the opening of workouts, the big questions were Bo Diaz's knees and his attitude. All winter long, he had read and heard he was on the trading block. Then the Phillies announced they wouldn't deal him until they could better ascertain his physical status. The moody Diaz couldn't be happy with all this.

To everyone's surprise, however, Diaz arrived in good spirits and in surprisingly strong condition. He was able to catch from the first day on. And he worked hard, volunteering for drills and showing every indication of being ready to challenge for the starting job.

Nevertheless, Felske has him into his office for a private meeting. Diaz tells Felske that he is ready to do whatever the club wants him to do. He wants to play and won't like second-string status if he ends up remaining with the Phillies. But Diaz assuages Felske's concerns by assuring the new manager that he will make no waves.

Diaz's obviously advanced recovery from his knee problems made the Phillies feel comfortable about both their catching situation and their trading situation. Diaz's market value will obviously be greater the healthier he is. And if Diaz shows he is all the way back and playing like he did in 1982 and 1983, the Phillies will have the pleasant prospect of having two proven catchers available.

The only early problem stemmed from the murky world of immigration regulations. The Phillies had been looking forward to seeing Dominican reliever Ramon Caraballo for the first time. However, their first look at Caraballo was delayed for a week; when Caraballo went to the airport, he was denied exit from the country because his visa was not in order.

Minor-league coordinator Larry Rojas had to spend three days on the phone with various U.S. and Dominican officials trying to unravel the mess. Caraballo was meanwhile stuck in Santo Domingo. The breakthrough finally came after all government offices went back to work following a Dominican holiday. Rojas went to the Tampa airport to pick up Caraballo, who was tired and disheveled after his tedious ordeal. And as a footnote to the travels of Ramon, on his first day of workouts he mistakenly reported to Jack Russell Stadium instead of the Carpenter Field minor-league complex where early workouts were held. He had to hitch a ride with a stadium worker in order to finally report to the Phillies.

WEST PALM BEACH, FLORIDA—When Eddie Haas, his coaching staff, and the front office first meet to talk in generalities about the 25-man roster with which the Braves will leave spring training, they decide to carry 10 pitchers, two catchers, eight infielders, and five outfielders. To reach these numbers, they will have to trade a catcher (Bruce Benedict or Alex Trevino), either return Bob Horner to the disabled list or trade Ken Oberkfell, and make some tough cuts among the pitchers and outfielders. But Haas knows who he wants to be his infielders: Chris Chambliss, Gerald Perry, Glenn Hubbard, Rafael Ramirez, Bob Horner or Ken Oberkfell (but not both, he thinks at this point), Randy Johnson, Paul Runge, and Paul Zuvella.

It will become more complicated than this.

March 2

ST. PETERSBURG, FLORIDA—It is the Mets' considered opinion that financial security will bolster Darryl Strawberry and help him become the player he can be. With that in mind, the club does what no other club has done—they give a player with less than two years' experience a multi-year contract, the average annual value of which will exceed $1 million.

Last night, Strawberry's agent, Richman Bry, met with Al Harazin late into the night, creating the framework for a five-year contract that will cost the club $5.4 million and provide Strawberry income well beyond his playing days. Bry explains the package to his client, who is delighted with the security it provides. Strawberry, married two months ago, is an expectant father. "I have to be pleased with the way it secures the future for my family," Strawberry says today. "It will be nice to go out and play and not worry about money."

One-third of the value of the contract, $1.8 million, is deferred with interest and, according to Bry, it will provide Strawberry approximately $500,000 annually for 30 years after he retires.

The contract won't be signed for 10 days, on Strawberry's 23rd birthday, but other clubs are already stunned by the Mets' actions. Strawberry is 22 days short of qualifying for salary arbitration, but despite his lack of negotiating power, the Mets give him a contract that dwarfs the contracts of other players with so little service.

The terms of Strawberry's contract are a signing bonus of $100,000 and salaries for 1985, $500,000 ($100,000 deferred); 1986, $900,000 ($300,000 deferred); 1987, $1.2 million ($400,000 deferred); 1988, $1.3 million ($500,000 deferred); and 1989, $1.4 million ($500,000 deferred). The salary for 1990 is established, though not guaranteed, at $1.8 million, $700,000 of which would be deferred if the club exercises its option. (All deferrals are with interest.) Like many other players, Strawberry is willing to accept a low salary, relative to the full value of the contract, in 1985. Should a strike interrupt this season, the wages Strawberry loses will be at this "reduced" rate.

In addition, there are a series of incentive bonuses: $100,000 for winning the Most Valuable Player Award; $50,000 for placing second, $25,000 for placing third through fifth; $100,000 for winning the World Series Most Valuable Player award; $50,000 for winning the playoff Most Valuable Player award; $25,000 for election or selection to the all-star game. A sum equal to the money earned by winning any and all of the Most Valuable Player awards is to be added to the 1990 salary and guaranteed, if the club exercises its option.

The fear among other clubs is a result of the nature of the arbitration process. While Strawberry has shown awesome potential, his actual performance in his first two seasons has been great but human—26 homers each year, 74 and 97 RBIs, and batting averages of .257 and .251. For this he is to be rewarded at a million-a-year rate. Agents for young players are sure to cite these numbers over and over in battles with every other team. The actions of one team today have a ripple effect on the salaries of every other team.

The Mets also sign Ron Darling to a one-year contract for $165,000. The contract includes incentives that will give Darling a chance to earn the $200,000 he wanted.

TAMPA, FLORIDA—With spring training camps opening everywhere, the muddled labor situation drags on without any apparent progress. The already complicated negotiations were thrown into even more confusion when, at the urging of commissioner Peter Ueberroth, the owners asked the players to place a moratorium on discussion of the issues in order to study what the owners claim to be serious financial problems.

The Players' Association hurriedly calls a meeting of all player representatives to brief the players on this latest turn of events. But there isn't much to discuss. The players are as unsure of the motives behind the owners' decision as many owners are. But they are also not ready to rattle the sabers and set a strike date, preferring to wait out the latest twist indefinitely.

WEST PALM BEACH, FLORIDA—Eddie Haas is awakened by a ringing telephone in his hotel room. The familiar voice on the other end is Bob Horner's. But Horner is not talking in his characteristic, subdued tone.

Quickly, Horner tells Haas that he had decided not to wait until Monday for his decisive examination by Dr. Carter, that he saw the doctor yesterday instead. Horner was given the doctor's permission to report to spring training. "I'm coming down on the next plane," Horner tells Haas. "I want to be at tomorrow's work-out."

The Braves have a hard time believing this. "I guess it's about time we got some good news with him," Mullen says about Horner.

Haas says, "He says he's ready to play, and it'll be good to see him in a baseball uniform." "It's a miracle, if it's true," Turner says.

March 3

WEST PALM BEACH, FLORIDA—Indeed, Bob Horner is at Municipal Stadium for the Sunday afternoon workout. It is another three-hour workout, as all have been under Haas, and Horner takes part in all facets.

In the field, he shows the rust of nine months of inactivity. On the bases, he runs well at a trimmer-than-usual 212 pounds. And all eyes are on him as he steps into the batting cage to hit against coach Bobby Wine, to face his first pitches since May 30, 1984. On his first swing, he tips the pitch. On his second and third swings, he does the same. But before he has taken his 28th and last swing of the day, he has sprayed a few line drives around the field, thoroughly encouraging himself and his teammates.

"He was swinging the bat as well as anybody in camp," Rick Camp says. "A couple of months ago, they were talking like his career was over. Now we might have a pretty good team." Dale Murphy adds, "He just walks in here and starts hitting. It makes you shake your head." And Horner says, "It wasn't a dazzling display, but it certainly was a start. It felt great. There was no pain. I've got five weeks, and there's no reason in the world I shouldn't be ready. I think I'll be in the opening-day lineup. I do, I do."

Before leaving Dallas, Horner recalls, he was told by Dr. Carter "there's no reason I can't do anything I want . . . the wrist has progressed that far. There's no question Dr. Carter saved my career. It was looking like I was on the down-and-out. Realistically, if I'd had this injury three years ago when they didn't have this particular operation, I'd be out this season. I'm very fortunate.

"I couldn't be any happier," Horner says, leaning contentedly against the batting cage. "I've had a lot of doubts. I thought a lot about my career maybe being over. I just wanted another opportunity, win, lose, or draw. To be this far along is more than I could have asked for."

CLEARWATER, FLORIDA—It is the first day for the entire Phillies ballclub to report and all seemed bright. Virtually every player reports in excellent condition, led by Mike Schmidt, in the best shape of his career after a rigorous off-season training program to strengthen his cranky leg muscles.

New manager John Felske presides over his first team meeting. With Giles listening and the entire Phillies front-office staff in attendance, Felske lays down his basic credo of unalterable rules.

"I don't believe in a lot of rules, I don't believe in treating you people like kids," Felske tells the players. "I'm easy to play for if you do two things. Be on time is the first. We won't ask to have you here in the middle of the night, but if everybody has to be here at a certain time then everybody should be here with no exceptions. And that will be true for the whole season.

"And when you put on the uniform, I want a total effort. I don't care who you are, if you don't hustle for me you'll hear about it. And if it happens a second time, you just won't play. It's that simple. We owe a lot of people our total effort—our teammates, the owners, and the fans. And I just won't tolerate anything less."

On this blisteringly hot Sunday afternoon, the Phillies go through a three-hour workout. Larry Rojas helps out, hitting fungos to catchers and throwing batting practice. However, he feels weak toward the end of the day and retreats to the clubhouse, where he begins sweating profusely and experiencing chest pains. A clubhouse man and trainer take one look at him and rush him to a nearby hospital where it is learned that Rojas has suffered a heart attack.

The attack is a mild one, caught in time, and Rojas ends up being hospitalized a little over a week. But the incident casts a shadow on the Phillies' first day of full workouts. "This isn't an omen, I hope," says Giles at his condominium where he entertains a group of media people while making periodic calls to the hospital.

TUCSON—The word came from Indians manager Pat Corrales: The only way Cory Snyder can make the Indians is as a second baseman.

In the winter, Corrales had considered using Snyder at third, a position more comfortable to him than second. Third baseman Brook Jacoby would be shifted to second, a position he had never played.

"Jacoby is my starting third baseman, period," says Corrales. "Cory will have to win the second base job in order to start the season in Cleveland."

MESA, ARIZONA—A mystery begins to develop in the Angels camp. First baseman Daryl Sconiers, who had called three days earlier to say he would be three days late in reporting, does not arrive as scheduled. His agent and members of his family say they do not know where he is. Mike Port says Sconiers can report whenever he wants, but that the meter will be running. The 26-year-old DH candidate and backup first baseman is being fined $245 per day.

March 4

WEST PALM BEACH, FLORIDA—His legs ache and his body feels heavy all over. But his wrist again functions fine as Horner takes another round of batting practice. "There's no pain, no pain at all," Horner says.

CLEVELAND—Cleveland bleacher fans die hard.

Bob Beckman, an engineering student from Cleveland Heights, has started a "Save the Bleachers" campaign. Beckman and his friends have passed around petitions and picked up 1,000 signatures in the first week. His goal is to present Peter Bavasi with 12,000 signatures on opening day, demanding the Indians reopen the bleachers.

No one is saying it publicly, but some members of the Cleveland front office have hinted that closing the bleachers was a publicity stunt by Bavasi. He succeeded in making that issue the talk of the town, instead of the more important question of who will own the team.

Supposedly, Bavasi plans to wait until right before the season to announce that the bleachers are open, at least for certain dates.

PHILADELPHIA—Throughout the last several weeks, the slow negotiations with the city of Philadelphia for a new lease dragged on. However, gradual progress was being made, and the call was finally made by club vice-president Dave Montgomery to have Giles return from Florida for the final agreement.

In exchange for various future concessions, the Phillies agree to extend their lease with the city past the year 2000. The city is thus assured indefinitely that the Phillies won't be tempted to explore suburban stadium alternatives in the future. And though the Phils will still pay among the highest rents in major-league baseball, they will receive some needed relief. It is good news for the Phillies' investors group, which is not anxious yet but needs some positive developments after increasingly lackluster profit-loss figures.

March 5

WEST PALM BEACH, FLORIDA—Gary Carter, with the permission of the Mets, returned yesterday to his Palm Beach Gardens home on the East Coast of Florida. He requested the day's leave to attend a dinner and spend time with his family.

This morning, he is ready to fly across Florida to return to camp, but his 7 A.M. flight is cancelled. What to do? How will Carter get to camp for the 10 A.M. workout? Being resourceful and having the resources, he charters a plane for $465. The Carter Charter and a quick drive from Tampa Airport to the Mets Payson Complex get Carter to camp only 30 minutes late. He is apologetic. The club is impressed with his perseverence.

Meanwhile, Carter's former teammates, the Expos, are impressed with the effects of his absence from their camp. "We're better off without Gary Carter," Andre Dawson says. "We'll be a looser club now that he's gone. A lot of guys thought Gary wasn't a team player. That he was looking out for himself. A lot of guys got tired of his crying day in and day out. He always blamed somebody else. Carter hustled the most when we were on national television, and we weren't the only guys in the league that thought that."

Carter is stung by the criticism, but responds without rancor. "I never knew they felt that way," he says. "No one said things like that when I was there."

ST. PETERSBURG, FLORIDA—Dawson's comments create yet another news angle in the Mets camp. Newspaper reporters from New York and other major-league cities; free-lance writers from everywhere; and network, local, and New York television crews have converged on the Mets camp in numbers that exceed even the coverage afforded the championship Yankees team of the late 1970s.

Carter is a story, of course. But so is Gooden and Hernandez and Strawberry and Orosco and new man Howard Johnson and Dave Johnson and the team itself. "I have so many requests for players' time," says Jay Horwitz, the public relations director, "it's like it's an auction."

The attention begins as an inconvenience that most players this side of Dave Kingman have learned to tolerate. It becomes a burden, particularly when camera crews request—and in some cases, demand—exclusive time with the higher-profile Mets. And the attention becomes an obstacle when Gooden, in particular, can't go about his business because an inconsiderate camera crew is taping Gooden as he dresses. A microphone on a long boom rests on the floor near his locker to pick up the sounds of his dressing.

Johnson is distressed by the situation and considers closing the clubhouse to all media before workouts. And this is all happening at a time when commissioner Peter Ueberroth is admonishing clubs that have restricted media access and ordering open clubhouses everywhere in baseball.

Johnson confers with the beat writers and is dissuaded. The clubhouse remains open, Horwitz is instructed to "protect" Gooden.

But there are other, more subtle and self-imposed restrictions. Rusty Staub privately cautions his peers about their public remarks. Staub notes that the 25-player roster and starting lineups are all but established, so that the camp offers little competition for jobs and few hard news stories.

Aware of the politician's credo—"Never screw up on a slow news day"—Staub tells his teammates, "It's a slow camp for us. It's even slower for them [the media]. Be careful what you say."

MESA, ARIZONA—Daryl Sconiers misses his fifth straight workout, his fine climbing to $1,225.

March 6

CLEVELAND—Ernie Camacho decides to be a team man and signs a one-year contract worth $125,000.

"I did it for unity," says Camacho. "I could have waited, but they weren't going to change anything. All the established pitchers were signed but me. I was in a corner all by myself and I didn't like it."

Meanwhile, the Major League Players' Association released data showing that the Indians had the lowest paid team in 1984 with an average salary of $159,774.

Here is a breakdown, along with the base salary for each player for 1985:

PLAYER	1984 SALARY	1985 SALARY
Chris Bando	$ 106,000	$ 225,000
Rick Behenna	48,500	50,000
Tony Bernazard	365,000	365,000

PLAYER	1984 SALARY	1985 SALARY
Bert Blyleven	650,000	750,000
Brett Butler	265,000	450,000
Ernie Camacho	40,000	125,000
Joe Carter	60,000	120,000
Carmen Castillo	60,000	110,000
Jamie Easterly	265,000	280,000
Steve Farr	40,000	50,000
Mike Fischlin	153,000	180,000
Julio Franco	200,000	430,000
Mel Hall	162,900	295,000
Neal Heaton	190,000	225,000
Brook Jacoby	91,000	134,000
Mike Jeffcoat	50,000	60,000
Roy Smith	40,000	60,000
Pat Tabler	115,000	275,000
Andre Thornton	370,000	1,100,000
George Vukovich	235,000	350,000
Tom Waddell	40,000	112,000
Jerry Willard	40,000	65,000

ST. PETERSBURG, FLORIDA—Andrea Kirby, a news and feature reporter with Channel 5, a Metromedia affiliate in New York, begins a three-day program for six players, selected by the club, to help them improve their media "presence." Her students are Dwight Gooden, Darryl Strawberry, Doug Sisk, Jesse Orosco, Howard Johnson, and John Christensen. Attendance is optional. Gooden attends the first session and learns to improve his eye contact, but doesn't return. Four others complete the course and diplomatically say they benefitted from it. Sisk identifies it as a waste of time.

Kirby says her greatest achievement is having helped Orosco overcome his reservations. "Jesse admitted he was intimidated," she says. "But now he's over that. It was plastic surgery. We didn't change them. We talked about their responsibilities to the media, the media's work, and the relationship between the two."

Ron Gardenhire, second to Rafael Santana on Dave Johnson's depth chart at shortstop, bemoans the recognition—or lack of it—afforded him. "Nobody's ever said 'Gardy's got a lot of talent.' They just say 'He'll run through a brick wall for you.' They say Darryl has talent and Keith has talent. But I'm just a threat to a brick wall."

March 7

MESA, ARIZONA—Ken Forsch has just finished pitching batting practice. Third baseman Doug DeCinces, an impressed observer, shakes his head and says, "He was awesome. It made me realize again just how much we missed him last year."

Forsch appears to have regained his berth in a rotation that includes Geoff Zahn, Ron Romanick, and Mike Witt. "I warmed up hard for 10 minutes today and then threw 15 minutes of BP," Forsch says. "That's 25 minutes full out. No apprehension or discomfort."

ST. PETERSBURG, FLORIDA—It is time to be drilled in the procedures of rundowns. So here are the Mets, playing a schoolyard game. Pitchers and outfielders are drafted to serve as victims in loosely choreographed "pickles."

When the drill is complete, Keith Hernandez is impressed. "This is the drill that no one ever takes seriously. It always deteriorates into a giggle session." But none of the Mets laughed during the workout. "An indication we're being serious about our work," Hernandez says.

"No one looks forward to those drills, but we do them because we know it's necessary. Spring training itself is a necessary evil. But we recognize this year could be special for us, and everyone seems to be willing to work toward making that happen."

Ron Darling changes his uniform number from 44 to 12. "Forty-four," he says, "is a hitter's number."

WEST PALM BEACH, FLORIDA—Bob Horner continues to take batting practice without difficulty, and he continues to talk confidently about being in the opening-night lineup. Although cautious, the Braves are beginning to think that he just might be there. And so they begin to wonder what ramifications this will have on their roster.

What, they wonder, should they do with Ken Oberkfell, the infielder obtained to replace Horner last season? There will be opportunities to trade him—within days of Horner's return, the Orioles and Giants called to ask about Oberkfell—but the Braves know all too well about Horner's fragility and are leaning toward keeping Oberkfell as an insurance policy.

"I'm not ready to become a utility player," Oberkfell says. "I think I can still be valuable to somebody, even if it isn't here."

Meanwhile, Paul Zuvella has been working hard and impressing all observers through the first week of full-squad drills, and starting shortstop Rafael Ramirez only arrived today. He first telephoned from his native Dominican Republic and said he was being held up because his wife was having difficulty obtaining a visa to enter this country. And then, a few days later, he telephoned to say that his credit cards had been stolen and it would take him a few days to get this straightened out.

The Braves were growing impatient. Haas fined Ramirez $500 when he finally arrived. And privately, front-office people express disappointment that Ramirez has not responded more favorably to his new contract.

TUCSON—Cory Snyder's debut at second base will be one he'll always remember—for all the wrong reasons.

In the Indians' first intrasquad game, Snyder makes two throwing errors in five innings. For good measure, he strikes out in his only two at bats.

"Cory will be all right," says Corrales. "No one bit him out there. He lived. He'll get more chances."

March 8

MESA, ARIZONA—Yvonne Sconiers, the mother of AWOL first baseman Daryl Sconiers, is reached by telephone at her Fontana, California, home. She says that she talked to her son by phone the day before and that he is fine, but that she did not know where he is or when he will report. Mike Port is asked if the club will consider hiring an investigator.

"That's something for Sconiers's family or his attorney to decide," Port says. "If I hire an investigator it will be to find a pitcher."

WALNUT CREEK, CALIFORNIA—Contra Costa County district attorney Gary Yancey announces he will not file a felony cocaine possession charge against Washington, but he does file a misdemeanor charge of possession of less than one ounce of marijuana. A guilty verdict will mean a maximum $100 fine. But it also could mean a one-year suspension from baseball by the commissioner's office.

Ex-commissioner Bowie Kuhn had laid out a policy that "any player convicted of or pleading guilty to possession of a controlled substance will be suspended without pay for one year." Bob Wirz, a spokesman for new commissioner Peter Ueberroth, says that Ueberroth has not rescinded Kuhn's policy, but its implementation will be "subject to the discretion" of Ueberroth. This means that the Braves must continue to wonder about their right fielder's future.

According to district attorney Yancey, the marijuana was found in a plastic bag "located in plain view next to the driver's seat" when Washington was stopped. Yancey says he did not file cocaine charges because there was "insufficient evidence Washington had knowledge of his possession of the narcotic."

Washington, meanwhile, says he will plead not guilty to the marijuana possession charge. He is free to remain with the Braves in spring training, and his lawyer will enter the not-guilty plea at a hearing on April 12 in California. At that time, a trial date will be set. Now, the Braves at least know they will have their right fielder for the start of the season.

CLEVELAND—If you ask enough people, someone will eventually say yes.

That was Peter Bavasi's approach to hiring a new general manager for the Cleveland Indians. What seemed like a cast of thousands passed up the golden opportunity to be an executive for an ownerless team. But Bavasi persevered and stayed on the telephone. To his credit, Bavasi started his search in baseball's top drawer and worked his way down until he discovered Joe Klein.

Klein comes to the Indians with the same basic background as deposed farm director Bob Quinn. He played in the minors for seven years and managed down on the farm for ten more. He then moved up to assistant farm director of the Texas Rangers. In 1980, he became the Rangers' minor-league director and finally took over as the Rangers' general manager in 1983.

Klein's tour of duty as the Texas general manager will be remembered for two disastrous trades. The first sent Jim Sundberg to Milwaukee for Ned Yost. Sundberg had two disappointing seasons with Texas prior to the deal, but regained his all-star form in Milwaukee. Meanwhile, Yost batted .181 and lost his job as the Rangers' starting catcher after two months.

In Klein's defense, he was forced to deal Sundberg because the catcher had a sharp personality conflict with Texas manager Doug Rader. Rader lobbied hard for the Yost-Sundberg swap.

The second deal is harder to explain. He sent promising young pitchers John Butcher and Mike Smithson to Minnesota for Gary Ward. Butcher and Smithson were two big reasons Minnesota made a surprise run at first place in 1984. Ward got off to a terrible start with Texas and the Rangers languished for all of 1984. But Klein didn't last the season, as he was sacked two months after the Ward deal.

When Klein was the Rangers' farm director, he turned out such young pitchers as Len Barker, Dave Righetti, Ron Darling, Walt

Terrell and Roger Nelson, all of whom were traded out from under him by former Texas owner Brad Corbett.

Like Quinn, Klein is respected as a farm director who did reasonably well with few resources. In Cleveland, Klein is a fresh face. At 42, he has the enthusiasm and dedication Bavasi wants.

"Joe is a good baseball man and a pretty driven guy," says Bavasi. "The guy we need in this position must have a blind commitment to restoring the Indians, and Joe does."

Originally, the man hired as vice-president of baseball operations (Klein's official title) was supposed to be directly under Bavasi and over vice-president of baseball administration Danny O'Brien. But O'Brien was general manager in Texas when Klein was farm director.

"Dan and Joe worked together in Texas and Dan was the boss there," says Bavasi, "so I thought it would be appropriate if we kept it that way here. But Joe's job description has not changed."

Klein is in charge of baseball matters such as trades. O'Brien is in charge of the baseball budget. "Dan is responsible for the ultimate financial success of the baseball budget," says Bavasi.

"I see this as the purest baseball job you can get," says Klein. "For example, say I decided it was time to negotiate with a player on a long-term contract. I'd recommend it to Dan and he would get it done.

"I'll have the ultimate responsibility for making trades, but it won't be a one-man decision. I can't see myself making a trade that no one else wanted to make."

So the Indians' brass has an interesting background. Depending upon who is doing the talking, Bavasi either left Toronto or resigned before being fired as president of the Blue Jays.

O'Brien was fired as general manager in Texas and Seattle, and Klein was rudely booted out in Texas. Of course, being fired isn't necessarily an indictment in baseball, considering all the fine people who have been axed at some point in their careers. And as Bavasi has discovered, a man with a solid baseball position was not about to leave it for the Cleveland Indians.

16 *The Games Begin*

March 10

CLEARWATER, FLORIDA—Carpenter Field is really a complex of four full-sized baseball fields. Atop them is a catwalk from which you can oversee what goes on everywhere. And that is where Giles, Owens, and scouts Hugh Alexander and Ray Shore perch daily to watch the Phillies work.

Decision-making began almost as soon as the first ball was thrown. The Phillies had to assess the physical condition of such people as Bo Diaz, Darren Daulton, Tony Ghelfi, and outfielder Garry Maddox, who had off-season back surgery. And opinions had to be quickly formed about the collection of people auditioning for jobs in the Phillies' bullpen, the obvious area of greatest need.

So Giles and his coterie of veteran baseball men concentrate on the injured and on the unknown pitchers.

The injured people all arrived in much better condition than could have been forecasted. Diaz, Daulton, and Ghelfi all appeared close to 100%, albeit rusty. And Maddox, having gone through the same off-season conditioning program as Schmidt, was in his best condition in years.

However, the pitching is more of a mixed bag. In the early days, the most impressive newcomer was Arturo Gonzalez, a tall right-hander plucked out of the Mexican League. Having pitched winter ball, he was far ahead of most other pitchers in arm strength and pitching condition. Gonzalez was throwing hard from the first day and the Phillies saw a glimmer of promise.

But Ed Olwine, the draft choice out of the Mets' organization, does not look impressive. Neither does Joey McLaughlin, a free agent signee and non-roster player. Young Ramon Caraballo, once he finally arrived, showed glimpses of the ability that stamped him as a prospect of some hope. But he obviously is too raw to help right away. And he arrived with a tender elbow aggravated by continuous winter-ball work and rigorous workouts with the Phillies.

So it is quickly apparent that the Phillies will again test the trade market. But they will find it difficult to get that elusive reliever.

Shore is dispatched to start roaming through the various spring training camps in the first week of exhibition games. He zeroes in first on the Toronto Blue Jays, who are interested in Diaz and have surplus relief pitching.

Little auditions are arranged between the teams. The Phillies schedule Diaz to catch a few innings of an intersquad game on a day when Blue Jays scouts can be in attendance. And Toronto agrees to pitch young reliever Tom Henke in a morning B game against the Phillies so that Shore, Alexander, and Owens can watch him up close and personal.

Cincinnati is another club interested in Diaz, and their special scout Jimmy Stewart becomes a regular at the Phillies' camp throughout the spring's first weeks. However, the Phillies have little interest in what the Reds have available, and their talks with Cincinnati sputter.

March 12

ST. PETERSBURG AND ORLANDO, FLORIDA—Today, two events present a striking contradiction. The Mets and Darryl Strawberry sign the contract that will cost the club $5.4 million on the same day that the Player Relations Committee, the negotiating arm of the 26 club owners, announces that baseball's finances are in such bad shape that the industry's net operating losses could exceed $150 million by 1988 if management and the players' union don't curb inflation.

The Committee's report states that 18 of 26 clubs lost money in 1983—$66 million total, or $2.5 million per club, and that five of the eight clubs that operated at a profit reported gains of less than $1 million.

The information is presented to the players' union, which requests greater detail.

CLEVELAND—Peter Bavasi shows he is a man of the people—kind of. He also bleeds the bleachers issue for one more headline.

Bavasi announces that the bleachers will be open for all day games. "The fans spoke and we listened," he says. "This is what they asked for. Most of the fans who complained said they liked to sit in the sun. So we have given that opportunity.

"The guy who plays the drum (John Adams) put it best when he said 'This is my team. The fans own the Indians.' The fans want the bleachers open afternoon games and that's what we'll do."

CLEARWATER, FLORIDA—The exhibition opener attracts a sellout crowd that includes such celebrities as Harry Reasoner, who is still working on the Dwight Gooden piece for "60 Minutes."

Though just another stop on the way to the new season for most veterans, the opener is not just another afternoon for all those various Phillies wondering about their status.

Chief among them is young shortstop Steve Jeltz. On the surface, he has nothing to worry about. Last September he was recalled from the minors and handed the shortstop job for the entire month as veteran Ivan DeJesus was benched. And Jeltz played well, showing excellent defensive skills and occasional offensive punch.

But when you're a young player with limited batting ability trying to win a job from a veteran making $600,000 a year, nothing is ever definite. Jeltz might be assured of remaining with the club as a utility man if he doesn't win a starting job. But that is the most precarious of major-league existences.

So Jeltz felt the pressure as he started at short in the exhibition opener. And he proceeded to make three errors to open a season in which the biggest Phillies objective was to improve their awful defense.

Jeltz would later shake his head about the nightmarish opening to his spring bid for a starting job. "I know I can pick it, I never worry about that part of the game," he says. "But I had one ball that came up tough off this terrible infield. Then I tried to hurry a throw. Then I tried to turn a double play that I should have not even tried. Man, what a day. But the thing is that John (Felske) never said a word. He knew how I felt. And I knew I wasn't going to be buried after just one game."

Felske inspires similar security among the several other younger Phillies trying to win jobs. "Everybody here knows the score, they know their situation," says Felske. "I'll talk things over with each and every one of them. But I'm not going to jump on them for mistakes right away. The kids are under enough pressure. What I want is to see how kids like Jeltz respond to problems."

Felske, his coaches, Giles, and the Phillies' top executives meet after the game, and begin talking about Diaz.

Throughout the winter, Felske had quietly argued that the Phils should relinquish Diaz only reluctantly, that they should trade him only if they were offered the most attractive pitcher. "What's wrong with having two top catchers? Where is it written that you can't have two No. 1 catchers on the same team?" Felske would say over and over at the meetings.

Now, with Diaz obviously rounding into top condition and playing well, Felske's arguments are being heard. And in typically abrupt and quick-trigger fashion, Giles proceeds to announce that Diaz is off the trading block. "Bo Diaz is staying with us; he is not going to be traded," declares Giles.

The announcement is greeted cynically in the Phillies clubhouse. Says one veteran, "It makes sense to keep Bo. But who can believe announcements like that after all the moves they've made in the past?"

Nevertheless, with Diaz ostensibly off the trading block, speculation now shifts to who will be offered for that elusive reliever.

March 13

TUCSON—The Cory Snyder report: 1-for-10 with four strikeouts and a dozen feeble swings.

"So far his hitting has been more of a problem than his play at second base," says Indians manager Pat Corrales.

The good news is that Snyder's father drifted into the background after he was barred from the clubhouse by Corrales. He has returned to his home in Salt Lake City, leaving Cory on his own.

SARASOTA, FLORIDA—Significance is in the eye of the beholder and, apparently, not in the eyes of the participants. So it is that neither the best pitcher in the history of the Mets nor the Mets' best current pitcher are particularly moved by facing each other. The White Sox versus the Mets. Tom Seaver versus Dwight Gooden. So what, they say.

Both perform the way duelling stars are supposed to. Gooden allows two hits and a walk while striking out one in his three innings; Seaver goes five innings, allowing one hit and no runs. Each offers polite but almost perfunctory acknowledgment of the other's work. "I wouldn't mind meeting him," Gooden says. "You don't have to meet him to know what kind of pitcher he is," Seaver says.

March 14

WEST PALM BEACH, FLORIDA—The Braves now know two-thirds of their opening-night outfield—Dale Murphy in center, Claudell Washington in right. And in left?

The Braves had such difficulty there last year that many fans called for them to make a deal (Jim Rice?) during the offseason. But they didn't, and Eddie Haas is looking closely at the same players who failed Joe Torre last year: Brad Komminsk, Terry Harper, Albert Hall, and Milt Thompson. Komminsk and Thompson, from the first workout, were hitting the ball well and playing with confidence. It appears to be a two-man contest, and Haas has mentioned the possibility of platooning the two at the position.

Meanwhile, the Braves' three high-priced catchers were all off to slow starts. Through two weeks of exhibition games, they had not thrown out a single base runner or driven in a single run. Since the deal for Cerone was made, Benedict has been on the trading block. But Trevino is not impressing Haas and his coaching staff, and Haas informs the front office that he'd just as soon trade Trevino and keep Benedict as a backup to Cerone.

John Mullen quickly gets the word around to scouts that Trevino might be available. The California Angels have a good report on Trevino from their new TV broadcaster, Joe Torre, and say they'd like to talk about a deal. The Pittsburgh Pirates, looking for a backup catcher to Tony Pena, also express some interest. The Braves are confident of dealing Trevino by the end of spring training. But his four-year, $2.2 million contract, signed one month after he joined the team last summer, is an obstacle.

MESA, ARIZONA—Left-hander Pat Clements, apparently determined to solve what Mauch considers the club's most pressing need and keep it out of the trade mart, makes his Cactus League debut, working 2⅔ shutout innings against Milwaukee.

"He was outstanding," Mauch says. "He got every left-hander out. He did everything we asked of him."

Another week, and the Angels have still not found Daryl Sconiers, who has now been fined $3,675.

March 15

CLEVELAND—Pat O'Neill, the Indians chairman of the board, says nothing is happening on the sale front.

"I don't know when the sale of the club will be completed," says O'Neill. "Tomorrow wouldn't be too soon for me, but it seems like it will take quite a while. We are at 20,000 feet and holding."

The only news O'Neill has is that Dave LeFevre will not be elected to the team's board of directors to replace Gabe Paul.

"LeFevre is still in the picture," says O'Neill. "We've had no new serious bidders for the team so we are talking to the old ones, and that includes Dave LeFevre."

Meanwhile, LeFevre is in Tucson to observe the team as if he owned it. "We're still working towards the purchase of the Indians," he says, "but it takes time."

March 16

TUCSON—Are Cory Snyder's days at second base over? Pat Corrales says that isn't the case, but the manager uses Snyder at third base today for the second straight game.

"Cory looks better at third than second," says Corrales. "I think he is getting a little better and more confident each day. The real question is his hitting. If he hits, I wouldn't be afraid to put him at second. He wouldn't embarrass himself at second, but he has to cut loose at the plate."

WEST PALM BEACH, FLORIDA—Leo Mazzone, a new member of the Braves' coaching staff, has watched Paul Zuvella for three weeks. He needs to see no more before making the pronouncement, "He does everything right."

March 17

YUMA, ARIZONA—Ken Forsch leaves an exhibition game against San Diego after only one inning with an inflammation in his elbow. It is not believed serious, but it is not known when Forsch will be able to pitch again.

MESA, ARIZONA—Nick Lampros, a San Jose, California, attorney who represents Daryl Sconiers, calls Mike Port and says he expects Sconiers to be at the Angels' training base tomorrow. There are no details given about Sconiers's absence, which has spanned 17 days.

CLEVELAND—Bob Quinn gets his first nibble on a job since being fired as farm director of the Indians. Ironically, Quinn contacts the Kansas City Royals about a position as assistant general manager—the same job Joe Klein had before leaving the Royals for Cleveland.

The Royals appear to be interested in Quinn, but no decision is immediately forthcoming.

WEST PALM BEACH, FLORIDA—Across the state in St. Petersburg, the St. Louis Cardinals are having difficulty in their negotiations with shortstop Ozzie Smith. They have begun to look around the big leagues for another shortstop, in case they are unable to sign Smith and have to deal him. Dal Maxvill, who opened the spring as the Braves' third-base coach but has since left to become the Cardinals' general manager, knows all about Paul Zuvella.

Maxvill calls John Mullen to ask if the Braves would be interested in dealing Zuvella, perhaps for Ken Dayley, the ex-Braves pitcher who was having a good spring with St. Louis. No way will Zuvella be traded, Mullen tells Maxvill. "He's an important part of Eddie's plans."

March 18

TUCSON—Sometimes the business of showcasing a player is a subtle process. More often, it's like today's experience for Mike Jeffcoat.

The Indians hope to interest the Boston Red Sox in Jeffcoat. Red Sox scouts are in attendance at today's game. Jeffcoat pitches two scoreless innings against the San Francisco Giants. He prepares to leave the dugout to pitch another inning but is stopped by Pat Corrales.

"You're through for the day," says Corrales.

"What do you mean?" asks Jeffcoat.

"Take a shower, you're not pitching any more today."

"Why not?" asks Jeffcoat. "I was supposed to pitch three innings. That was what I was told."

"Look, you pitched two good innings," says Corrales. "You're being showcased today and you looked good so let's not go another inning and take a chance on messing it up."

MESA, ARIZONA—Daryl Sconiers, in a brief visit to the Angels training base, says his absence stemmed from a "substance problem" he thinks is under control. He and attorney Lampros leave for Los Angeles, where Sconiers's condition is to be evaluated by Dr. Gerald Rozansky, head of the Life Start program at Centinela Hospital Medical Center. Neither Sconiers nor the Angels identify the substance or the duration of Sconiers's involvement with it. Mike Port says the fine of $4,165 will stand.

March 19

WEST PALM BEACH, FLORIDA—Almost a month into spring training, there remains a two-man contest for the first-base job—Chris Chambliss versus Gerald Perry. Today, Chambliss watches as Perry homers and doubles in an exhibition game. But Chambliss, too, is having a good spring.

Lighter than a year ago, he looks like he has regained some of the range he had lost in the field, and he is swinging the bat well. Haas begins to talk up the notion that, although both are left-handed hitters, both Chambliss and Perry could play frequently at first base. He points out that both would be assets as left-handed pinch hitters.

Both Chambliss and Perry make it clear that they want a full-time starting position, and the battle continues.

TUCSON—"I don't care what anyone says, Cory Snyder can play second base," insists Indians manager Pat Corrales. "But if he doesn't make it here this year, he'll probably never play second on a regular basis. That's because he is more natural at third."

Corrales is tired of hearing scouts criticize Snyder's play at second base. "The hell with them. These are the same guys who said Cal Ripken couldn't play shortstop. Let them run their clubs and we'll run ours. The only reason they said those things about Cory is because he is 6-foot-3. But his frame isn't as big as Bobby Grich's. Besides, who wrote the book on what a second baseman is supposed to look like? Does he have to be a little, short chubby guy to make a quick pivot?"

Nevertheless, Snyder is only batting .222 on a team hitting .305 in Arizona.

"I'm going to play Cory as much as I can, even if he doesn't make the club this spring," says Corrales. "I want him to get his feet wet and exposed to the majors."

March 21

CLEARWATER, FLORIDA—Keith Hernandez, Gary Carter, Wally Backman, and Ron Gardenhire are absent as the Mets lose, 6–5, to the Phillies. Each absence is excused—Hernandez is in Pittsburgh, testifying before a grand jury investigating drug trafficking in the Pittsburgh area; Backman is recovering from oral surgery; and Gardenhire is home in Wichita with his wife and new baby.

Johnson has no problem with their reasons. He is upset by Carter's absence—though not at Carter himself—and makes his annoyance public.

Carter had a commitment to be in New York to tape a commercial for *Newsday,* the Long Island newspaper. Johnson and Frank Cashen originally had not approved his absence. But when the newspaper reinquired, a commitment was made without the knowledge or approval of Carter, Cashen, or Johnson. "I don't like people missing camp," Johnson says, though he acknowledges that Carter probably wouldn't have played against the Phillies. "If I'm mad at anyone, it's not Frank. It's above Frank."

"I never would have gone if I knew it would cause so much commotion," Carter says.

On the other side of Florida, a newspaper account of the minor incident involving Carter is thumbtacked to the Expos clubhouse bulletin board. Carter's quotes are marked, and the words "I" and "me" are underlined. The Expos, who had referred to Carter as "I-me," had expressed dissatisfaction—or was it jealousy—about the many endorsements afforded Carter when he played in Montreal.

PALM SPRINGS, CALIFORNIA—The Angels' base of operations shifts to California for the second half of the spring schedule. The change of scene brings no change of fortune for Ken Forsch.

Forsch tries to throw on the sidelines, but still experiences soreness in his elbow. There is a growing feeling that Forsch will have to open the season on the disabled list, creating a vacancy in the Angels rotation.

Both Port and Mauch, however, say they are impressed with the pitching of farm prospects Urbano Lugo and Bob Kipper. The indication is that they would rather promote from within than trade for a veteran.

March 23

TUCSON—Manager Pat Corrales has learned that miracles don't happen, at least not to the Indians.

During the winter, Corrales entertained springtime dreams of taking a kid who never played a professional game, who had never played anything but shortstop or third base, and making him into a big-league second baseman in six weeks.

It was Corrales's attempt to catch lightning in a bottle. But there was barely a spark.

Cory Snyder is batting only .182. His performance at second isn't frightening, but it certainly isn't major-league caliber.

"Basically, Cory didn't hit," says Corrales. "That's what it came down to. If he had hit, we could have lived with him at second."

Instead, Snyder will live in Waterbury, Connecticut, and play third base in the Class AA Eastern League.

"Cory has great ability," says Corrales. "But he needs to play every day, get his feet on the ground and relax a bit. You have no idea how much pressure is on a young guy who never played pro ball before."

"This is the first time in my life that I pressed and became tense," says Snyder. "I'm a little disappointed in myself. Maybe I didn't do as well as I could have done."

"I'm sure that Cory will be fine once he starts playing every day," insists Corrales. "He has too much talent to let this get him down for long."

"Getting out was hard to take," says Snyder. "I can't say anything bad about Corrales because he didn't do anything wrong. It wasn't my fault or his fault. It just worked out that way.

"I am glad that I'll be playing third base. I feel more comfortable there. Now I can concentrate on my hitting without worrying about learning a new position."

WEST PALM BEACH, FLORIDA—Brad Komminsk, who Hank Aaron once said "can do some things in this game that no one else has ever thought of doing," appears to be running away with the left field job. As a rookie last year, Komminsk flopped miserably, unable to hold up the weight of Aaron's and others' assessments. But this spring, he looks like the player who had terrorized the minor leagues.

He has a team-high 15 hits, including four for extra bases, and is batting .319. "I feel like I'm more in control," says Komminsk, who, indeed, is taking control in left and making Eddie Haas talk less and less of platooning at the position.

March 24

TUCSON—For the Indians, it will be the hardest cut of the spring.

Andre Thornton, the highest paid player in Indians' history and the cornerstone of Peter Bavasi's restoration of the franchise, feels his left knee buckle. Immediately, Thornton knows there is trouble. The same thing had happened to him in the spring of 1980—only then it was the right knee.

"I'll probably need surgery," says Thornton. "I hope it will be arthroscopic. Guys can bounce back from that procedure in three-to-four weeks."

Thornton is examined here by Dr. Richard Toll, who says that Thornton has torn cartilage in his lefts45knee.

The good news is that there is apparently no ligament damage, which would have meant repair by standard surgery and would have kept Thornton out for most of the season.

"I think I hurt my knee during the first week of camp," says Thornton. "I had the knee looked at and it appeared to be only a strain. I took some anti-inflammation drugs and it took away the symptoms for a while. But after a few weeks, I knew it was gone. I swung the bat and I couldn't really push off my knee. Every time I ran, I felt the knee trying to lock up on me."

Thornton is confident of making a strong comeback.

"The only thing I dread about the knee is the pain, both before and after surgery. I have reason to be optimistic. I was looking forward to the season. I was excited and I still am. I worked hard all winter and I wanted us to get off to a good start together. I do feel bad for the team. We need each other very much."

Down the Stretch

March 25

PALM SPRINGS, CALIFORNIA—Pat Clements pitches another perfect relief inning for the Angels in an exhibition victory over Seattle, apparently cementing his hold on the left-handed bullpen seat. Asked if he would have any qualms about opening the season with Clements, Mauch says, "I'd be tickled to death. He's the one thing we've been looking for all spring."

Is a trade still possible? "There's some names out there," Port says, "but none excite me. None has done a better job than Pat Clements has this spring."

WEST PALM BEACH, FLORIDA—Paul Zuvella has kept it up, getting a hit or two every start, playing flawlessly in the field, and by this point he has clearly become the standout of spring training. He has committed only one error all spring while playing three positions, and he is leading the team in batting average and RBIs. He is hitting .339.

"He is a big-league ballplayer," John Mullen says. "He has made this club."

But at the same time, the numbers game has heated up in the Braves camp, as it does about this time every spring. There are two major complications.

First, Trevino still has not been traded, and the Braves suspect that other clubs are waiting to see if they will release him and eat his $2 million contract. If this happens, then another club can sign Trevino for the minimum salary. "Everyone wants to see if they can wait us out and get him for nothing," Mullen says. But Mullen insists that if Trevino is not traded, he will open the season on the Braves roster and the team will simply go with three catchers for a while.

Second, while Horner has been impressive enough to make the Braves think he might be on the opening-day roster, they do not feel confident enough of his recovery to trade Oberkfell. Mullen recognizes the possibility that the Braves might open the season with both Horner and Oberkfell on the roster.

The 25 spots are overbooked already.

Another item in Bob Horner's comeback. On an off day for the Braves, their first of the spring, Horner telephones Haas and says, "I'd like to pinch hit in the game tomorrow." Fine, says Haas. "You're calling the shots right now."

March 26

WEST PALM BEACH, FLORIDA—For the first time in nearly 10 months, Bob Horner faces a pitcher from an opposing team. He pinch hits for second baseman Glenn Hubbard in the sixth inning of the Braves' 6–2 win over Baltimore. He watches one sinker from Nat Snell miss the strike zone, and then bounces the next one to third baseman Fritz Connally. "You have to walk before you can run," says Horner, who says he plans to start at third base tomorrow.

March 27

WEST PALM BEACH, FLORIDA—Horner appears in the starting lineup for the first time since May 30, 1984. He handles two routine chances in the field and goes 0-for-3 at the plate: a strikeout, a broken-bat grounder, and a soft fly to right center. He plays five innings.

"It didn't look like much," he says afterward, "but it meant everything to me. I'm very excited about what is happening. I was swinging the bat well, and I wasn't hesitating."

Meanwhile, Mullen says the team will make a determination on March 31 whether Horner will open the season on the active roster or the disabled list. "There's no decision to it; I'll be playing," says Horner. "If that's so, it would really be something . . . considering what we were thinking in December," adds Mullen.

PALM SPRINGS, CALIFORNIA—Gene Mauch makes it official: Reggie Jackson will play 130 to 135 games in right field, erasing the candidacy of Mike Brown, who will become part of a DH platoon. Mauch, confident that Jackson's involvement on the field will make him more productive at the plate, cites his spring average of .368 and says, "If there's a connection between the way the man is hitting and the fact he's playing right field, then damn right he's the right fielder."

They are talking about Gene Mauch in the Angels' clubhouse. They are talking about his intensity and how it seems better suited to the needs of a basically unemotional team than the relaxed manner of predecessor John McNamara.

"Gene Mauch brings something we need . . . some drive, some push, some demands," says Reggie Jackson.

"We have a quiet club," notes Doug DeCinces. "A lot has been said about that recently. I think Gene's outward intensity will change that. I also anticipate our younger players will be more mentally prepared to play now because Gene talks baseball from the time he arrives until he leaves. He's had great success with young players."

Jackson adds, "Baseball in California is entertainment. I don't even look on it as a job. There's not the life and death atmosphere to it that you find in the East. It's harder to develop a killer instinct. It's pretty rather than gritty.

"You've got fans who have to decide between the ballpark and going sailing. You've got girls walking around the stadium in bikinis.

"We'd come in with the Yankees and think, hey, it's the Angels. They don't slide hard, they don't play hard. I mean, it's tougher for a manager to develop the type of work ethic that will carry a team through a 162-game schedule, but I have respect for the business-like way Mauch goes about it.

"He projects an uneasy air, and that's good. You need to feel that you have to play to a certain level for approval. I stretched a double into a triple the other day, and he didn't say good hustle, he didn't say anything.

"He looked at me as if to say he expected me to be on third, as if to say, 'What next, old man?'

"He recognizes that winning is a long, plodding effort and he's always looking for the little ways to beat you. I have the feeling that he stays up all night thinking about how to get a bunt down.

"I told someone that if Gene Mauch lost his wallet in the desert and you watched him walk back into the desert to find it, you'd believe he knew exactly where he was going, where he had lost it. You believe what he says because the image he projects doesn't give you reason to doubt it."

ST. PETERSBURG, FLORIDA—Ed Olwine, the pitcher the Phillies selected from the Mets organization in the December draft, is returned to the Mets after compiling a 16.29 earned run average in four spring training appearances. Meanwhile, the Mets send the almost forgotten Jose Oquendo to their minor-league complex so that, in Johnson's phrase, "He can get enough work." Though Oquendo is not officially demoted, this assignment marks the beginning of the end of his Mets tenure.

In another minor personnel move, Frank Wills, acquired in the Tim Leary trade, is dealt to the Seattle Mariners for a 23-year-old right-handed pitcher named Wray Bergendahl, whom the Mets assign to Class A. Wills went through the spring virtually unnoticed, compiling a 7.50 ERA in six innings.

WEST PALM BEACH, FLORIDA—The word is around camp that Brad Komminsk has won the left field job. Eddie Haas hasn't told Komminsk that the job is his, but Haas has told his coaches and the front office, who told a few people, who told a few other people. . . . And besides, it is obvious.

His competitors have no argument. "He's won it; we all know that," says Milt Thompson. Albert Hall adds, "He's had a great spring and deserves it."

PALM SPRINGS, CALIFORNIA—Dr. Gerald Rozansky says the evaluation of Daryl Sconiers's involvement with chemicals, having already spanned more than a week, will take another two or three. Mike Port says it is now obvious that Sconiers will be unable to open the season with the Angels. He says Sconiers will be put on a restricted list.

CLEARWATER, FLORIDA—The Phillies had opened spring training with Len Matuszek holding the first-base job and no apparent competition in sight. However, Matuszek proceeded to play miserably all spring, hitting in the neighborhood of .150 while fielding poorly. Compounding things was Matuszek's morose attitude. A chronic worrier, Matuszek moped through his spring slump, and his presence around the clubhouse more and more resembled the classic appearance of a dark cloud.

As a result, teammates had little sympathy for Matuszek's struggle. And the situation became more and more evident to Felske and his coaches. Giles, never a big fan of Matuszek, is looking for alternatives. The idea of putting John Russell at first is mentioned, but nothing comes of it. Yet.

Russell is one of the darlings of the Phillies' organization, a former first-round pick in the amateur draft and a powerfully-built right-handed hitter who promises many home runs in the future.

Russell had come to spring training vying for the right field job, but that job was quickly won by Glenn Wilson, who, wearing new glasses and exuding new confidence, was perhaps the Phillies' top spring training performer.

Today Felske calls Russell into the office for a talk in which Felske tells Russell that he will probably start the season in the minors. Russell knew such news was coming, but he nevertheless is disappointed. "Heck, I can play in the majors, I'm ready to play here, and I'm not going to be helped by going to the minors," says Russell.

However, Russell's fortunes will soon change.

March 29

CLEARWATER AND VERO BEACH, FLORIDA—At the Dodgers' camp in Vero Beach on the east coast of Florida, trade rumors have been flying all spring. Los Angeles is obviously in need of offensive help, with third base long considered their problem position.

Rumor after rumor has floated in and out of camp with such frequency that Dodgers players have started joking about trades. On this afternoon, pitcher Bob Welch overhears a conversation involving a club official and an unidentified person. Welch thinks he hears that the Dodgers are talking about dealing himself, reliever Tom Niedenfuer, first baseman Sid Bream, catcher Jack Fimple, and top-rated prospect Ralph Bryant to the Phillies for Mike Schmidt.

Welch can't keep the news to himself. During the course of a radio interview with a Los Angeles-based reporter, Welch mentions the rumor. Without attempting to get much substantiation, the radio reporter gets the rumor on the United Press International wire service.

It becomes the lead story on most 11 P.M. newscasts in Philadelphia. However, Bill Giles goes to the dog track and doesn't hear a thing until he is called at his Clearwater condo at 12:15 A.M. "Say Bill, can you confirm or deny that you're talking to the Dodgers about trading Schmidt for five guys?" he is asked.

For two minutes, Giles who won big at the track that night,

just giggles. "What is this, a practical joke?" he asks. "No Bill, it's on the wire and will be in every newspaper in the country tomorrow," is the reply.

Giles then stops laughing and denies any deal involving Schmidt has ever been discussed. "It's the most ridiculous thing I've ever heard," he says. "I can't believe it. We have never or would we ever discuss trading Mike Schmidt. He's our franchise and we're going to live and die with him."

The Schmidt rumor will have about a two-day life span, the Phillies taking it all with a sense of humor. "I wouldn't know Ralph Bryant if he came into my bedroom at midnight," declares Alexander. Says Felske, "Right now, we're still uncertain where we'll play Fimple."

Further investigation reveals exactly how Welch heard what he heard. He had thought he had heard the name "Schmidt," when actually the Dodgers were talking about a deal in which the key player was named "Smith"—Ozzie Smith of the St. Louis Cardinals.

March 30

CLEARWATER, FLORIDA—Giles loves the dog track. St. Petersburg has the premier dog-racing facility in the world, beautiful Derby Lane, where the dining is superb and the quality of racing first-rate.

Giles convenes ongoing meetings of various Phillies staffers at the track. He loves to gamble, but he also finds the loose atmosphere of the track a good place to get unsolicited and frank opinions about personnel and possible player moves. And more and more, he is convinced he has to do something about first base. And as a result of some track-side analysis, Felske decides to play John Russell at first base for a couple of days.

The position isn't new to Russell. He played there for two weeks during the fall Instructional League program. And Russell plays well when inserted into the lineup there. He hits a home run and plays the position more than adequately defensively.

"I don't know what is going on, but it's like I've come back from the dead," Russell says. "I don't know if this is a shot to stick, but whatever it is, I'll give my best."

March 31

CLEARWATER, FLORIDA—Bill Giles spends a long Sunday closeted with Alexander and Owens as they work the phones to try and move Len Matuszek to another team. "I'll tell you this," Felske tells the trademasters, "if we've decided John Russell is our first baseman, I can't have Lenny moping around. It would be tough on everyone. You gotta move him if you can."

The Phillies quickly zero in on Toronto as their target. The Blue Jays are looking for left-handed hitting help, and have shown some occasional interest in Matuszek in the past. Late today, the Blue Jays say they will take Matuszek, and offer the Phils a list of minor-league prospects from which to choose as payment. The Phillies then counter with two specific names—pitcher Matt Williams and power-hitting first base prospect Fred McGriff. Toronto says no to relinquishing either, and Blue Jays general manager Pat Gillick supplies another list of prospects. At this point, Giles says he'll sleep on things and get back in touch in the morning.

WEST PALM BEACH, FLORIDA—Paul Zuvella's average is up to .350. Still only one error. Still the most impressive player in camp.

But the Braves decide today that Horner definitely will open the season on the roster, as will Oberkfell. Carrying both Horner and Oberkfell takes away one opening in the infield. And more and more it appears that Trevino might not be dealt before opening day, forcing the Braves to go with three catchers.

In that case, they will have to cut their pitching staff from the ideal ten to nine, or their supply of infielders from eight to seven. For the first time, Mullen admits, "Zuvella may not be on our team opening day, but he will be a big part of this team."

One factor working against Zuvella is that he has options remaining, meaning that the Braves can send him back to the minors without complication. Paul Runge, another rookie infielder having a less impressive spring, is out of options and cannot be returned to the minors. So he has made the team. This means that Zuvella and Randy Johnson are battling for the last infield spot, assuming the team carries eight infielders. And this is no contest; Zuvella is clearly a better player than Johnson at this point.

A few other decisions linger. Will Chris Chambliss or Gerald Perry, both having solid springs, be the starter at first base? Exactly how will the bullpen be aligned in the pre-Sutter innings? And will Steve Bedrosian's still-troublesome shoulder and Len Barker's elbow be sound enough to allow them to join Rick Mahler, Pascual Perez, and Craig McMurtry in the starting rotation?

The season will open in nine days. "It looks like this is going to be a pretty good team," Eddie Haas says.

April 1

CLEARWATER, FLORIDA—Giles arrives at the Jack Russel Stadium offices at 8:30 A.M. armed with two briefcases and a carton of cigarettes. "Yep, it's a two-briefcase day," he says with his characteristic giggle. "This one is my usual stuff. This one has my trade stuff, all the player reports we have. Yeah, this should be a long day."

Giles loves nothing better than wheeling and dealing. So he relishes what is in store for him this Monday morning.

He hunkers down in the newly built office and works the phones, with Alexander and Owens at his side. They know a deal with Toronto is likely. But they make one more round of calls just in case they can dredge up a better deal for Matuszek.

However, by noontime they decide to close the deal with the Blue Jays. They get Gillick on the phone, and Gillick provides a group of names from which he says the Phils can have three. Giles and his aides consult their scouting reports and settle on a trio of minor leaguers: pitcher Dave Shipanoff ("We liked the fact that he's been scouted as being a hard thrower, something we need in our minor-league system," says Giles); infielder Jose Escobar ("According to the reports, he has outstanding defensive skills and we don't have those kind of skills coming up in the system right now," says Giles); and outfielder Ken Kinnard ("I look at the reports and I see that he's a young switch-hitter with better than average speed," says Alexander. "Now, the son of a bitch might never play in the major leagues but when you can switch-hit and run, you sure as hell have a better chance of making it than someone who can't do those two things.").

So the deal is closed, with official announcement scheduled for 5 P.M. But there is one problem: Matuszek has gone with the team to Sarasota, some two hours away, for an exhibition game with the White Sox. He does not know a deal has been made.

Moments before game time, Giles calls the Sarasota ballpark and tells Felske the news. Felske in turn tells Matuszek, and assistant public relations director Vince Nauss drives Matuszek back to Clearwater. "There's no sense having Lenny stay here all day watching a game in which he plays for neither team," says Felske.

TUCSON—Joe Klein has made his first trade. Well, we assume it is Joe Klein's deal. Right now, the Indians have more general managers than starting pitchers with Phil Seghi, Dan O'Brien, and Klein all in Tucson. What's more, Peter Bavasi is not immune to sticking his nose into the player personnel department.

Anyway, it is Klein who announces the transaction—Jay Baller to the Cubs for Dan Rohn. Not the kind of trade that knocks the world off its axis, but it might say something about the new folks running the Indians.

It was Baller—not Julio Franco—who was termed the "key player" when the Indians traded Von Hayes to Philadelphia at the 1982 winter meetings. In exchange for Hayes, Gabe Paul and Seghi convinced Philadelphia to part with George Vukovich, Manny Trillo, Jerry Willard, Franco, and Baller.

"Baller was the last guy added to the package," said Paul then. "Without him, there was no deal."

At 6-foot-6, with a 90 mph fastball and a killer slider, the

Indians billed Baller as another Goose Gossage. But Baller flopped in two spring trainings and threw a ridiculous number of wild pitches in the minors.

Nonetheless, Paul and Seghi clung to the belief that Baller would one day be something special. After all, he walked into spring training in 1985 only 24 years old. It took Jim Kern until he was 27 to harness his control.

But in the process, Baller not only failed to make the Cleveland roster, he ran out of minor-league options. Rather than send him to the minors for another year where he would be a "frozen" player, Klein swaps Baller to the Cubs.

"We didn't have time to wait for Baller," says Indians manager Pat Corrales. "Jay has made some strides, but he's not ready. Besides, we couldn't bring him back from (Class AAA) Maine without getting waivers on him. Any team could have taken him from us for $25,000, so we decided to get something for him while we could."

And what did Klein get for this mountain of a pitcher? The mole hill of big leaguers.

"I'm the smallest player in the majors," says Rohn. "I've checked around both leagues. I'm 5-foot-7. Danny Gladden of San Francisco is pretty close to my size, but I'm smaller."

Rohn may be small, but he's also old for a prospect at 29. In 1984, Rohn batted .269 in Class AAA and .129 in 25 games with the Cubs.

"Based on our scouting reports, Rohn's best position is second base," says Klein. "But what he really does best is hit the ball. We actively sought him out."

It's known that Seghi objected to the deal, but he was overruled by O'Brien and Klein.

"All I know is that I'm happy to get out of here," says Baller. "Do you think I wanted to go to the minors and bring in the gold for the Maine Guides?"

WEST PALM BEACH, FLORIDA—Randy Johnson, a two-year big-league veteran, is sent to Richmond. Trevino still has not been traded. The roster stands at 26 players, one more than the opening-day limit. The Braves still hope to unload Trevino before the season opens April 9; otherwise, they will have to send a pitcher, possibly Craig McMurtry, to Richmond; or send Zuvella, their leading hitter and fielder of spring training, to Richmond.

"You have to understand," Mullen keeps saying, "it'd be temporary if we did that."

ST. PETERSBURG, FLORIDA—Roger McDowell, a right-handed rookie with a natural sinker, is told he has won a position on the opening-day roster. He has pitched 17⅔ innings and allowed two earned runs. His presence almost assures Doug Sisk that he will be used in the unwanted role of long relief. McDowell is to be the set-up man for stopper Jesse Orosco.

Johnson will use Sisk in "longer" relief to accommodate McDowell. Cashen has fears that McDowell's surgical right elbow will not respond well to the uneven demands of long relief.

At first, Sisk doesn't believe a change of assignment is forthcoming. "Why would they mess with success?" he wonders. And when it happens, he is displeased. "Why are they messing with success?"

CLEARWATER, FLORIDA—With the first-base situation clarified, the Phillies still have roster problems to solve before they open the season.

One involves the bullpen. When Al Holland arrived for camp on February 25, he weighed in at a whopping 242 pounds. Publicly, the Phils downplayed Holland's condition, but privately, they were aghast.

"Here's a guy who is a free agent after this season, who could be looking at being a million-a-year pitcher," says one teammate. "Never mind professional pride. Just look at it from the money angle. You'd think in this, of all years, he would have worked to be in shape. Instead it looks like he spent the winter in a Mister Donut shop."

Holland's weight problem obviously hurt his ability to throw.

He was forced to wear a rubber suit (called a heart-attack jacket by players) during workouts to lose weight quickly. He did in fact lose 10 pounds in a week, but became so weak by the fast loss that he didn't have the necessary strength to throw the hard fastball he needs to be successful.

Holland's weight also affected his control. He had always pitched from a stretch position because he saw the plate better that way and was able to generate more power. But because of his weight problems, he couldn't generate the power anymore from the stretch, so he adopted a full windup to try to compensate. That resulted in his pitches being high in the strike zone. And with his fastball off by several miles per hour, the result was that he was hit hard.

Concerned about Holland, and having already decided they wouldn't re-sign him no matter what kind of success he might have, the Phillies quietly start shopping Holland. And they begin focusing on the Pittsburgh Pirates, who are in need of left-handed relief help and have some surplus pitching to offer in return. The Phillies immediately seek Pirates right-hander Don Robinson, but are quickly turned down. They also inquire about young right-hander Cecilio Guante; scout Ray "Snacks" Shore watched him for five outings in Florida, since Guante had arm problems in 1984. Guante is healthy, but the Pirates don't want to deal him.

Then surfaces the possibility of acquiring 38-year-old Kent Tekulve, for a decade one of baseball's premier relievers but coming off a poor 1984 season in which he was removed from his customary closing role. Alexander likes the idea of acquiring Tekulve. "I'll tell you, the guy can still get people out," he says. "He wasn't that bad last year, it was more a case of him pitching for a bad team. I don't have anything to do with contracts or any of that stuff. All I know is that skinny guy could help us."

Pittsburgh begins to scout Holland regularly, dispatching legendary scout Howie Haak to watch Holland over the course of 10 days. Haak recommends that Holland could help the Pirates, and a deal begins to look more and more likely. But opposing it is Pirates manager Chuck Tanner, who is not enamored of Holland and is also very close to Tekulve, for whom he has great respect.

So the Pirates back down at the last moment; Holland will open the season with the Phillies.

Another lingering question is resolved with Felske's official announcement that Steve Jeltz will be the club's starting shortstop. Felske tells that to DeJesus, who understands the decision and accepts it grudgingly.

Jeltz tries to low-key the news. He tries to play it all cool, but after prodding, his satisfaction bursts forth.

"I've dreamed ever since I can remember of being a big-league player, and when they called me up last September, I thought I'd almost cry," says Jeltz. "Now, I hear I'm going to be the man on opening day and it's something I can't hardly put into words.

"From the start, all I could do here was to work hard, to give my 100%. But I knew the decision was going to be made by someone else and all I could do was play my best. If that was good enough, then I knew I'd start.

"Now I hear it's me and I feel great. I've worked hard to get here. And no matter what happens down the road, I'm not going to stop working. I can't be satisfied. This is just another step on the way for me and I know if I don't do the job, then they'll find someone else to do it instead of me."

April 2

ST. PETERSBURG, FLORIDA—The move that has been anticipated for months finally occurs: The Mets deal Jose Oquendo. The player who once was considered the club's shortstop for the remainder of the decade is dealt to the Cardinals for a shortstop of similar "good glove, weak bat" reputation, Argenis Salazar.

Cashen suspects he has helped Oquendo's career because he has heard the Cardinals are about to deal Ozzie Smith. If Oquendo were to emerge as the Cardinals shortstop, it would create a wonderful piece of irony—Oquendo starting for the team that traded away Rafael Santana, and Santana playing for the team that traded away Oquendo.

April 3

WEST PALM BEACH, FLORIDA—Paul Zuvella knows what is going on with the numbers. He knows there are still 26 players in the big-league locker room. He knows the Braves are having trouble trading Trevino, although they now have apparently agreed to assume about half of the financial obligations of his contract. Zuvella knows he could be a victim. He is hitting .339 (20-for-59) with 13 RBIs. Today, in an 8–4 win over Texas, he has two hits, three RBIs, and another flawless day at shortstop.

Before the game, he has a decision of his own to make. A truck is leaving West Palm Beach for Atlanta, carrying the personal possessions of the big-league players. Should Paul Zuvella put his possessions on the Atlanta-bound truck, or not?

He asks Mullen. "It's up to you," Mullen says, "but why don't you send them to Atlanta?" Zuvella is elated. He sends his belongings to Atlanta.

With just four exhibition games remaining, Chris Chambliss has his average up to .365, and Gerald Perry's has dropped to .180. Any more questions about who'll start the season at first base?

Chambliss, written off as over-the-hill by many in the Braves' organization last season, has shown this spring that the assessments were perhaps premature. "I worked hard during the offseason," Chambliss says, "and I came here to prove I can still play. I know I can still hit; I've always been able to hit, and you don't just suddenly stop knowing how."

But Chambliss knows that, his opening-night starting nod notwithstanding, he is unlikely to play the 140–150 games he'd prefer at first base. Eddie Haas has made it clear that both Chambliss and Perry will get extensive playing time and insists, "It can work with two guys playing the position. Don't make that big a deal out of who starts opening night, because both will play a lot." But the fact remains that Chambliss has won the right to start opening night, and if he can continue hitting during the regular season as he did in spring training, he could well force Haas to keep him in the lineup.

April 4

TUCSON—Dan Rohn will only have to worry about being the smallest player in the International League. He is sent to the Class AAA Maine Guides.

The move further illustrates that the Baller–Rohn deal was nothing more than a dump job on the part of the Indians, and a highly questionable one at that, since Cleveland lost five years and 10 inches of height in the trade.

WEST PALM BEACH, FLORIDA—Eddie Haas decides that Rick Mahler will start the opening-night game in Philadelphia. Beyond that, Haas admits that his pitching plans are still somewhat in disarray, although it appears that Pascual Perez will be the number two starter. Len Barker and Craig McMurtry have both had horrible springs, and Haas is wondering if perhaps Barker should start the year on the disabled list, or McMurtry should start it in the minors. These decisions will be tabled until the eve of the opener. Rick Camp, who has had a so-so spring, has moved closer to a starting job just by default, and Steve Bedrosian, his shoulder bothering him less each day, is also moving toward a spot in the rotation.

April 5

WEST PALM BEACH, FLORIDA—Claudell Washington receives word from his attorneys that prosecutors in Walnut Creek, California, have agreed to a trial date of July 3, which is an open date on the Braves' schedule after a series in San Francisco. This means Washington will be available to the Braves for at least the first three months of the season. Yet he admits, "I'm having a hard time concentrating fully on baseball right now."

ST. PETERSBURG, FLORIDA—All the weight lost by southpaw Sid Fernandez seems to have gone right onto his ERA. Fernandez has struggled all spring, and with his earned run average at 8.38, there is no place for him in the starting rotation. The Mets decide to send him down for the start of the season, weighing the potential damage the decision might have on his delicate psyche against the potential damage his lack of control might have on the team behind him.

Fernandez is told this morning, "He took it like a man," player personnel director Joe McIlvaine says, "last year, he took it like a child."

Optioning Fernandez is one of several moves the Mets make in setting their opening-day roster. Lefty Bill Latham and Roger McDowell, both rookies, are told they've made the club. Terry Blocker, an outfielder who had been optioned to Tidewater, is recalled to replace Ray Knight, who has undergone arthroscopic surgery on his ailing elbow.

The Mets will go north with four rookies—McDowell, Latham, Blocker, and John Christensen—and a pitching staff whose elder statesman (Bruce Berenyi) is just 30 years old. The average age of the roster is 27.8 years old.

April 6

WEST PALM BEACH, FLORIDA—Still no deal for Alex Trevino. Still no plans to release him. And while he is being shopped around, he is hardly being showcased: He hasn't had an at-bat since March 16.

TUSCON—Almost nothing has been said in the Indians training camp about Julio Franco's fielding. That's because there was nothing to say except, "Good job, Julio."

In 1984, Franco led all big-league shortstops with 36 errors, eight more than he made in his rookie year of 1983. But in the first 18 spring games of 1985, Franco was charged with only two errors, and it appeared the 23-year-old shortstop was maturing in the field.

Then came two spring games in which Franco booted four balls. There was nothing tricky about the plays; grounders were hit right at him and Franco butchered them.

"The main thing is his concentration," says Indians manager Pat Corrales. "Julio just isn't paying attention, but he is also having some trouble with his footwork and mechanics."

The Indians stun everyone by sending out another SOS signal for Brian Doyle. After a 6–3 loss to the Cubs, Corrales, Doyle, Franco, and coach Ed Napoleon take over the infield at Hi Corbett Field. Napoleon hits ground balls, and Doyle stands near Franco and occasionally stops the action to offer some suggestions about his footwork.

Meanwhile, Corrales watches, his arms folded across his chest.

"I wanted to get Brian in here because Julio is a crucial part of our club," says Corrales. "It wasn't that the errors were bothering me that much. Rather, I think they were starting to get to Julio mentally. I wanted his head clear and his confidence back when we opened the season in Detroit. We had to get the doubts out of his head."

"Players can't see themselves," says Doyle. "Julio got into some bad habits and didn't realize some of the things he was doing. I'm here to be Julio's eyes, his mirror."

"Basically, it centered on the position of Julio's glove," says Corrales. "Brian spotted it right away. We worked on correcting it."

Franco is surprisingly open to the advice. It's hard to guess how Franco will react to any hint of criticism or rejection, but he usually displays initial anger and then is repentant the next day.

"I think I'll be OK," says Franco. "Just got to work harder."

"Defensively, Julio can be the greatest shortstop in the history of the game," says Doyle. "Remember, he's still a kid. He's still learning about his body and how to play the game. Give him time."

CLEARWATER, FLORIDA—The Phils are down to the wire on their final roster decisions. And the biggest has become who will win the last two spots on the pitching staff.

Felske and the coaches are convinced that young left-hander Don Carman has earned a spot on the club. With Holland iffy, Felske feels it is vital to have another left-hander in the bullpen. And Felske is impressed that Carman, who had always possessed what scouts called "a million-dollar arm and a 10-cent head," has finally matured into the pitcher the Phils hoped he would be.

"We had a lot of surprises in spring training—how well Diaz and Maddox and Ghelfi came back from injuries, how well Glenn Wilson came in and played, how good some of the minor-league pitchers looked," says Felske. "But Carman was one of the biggest and most pleasant developments. He just seemed to have grown up and become a man, and he has thrown great all spring. He's like a different person and deserved to make this club."

The question is who will have to go to make room for Carman. The decision is between two veterans—Bill Campbell and Pat Zachry. Both are remarkably similar. Both are right-handers who do not possess overpowering stuff. Both are in the final year of their respective contracts and earning the same $400,000. Both can be free agents after the season. Both have had decent springs, but neither looms as a key member of the bullpen.

So it becomes a matter of which one the Phils can more easily trade. And in the process of shopping for takers, the Phillies fall into one last deal.

Giles went to St. Petersburg on April 4 for an exhibition game with St. Louis in which the big news was how Steve Carlton would pitch. His shoulder was stiff all spring, and the Phillies had to see some improvement or Carlton would be scratched from his opening-day starting assignment the following Tuesday night.

Carlton ended up having a shaky seven-walk outing, but he threw well enough for the Phillies to name him their opening-day starter. Once Carlton left the game, Giles roamed the stadium looking for Dal Maxvill, the Cardinals general manager.

"I just wanted to find out what they were going to do about Ozzie Smith," said Giles. "We had been hearing that they were having trouble signing him, and with him being a free agent after the season, I was hearing the Cardinals were going to trade him. So I really wanted to know what was going on. We didn't have interest in Smith because of the money involved. I was really just looking for gossip."

Giles got more than gossip. He found out that the Cards indeed were concerned about signing Smith and could end up trading him. And, as a hedge, they were looking for a veteran shortstop just in case.

And Giles just happened to have DeJesus sitting on his bench, likely to be a malcontent later in the season if he wasn't playing, possessing a contract in which a team's obligation to him ended after the season because of club-option clauses, and very available to anyone who wanted him.

So Giles said he'd get back to Maxvill right away. He drove back to Clearwater with Paul Owens, and the two decided they would also try to unload either Zachry or Campbell on the Cardinals, thereby relieving their roster problems while at the same time losing another substantial salary.

The deal was closed in surprisingly easy fashion. St. Louis opted for Campbell over Zachry. And the Phillies didn't ask for much in return. They first inquired about Jeff Lahti, the reliever they almost had during the winter meetings in the ill-fated Lavalliere deal. But a reporter who was just making conversation told Giles that Lahti was headed for the disabled list because of a neck problem, and Giles backed off Lahti.

The Phillies then countered by asking for left-hander David Rucker, whose stuff impressed both Alexander and Shore. The Cardinals were amenable; this morning the deal is announced.

DeJesus and Campbell head for St. Louis in exchange for Rucker. For now, the Phils send Rucker to the minors, though he is not going to stay there for very long. With DeJesus gone, the Phillies re-sign Kiko Garcia, whom they had released a week ago.

After a winter of near misses and assorted setbacks and surprises, the Phillies have finally constructed their opening-day roster. It proves to be one of the youngest in the major leagues; the opening-night lineup (minus Carlton) possesses just one player—Schmidt—with more than three years' experience and a multi-year contract. It is also largely a home-grown lineup, with six of the starters having come up through the Phillies' farm system.

All this might change later. But at least at the opening of the season, Giles has made good his promise to try and build a team that fans could have around for a period of time. "From a marketing and economic point of view, it just makes sense to build your own club and try to keep it together," says Giles. "And to think this could be a club whose nucleus stays together for a while and grows up in front of the Philadelphia fans. And that could well be the best way to win back some of the fans we have lost over the last few years."

For better or worse, Giles and the Phils have rolled the dice for 1985.

April 7

TUCSON—The Indians' baseball winter comes to a close as they fly from the sun of Arizona to the snow of Detroit to open the regular season.

Andre Thornton, the man they spent so much of the winter trying to sign, is back in Cleveland recovering from arthroscopic knee surgery. The operation was considered minor, and Thornton hopes to be back in the lineup by early May.

But his injury also seems to be yet another example of the Indians' inability to get a break unless it is a bad one. This is a franchise that hasn't been very good, nor has it been lucky. That's a deadly combination.

The biggest question—who will buy the franchise—remains unanswered. Dave LeFevre has assumed control of the club, hiring Peter Bavasi, Joe Klein, and Dan O'Brien to run the front office. LeFevre was also the force behind the re-signing of Thornton.

"Isn't it marvelous how Dave spends the O'Neills' money?"

says one member of the Tribe's front office. "He has the best of both worlds. He's running the show and not paying for it."

Of course, someone has to make some decisions, and the O'Neills are counting on LeFevre eventually clearing all of his legal and financial hurdles to take over the Indians. But the fact remains that he owns only 5% of the team as the season opens.

The Indians didn't fire their manager, but sacked about everyone else right down to a couple of secretaries. If nothing else, the faces of the Indians changed.

Former president Gabe Paul retired to Tampa, still on the payroll as a "special consultant." Phil Seghi no longer has the title as the team's general manager, but has elected to remain with the Indians in Cleveland instead of following up on his planned retirement to southern California. Seghi's office is changed at the Stadium, moved from a prestigious spot up front to the back of the building.

Ex-farm director Bob Quinn went to spring training in Florida, visiting with 12 teams to remind them he was still alive and more than available. But Quinn's attempt to assume Klein's old job as a special assistant to Kansas City general manager John Schuerholz failed; Schuerholz abolished the position, so Quinn is out of work as the season opens.

Finally, Cory Snyder will open the season as a third baseman at Class AA Waterbury. Like so many of the Indians' dreams, the vision of Snyder moving straight from Brigham Young to second base in Cleveland was nothing more than a mirage.

ST. PETERSBURG, FLORIDA—The Mets complete their spring training schedule with a 6–1 loss to the Cardinals and a 13–12 record. Roger McDowell is voted the outstanding rookie of the spring, and Dave Johnson is content as he dresses for his trip north. "We had more things go wrong than I liked . . . more than I expected. But I like our solutions," he says. "I like our chances."

WEST PALM BEACH, FLORIDA—Zuvella plays two innings at second base in the Braves' final exhibition game. One at-bat, one hit. Two fielding chances, two perfect plays. His final statistics for the spring are a team-leading .350 batting average, a team-leading 13 runs batted in, and only one error in 20 games.

After the game, Zuvella is aboard the chartered flight that carries the Braves to Philadelphia for the season opener two days hence. Trevino is also on board. In all there are 26 players.

"I'm going under the assumption I've made this team," Zuvella says. "If that turns out not to be the case, I'll have to adjust to it. But I'm trying not even to think of that possibility."

Before the plane leaves for Philadelphia, Eddie Haas reveals his plans for the pitching staff. Mahler will be followed in the rotation by Perez, Rick Camp, and Bedrosian. Len Barker and McMurtry, if not optioned, will open the season as long relievers. Zane Smith will pitch long and middle relief. Veterans Gene Garber and Terry Forster will be the set-up men for Bruce Sutter.

April 8

ANAHEIM—The Angels reveal their opening-day roster. In the wake of the long winter and spring, a period of comparative inactivity by the new front office, the roster reflects the new emphasis on development from within.

Three rookies—relief pitchers Pat Clements and Bob Kipper and infielder Craig Gerber—make the team. The club has brought north seven rookies in the last two years. Ken Forsch is on the disabled list, his starting spot to be taken by versatile veteran Jim Slaton. Donnie Moore has established himself as the top man in the suddenly deep bullpen. There are numerous questions still to be answered, but Gene Mauch is characteristically confident on the eve of his 24th season as a major-league manager.

"I've eaten a lot of March words in April and a lot of April words in June," he says, "but I meant 'em when I said 'em. If these guys play to their capability, and I'm assuming they will, they can't be beaten."

If that happens the Little General will know he definitely made the right decision in responding to the fires in his belly, coming back from the certainty that he would never manage again, the indifference that gripped him following the death of his wife.

Mauch reflects again and says, "Part of it (the decision to return) was knowing the caliber of the people I would be working with. Part of it is that bumming around is all right until you start feeling like a bum. I had a plan for 40 years—all baseball and a little golf. I tried it the other way (the last two years) and I didn't like it at all."

PHILADELPHIA—Zuvella works out with the Braves at Veterans' Stadium on the eve of the opener, taking batting practice with the reserves, shagging fly balls as the regulars hit, taking infield practice at three positions.

In the locker room afterward, a reporter asks him if he's heard anything about the roster situation. "Why would I?" he asks, trying to convince himself he wouldn't, it seems. "I don't think they brought me here to send me to Richmond."

But when Zuvella returns to his room a couple of hours after the workout, a note has been slipped under his door. "See Eddie in Logan's," it says.

At first, Zuvella thinks this is a prank by one of his teammates, maybe his friend Paul Runge. Logan's, the hotel bar, is normally off-limits to the players. But Zuvella gets to thinking about it and decides it might not be a prank.

He goes to Logan's and peeks in the door. He spots Haas, and his heart drops. He approaches Haas, who gets up and walks toward Zuvella. "Let's go talk," Haas says. The two leave the hotel bar, walk through the lobby, get on an elevator and go to Haas's room.

Haas reiterates to Zuvella that he will be a significant part of this team—soon. But Haas tells Zuvella that, for now, there is a roster problem that can only be fixed by sending Zuvella to Richmond. Haas implies it will be for only 10 days, but points out that there are no guarantees. The team will continue trying to deal Trevino, Haas tells Zuvella, and as soon as that happens, Zuvella will be summoned from Richmond.

"I don't really know how to react," Zuvella says later. "I understand the situation, and I understand they intend for this to be temporary. But what if they don't make a trade right away, and the team gets off to a real good start, which I hope it does? They might decide, 'Why change anything, we're going so good?' And then I'm stuck at Richmond. I don't think I have anything left to prove there."

And the Braves agree.

"This was such a difficult decision," Mullen says, "because Paul Zuvella made this team by 900 million lengths."

"It was the best decision we could make at the moment," Haas says. "With our pitching the way it is I didn't feel we could afford to go with nine pitchers."

So Zuvella goes to Richmond, and the Braves open the season with two pitchers who probably aren't in any condition to help the team right away and one catcher whom Haas clearly does not intend to use at all.

"Sometimes," Alex Trevino says, "this is a strange game."

DETROIT—It is a cold, blustery day at Tigers Stadium as the Detroit Tigers begin their defense of their World Championship. Outside the stadium, journalism students from Wayne State University conduct a poll for the *Detroit Free Press,* asking fans if, in the wake of the violent celebration following the last game of the World Series here, they feel the park is too dangerous to come to. "I'm here, aren't I?" one responds.

The skies threaten snow, but it is opening day, the 100-year-old American holiday celebrating the passing of another winter. Jack Morris stands on the mound as Brett Butler steps in for Cleveland to lead off another season. Morris scrapes at the rubber, raises his arms over his head, looks down at the ground, lifts his left knee, drives, uncoils, and delivers . . .

Epilogue

August 1985

Paul Zuvella's detour into the minor leagues lasted just 10 days. On April 18, Alex Trevino was traded to San Francisco for minor league catcher-outfielder John Rabb. But when Zuvella returned to the Braves, he found Rafael Ramirez and Glenn Hubbard firmly entrenched in the middle of the infield. His promising spring had earned him only a utility role; through the middle of August, Zuvella had just 99 at bats, and was batting .192.

Even with Bruce Sutter in the bullpen and a surprisingly sturdy Bob Horner in the lineup every day, the Braves found themselves far out of contention. At the halfway point of the season, they were further under .500 than any Braves team since 1979.

The Braves' fall was hastened by a pitching staff that self-destructed. Rick Mahler had 15 wins by early August, and Steve Bedrosian pitched reasonably well despite intermittent shoulder problems, but the rest of the anticipated rotation was a disaster. Pascual Perez had won only one game by the All-Star break, and soon thereafter went AWOL for several days before being placed on the disabled list for the third time. Len Barker was on and off the disabled list as well, and had just one win and an ERA hovering just under 6.00.

The bullpen, even with the addition of Sutter, was erratic. Part of the problem was that the Braves had few save opportunities early in the season; when the work began to come, Sutter was far

288

from invincible. More times than the Braves could have imagined, Sutter inherited one- or two-run leads and turned them into tie games, or worse. And it did not escape notice in Atlanta that Sutter's old team, the Cardinals, was battling for a pennant with a no-name bullpen, or that the reliever lost in the compensation draft, Donnie Moore, was turning in an all-star season for his new club.

The pitching problems, while worse than expected, were not a complete surprise. The problems the Braves had scoring runs were. The problem came despite Dale Murphy's finest season, and Bob Horner's extraordinary comeback. Horner was on pace for a 25-homer, 90-RBI season, and his wrist had not troubled him at all. At midseason he could say, "I've forgotten all about it. I just feel like Dr. Carter saved my career. I don't know how I could ever have expected this season to go this well for me, personally."

But the season had gone so badly for the first-base duo of Chris Chambliss and Gerald Perry that Horner was shifted over to the position in mid-June. Chambliss's comeback spring proved an illusion; in early August he was batting .225 with just one home run. Perry, the "can't-miss" prospect, was doing a fine job of missing, hitting .190 with one homer and 7 RBIs. And with Horner playing first, third base was left to Ken Oberkfell; the Braves could only be thankful that they had resisted trading him, though for all the wrong reasons. They kept Oberkfell because they feared for Horner; they hadn't anticipated that Horner would be healthy and that Oberkfell would be out-hitting their other first basemen.

The other "can't-miss" prospect, Brad Komminsk, missed just as badly. His batting average was around .220, and his first home run came more than four months into the season. By then, he had lost the starting job to Terry Harper, who was providing some punch at .250, with 14 homers and 58 RBIs. The Braves were getting little offense from anyone in the lineup besides Murphy, Horner, and Harper; Claudell Washington was suffering a difficult season, with his trial date hanging over him. The trial was first postponed to late August, then postponed again until after the end of the season.

The Braves' other off-season move, the trade for Rick Cerone, was another failure. Cerone struggled to keep his average above .200, and had trouble throwing out runners. He found himself sharing the job with Bruce Benedict, who also had just two extra base hits in the first four months of the season. Compounding the problem was the fact that the young pitcher traded for Cerone, Brian Fisher, had become a mainstay of the Yankees bullpen. Fisher was drawing raves from American League scouts in the set-up role for stopper Dave Righetti, the exact spot the Braves were having so much trouble filling for Bruce Sutter.

And the grumblings about manager Eddie Haas grew louder and louder. Haas proved to have as much trouble communicating with his players during the season as he had had with the media over the winter. Rumors of his departure were rampant from mid-season on, and he was finally relieved of his job in late August. Bobby Wine took over, amid speculation that Ted Turner would bring back Phil Niekro as a player-manager for the 1986 season.

So many of the Braves' plans had gone awry: they had been certain that Chambliss and Perry would produce at first; they thought Komminsk would join Murphy and Horner in the middle of the order; they were sure that Sutter would make the bullpen unbeatable; they hoped for the best from their starting pitchers; they thought Cerone would provide power and defense behind the plate; they thought Haas would be the man who could make all these things happen. So many miscalculations, piled one on top of another, led to questions about the ability of the front office itself.

Had the Braves known over the winter that Bob Horner would have the kind of season he was having, they would have felt certain of being an exciting, contending team. They were neither. And they were already preparing for another winter at the drawing board.

Another team facing further decisions was the Phillies. They have long been known for their hair-trigger choices, but even by their standards it didn't take long for their various and sundry spring projects to come apart. The start of the Phillies' season resembled a Pentagon worst-case scenario.

Things started to unravel on opening night. Steve Jeltz made three errors at short and John Russell made two at first base to launch the club on its way to a 1–8 start. The Russell experiment at first base was the first casualty. Russell didn't hit at all in his first few starts, and with the rest of the club slumping, John Felske was forced to quickly bench the rookie and use veteran Tim Corcoran at first. Russell was ultimately sent back to the minors wth orders to play left field. He subsequently returned to the majors, but showed only brief flashes of his anticipated power.

Russell wasn't the only player tossed aside in the rough start. The mercurial Jeff Stone, a given in the offseason as the starter in left, played with only sporadic effectiveness. He demonstrated little of the base-running flair that had the Phils dreaming of a 200-steal season from the club. Stone fell into disfavor because of his lack of aggressiveness, his defensive problems, and his often lackadaisical work habits. He, too, was sent to the minors to await a summons toward the end of the season for what could be a make-or-break audition.

Steve Jeltz also played himself out of a job. He never hit consistently, and Felske and the rest of the team grew weary of his showboat tendencies in the field and led to several late-inning errors and cost the Phils a string of games. Felske had meeting after meeting with Jeltz, trying to browbeat the rookie into listening to advice and not straining to be flashy. But the conversations never had any effect, and Jeltz joined Stone and Russell in Portland.

Then there was poor Bo Diaz. He worked as hard as anyone in Florida to rehabilitate his injured knee and entered the season close to 100 percent. But in the second week of April, he suffered a broken wrist when struck by a pitch during an exhibition game against the Phils' Double-A Reading club. That sidelined him for six weeks. Then, just when the wrist was close to being fully healed, Diaz developed a kidney stone disorder that required surgery and kept him in the hospital for ten days.

While all this was happening to Diaz, Ozzie Virgil played well enough to earn a berth on the National League all-star team. This guaranteed Diaz a spot on the Phillies' bench, and trade rumors sprung up once again. The deal was delayed because of a recurrence of Darren Daulton's shoulder problems, but when Daulton was finally certified healthy, Diaz was traded to the Cincinnati Reds for a package that included shortstop Tom Foley. Foley's presence pushed Jeltz further into the background.

The Phils' off-season moves had virtually no impact. The Pat Zachry–for–Al Oliver trade proved a washout; Zachry was released early in the season, while the Dodgers traded Oliver to Toronto for—the circle remaining unbroken—Len Matuszek, whom the Phils had dealt to the Blue Jays in the spring. The Phillies hope they may have gained something from that deal, bringing reliever Dave Shipanoff up from Portland for a look in August.

As for the trade with St. Louis, Dave Rucker was a disappointment, though the Phils still hoped the lefty would ultimately develop further. Bill Campbell became a bit player in the Cardinals' surprisingly effective bullpen, while DeJesus sat on the St. Louis bench. The Phillies spent much of the summer lamenting the dissolution of the Mike Lavalliere–for–Jeff Lahti trade; Lahti suddenly became the ace of the Cardinals' pen.

The Phils never solved their own bullpen problems. They came out of Florida with their fingers crossed about Al Holland. But he started the season poorly, never throwing with his old velocity, and so the Phils revived their talks with Pittsburgh, and ultimately made the Holland-for-Kent Tekulve swap. Tekulve was inconsistent, but the Phillies got surprisingly good work from Don Carman. "Donnie earned his job in spring training, but none of us really had a line on what he might do," said Felske. "He might have been the best surprise of the year."

The most significant move of the year came in May. Faced with the same problem then bedevilling the Braves—inconsistent production from the first base spot—the Phillies shifted their own veteran third baseman, Mike Schmidt, to first. Schmidt was in the throes of a miserable slump, both at the plate and in the field, when the Phils decided to throw the dice and make the shift. They brought Rick Schu up from the minors to take over at third.

The move worked out well. Schu made his errors in the field, but also brought hard-nosed aggressiveness to the club. After starting slowly with the bat, Schu raised his average to around .280 while demonstrating occasional power. And Schmidt adapted quickly to his new position, playing it with verve and effectiveness.

It was not lost on the Phillies' decision-makers that the most successful of the youth projects was the one they didn't rush into the opening-day lineup. "We might have learned a lesson," said Felske. "In hindsight, we probably made a mistake with John Russell by rushing him into the lineup at a position where he wasn't really comfortable. That was probably too much to ask of a young player, because he worried about his defense. And his hitting suffered as well. It would have likely been better for us to start him in the minors and get his feet on the ground before bringing him up."

Not all the disappointments were on the field. Steve Carlton came down with a shoulder problem that put him on the disabled list for the first time in his career and cast his future in doubt. Joe Lefebvre twice needed further arthroscopic surgery on his knee, and his future was also in doubt, though he was doing some running by the end of the season. And attendance plummeted predictably following the Phils' awful start. But out of the dregs were some bright spots that justified at least some of the Phillies' winter judgments.

Juan Samuel's defense became at least steady and at times spectacular, as he reduced his errors by two-thirds while turning the double play consistently. Wearing new eyeglasses all season, Glenn Wilson became an all-star and was among the league leaders in RBIs. Von Hayes, his legal problems resolved out of court, had a brilliant start before tailing off into a merely solid year. Kevin Gross developed into one of the league's quality starting pitchers, and Jerry Koosman and Shane Rawley both pitched effectively.

And then there was John Felske himself, whose first-year won-lost record may not have been impressive, but whose handling of the difficult situation was. In stark contrast to the uncommunicative Eddie Haas, Felske's candor and public restraint never wavered through the Phils' disappointing first half. What made his frustration so acute was that so many of the Phils' losses came not as a result of the rookies' mistakes, but rather from the club's failure to hit in the clutch. This was particularly true of Schmidt, whose long first-half slump was the single biggest factor in the club's demise.

Felske somehow refrained from losing his temper in public, and won respect from most observers for how he handled the club. Even the impulsive Bill Giles showed no inclination to make his manager a scapegoat. "I don't think anyone could have handled what happened any better than John did," said Giles. "I think he impressed everyone with how he stayed upbeat and positive in what was at times the worst of situations."

"It would have been one thing if we had started the year adequately and then went bad," said Felske. "But with the way we started, we were immediately branded a bad team. And the crime was that there were countless games that could have been different with just a hit or a sacrifice fly at the right time. Sure I felt it. We had a lot of young players trying to prove they belong in this league. And just as they were trying to prove themselves, so I was trying to prove I belonged here as well."

It was a season in which a lot of people were trying to prove themselves. And the question marks that lingered all season promised another winter of decisions for the Phillies organization.

By the All-Star break, the Cleveland Indians were not only in last place, they were on a pace to lose 110 games. They had made 19 player moves, and 41 different athletes had worn a Cleveland uniform by mid-season.

Injuries ravaged the team. Andre Thornton missed the first month of the season because of arthroscopic knee surgery. When he returned, Thornton spent the months of May, June, and July trying desperately to shake the rust off his swing. The result was a .169 batting average and six homers at the break.

In May, Mel Hall was in a serious automobile accident and was sidelined for the season with injuries to his back and pelvis. At the time, Hall was the team's leading hitter at .311.

Players shuffled back and forth from Class AAA Maine at a mind-boggling pace. There was Jose Roman, Roman Romero, Bryan Clark, Benny Ayala and Leroy Purdy Smith III; to the fans, they were nothing more than footnotes to a disaster.

The Indians were being seriously ignored. They had but seven home crowds over 10,000 and were staring at a final season attendance total of slightly over 600,000.

It's hard to imagine that the situation could be much worse. Lousy team, lousy gate, lousy luck. But as has been the case with the Indians, it always could be worse and inevitably became so.

The team still didn't have a legitimate owner. The team remained with Steve O'Neill's estate, which still hoped to sell it. Dave LeFevre still hoped to buy it, but virtually no progress was made in that area. And the front office of Peter Bavasi, Joe Klein, and Dan O'Brien hadn't exactly distinguished itself.

In June, Bavasi stopped shaving.

"I'm going to grow a beard until we get out of last place," said Bavasi.

"Here's hoping Bavasi doesn't trip on it," wrote Sheldon Ocker of the *Akron Beacon-Journal*.

Klein and O'Brien had already swung into action, and almost ruined Julio Franco's confidence in the process. Franco is a notoriously poor fielder early in the season, and he went into the first week of May on a 56-error pace. But Franco was also in the American League's top ten in hitting and seemed on track to his first big-league .300 season.

That's when Klein had a brainstorm.

San Francisco had been pulling a Henny Youngman act and saying to anyone, "Take Johnny LeMaster, please." The Indians took him, thank you.

Cleveland was not dissuaded by LeMaster's lifetime .221 batting average or his 0-for-17 start in 1985. Nor were they bothered when LeMaster lost his job to Jose Uribe, a man so desperate to make the majors that he had changed his name three times in the last year hoping to find one that made him sound more like a big leaguer.

Johnny LeMaster could catch a ground ball, and the Indians were willing to pay his $450,000 salary (plus a $75,000 bonus for being traded) for him to do it in Cleveland. San Francisco got Mike Jeffcoat in exchange.

When LeMaster arrived in Cleveland, manager Pat Corrales announced that Franco would move to second base to make room for the new acquisition.

"Julio never play second base and Julio no play it now," said Franco after hearing of the deal. "Why do they always pick on Julio?"

Hitting coach Bobby Bonds saw that Franco was upset, and immediately ushered the shortstop into Corrales's office. After a half-hour conference with Corrales and Bonds, Franco emerged and told reporters he was a great team man and would do his best at second.

For the next eight days, LeMaster was the shortstop, and Franco played second. Tony Bernazard, Franco's closest friend on the team, was benched even though he was leading the team in RBIs.

The deal was assailed by the Cleveland media and fans. Even those who were critical of Franco's lack of concentration in the field thought the LeMaster deal reeked of panic.

Always aware of public relations, Bavasi clipped an article by Ocker from the *Akron Beacon-Journal* and gave it to members of the Indians' front office and coaching staff. The story demonstrated that Franco had more chances and more double plays per game than LeMaster in 1984. It also recounted Franco's fielding history in which he cut his errors exactly in half after the All-Star breaks in 1983 and 1984.

Finally, Bavasi sent a not-so-subtle hint that Franco be put back at shortstop. Maybe that's what Bavasi means when he talks about restoring the Indians.

Anyway, LeMaster spent 22 days in Cleveland before he was swapped to Pittsburgh for a couple of minor leaguers. LeMaster may have set a major-league record by playing for three last place teams in one month.

To Franco's credit, he pretty much stuck to the company line during the switch and did an acceptable job at second. But his batting average dropped over 50 points during his personal two weeks of turmoil.

After playing for relatively small stakes with deals such as Jay Baller for Danny Rohn, Mike Jeffcoat for Johnny LeMaster, and LeMaster for a Double-A nobody to be named later, Joe Klein took some bold steps into the world of big league trading.

Immediately, there was speculation that he might have ended up with both feet in his mouth.

Klein spent all spring trying to deal Bert Blyleven. The auction took several intriguing turns. Minnesota offered Tim Teufel, Dave Engle, and minor league pitcher Alan Sontag. Toronto dangled promising minor-league pitcher Tom Henke and other young players. St. Louis, Detroit, and California put together packages.

But Klein turned them all down. When the June 15 trading deadline dawned, Blyleven was still an Indian and his waivers (which would have enabled him to be dealt to the National League) had expired.

"We don't have to trade Blyleven," said Klein. "We can keep him all year. Nowhere is it written that we must trade Blyleven."

Klein continually put Blyleven's name in for waivers, but he was always claimed by several teams including Minnesota and Detroit. Finally, he decided to work out a deal with the Twins, who had the worst record (hence the first crack) of any team claiming Blyleven.

The Twins knew they could keep Blyleven from being traded anywhere else, and thus they were no longer in a competitive situation. They could now hang onto Teufel and Engle, and the talks turned to players in the Twins' farm system. As a result, Blyleven was dealt to Minnesota on August 2 for Curt Wardle, Jay Bell, Jim Weaver, and a player to be named later (expected to be Alan Sontag).

As expected, Blyleven was thrilled to go to Minnesota. After all, it was somewhere other than Cleveland.

"After the Angels, the Twins probably were my second choice," said Blyleven. "There were a lot of ups and downs in Cleveland. It was here that I went on the disabled list for the first time in my life. We didn't have much run production and when we did, we didn't pitch very well. All the trade talk got hard for me to deal with. But I won my 200th career game here, was well received by the fans, and made some good friends."

What about the players the Indians received for him?

"No comment," said Blyleven. "I got some ideas about what I'm worth, but I'm not a general manager."

The Minnesota players weren't thrilled about coming to Cleveland. "When my wife heard about the trade, she spent all day crying," said Wardle. "Personally, I don't have much reaction. I'm going to Cleveland. It's something that's a part of baseball."

At the time of the deal, Blyleven was 9–11 with a 3.26 ERA. He was leading the American League in innings pitched, complete games, shutouts, and strikeouts.

Wardle, a 24-year-old lefty, was 1–3 with a 5.51 ERA for the Twins. He allowed eight homers in 49 innings of relief. Also, 6 of the last 11 lefty batters he faced had hit safely.

Weaver, 26, had been a veteran of the Minnesota farm system. The outfielder was batting .239 with eight homers at Class AAA Toledo.

Jay Bell, the key to the deal according to Klein, was hitting .272 with 10 homers and 53 RBIs at Class A Visalia. But in 105 games, the 19-year-old shortstop had made a whopping 55 errors.

"Bell is a fine athlete with some speed and power," said Klein. "But he's a typical young shortstop and they make a lot of errors."

Bell was Minnesota's first pick in the June 1984 amateur draft.

"When I was running the Texas farm system, we had Bell on our list right next to Oddibe McDowell when it came time for the draft," said Klein. "He has real potential."

On the surface, it seemed the Indians received a Class AAA lifer (Weaver), a breaking-ball reliever who can't get lefties out

(Wardle) and a young shortstop with swiss cheese for a glove (Bell). Also, Sontag (a 22-year-old righty who was 11–7 at Class A) was expected to be in the package. None of that sent Cleveland fans scurrying to the ticket windows.

Weaver and Bell were assigned to the Cleveland farm system. For better or worse, Wardle took Blyleven's spot in the starting rotation. And at last, Blyleven had been traded.

There was one bright bit of news from the farm. Cory Snyder, who was hitting under .200 for Class AA Waterbury in the first six weeks of the season, was leading the Eastern League with 12 homers and 44 RBIs by mid-July. He was also playing a solid third base. "The kid is really starting to play," said Corrales. "Once he adjusts to pro ball, he's going to be something."

But by the time he does, will anyone in Cleveland care?

The surprising California Angels justified Gene Mauch's April optimism by taking the lead in the American League West and staying there throughout the first half of the season.

Perhaps even more surprising was the team's maintenance of their resolve to give the youngsters a chance. The youngsters, particularly the pitchers who included starters Mike Witt, Ron Romanick, Kirk McCaskill, and Urbano Lugo, and relievers Pat Clements and Stew Cliburn, augmented the all-star year being turned in by Donnie Moore to give the Angels a deep and impressive pitching staff. They were all the more surprising considering the fact that Geoff Zahn spent several months on the disabled list, and Ken Forsch was unable to pitch in a single game.

But old habits die hard. When the Angels returned to Anaheim on August 2 after a road trip that saw them lose five of their last six games, they learned that Mike Port had swung his first major trade. The deal with Pittsburgh sent Clements, pitcher Bob Kipper, and outfielder Mike Brown to the Pirates for pitchers John Candelaria and Al Holland, and outfielder George Hendrick. Designed to give the Angels maturity and stability down the stretch, the trade sent away three players in their early twenties for three in their thirties, and added some $2.5 million in guaranteed salaries to the payroll. Suddenly, the Angels' 25-man roster had 16 players over 30 years old.

The three veterans had been openly unhappy in Pittsburgh. Port could only hope that the change of environment would bring a change in attitude. There was a lot of money riding on that hope: Candelaria's contract runs through 1986, and Hendrick is signed through 1988. (Holland remains eligible for free agency at the end of the season.)

"We never said that we would build only with young players," Port said. "We wanted to get a better blend of young players to go with our older nucleus, and despite this particular trade, we've done that.

"When we look at this club position by position a few years down the road, we see a smooth transition with what we now have in our farm system. But we also wanted to position ourselves to win this year, and we think this trade will help us do that."

The key acquisition was Candelaria, who had a 124–84 record in 11 seasons with the Pirates, and was expected to give the Angels a proven left-handed starter down the stretch. Port and Buzzie Bavasi had talked with Pittsburgh about Candelaria for two seasons. It is believed that the trade came about only when the Angels, fearful that their lead was slipping away, agreed to take on Hendrick's contract commitments as well. Port insisted, however, that the Angels had good reports on Hendrick, and that they needed him to replace Brown. He also defended trading Brown, a part-timer behind Reggie Jackson in right, by noting that Brown was likely to spend 1986 in a similar role because of the expected return of outfielders Jackson, Juan Beniquez, Brian Downing, and the rejuvenated Ruppert Jones. Jones, a late free-agent signed by the Angels, emerged as the club leader in slugging while ranking right behind Jackson with 18 homers in early August.

Mauch said that he did not know about the final form of the trade until Port presented it to him as made, but it is believed that Mauch pushed for the deal, seeing the three veterans as important stepping stones to his first pennant in 24 years of managing. Many observers recall that the last time the Angels gave up a promising young player in a controversial trade—Tom Brunansky to the Twins for Doug Corbett—Mauch was in his first stint as manager and pushed hard for it. Corbett was a flop for the Angels in 1982, while Brunansky has become an important power hitter for Minnesota. These observers could only remind themselves of Mauch's praise of Kipper and Clements, see Mike Brown's strong start with the Pirates, and wonder if the Angels weren't making the same mistakes yet again.

And what of the New York Mets, baseball's newest glamour team? Would The Big Trade fit the final piece into The Big Picture? Would long-term security bring long-sought stability to Darryl Strawberry? Would success spoil Dwight Gooden? Midway through the 1985 season, the answers seemed to be maybe, quite possibly, and definitely not.

The Mets found themselves in a tight pennant race with the surprising St. Louis Cardinals. The Chicago Cubs were knocked out of contention by an extraordinary series of injuries that completely wiped out their starting rotation. The Mets, too, had weathered injuries, chiefly to Bruce Berenyi, who made three starts in April and was still awaiting his fourth in September; to Mookie Wilson, whose long absence opened a spot for the young kamikaze centerfielder Len Dykstra; and to Strawberry, who missed seven weeks because of a thumb injury suffered while making a diving catch, yet still had 21 homers and 21 steals by September 1. They had gone through such odd stretches as the one in which they scored 68 runs in 12 games after having scored 12 in the previous eight. They won one game in which they were held hitless for ten innings, and lost another—by nineteen runs!—in which they accumulated what was then their season high in hits. They won one 19-inning epic in which they twice gave up game-tying home runs when they were one strike from victory.

"We confuse you," second baseman Wally Backman said. "We do some strange things, don't we?" added Rusty Staub. And no one argued.

The Mets were the most schizophrenic team in the league. You knew what to expect from the others. You knew the Cardinals were going to run, the Dodgers were going to pitch, the Phillies were going to strike out, and the Giants and Pirates were going to lose—somehow. With the Mets, though, there was no clue. As Dave Johnson noted, "You can't take too much for granted with us—except for Dwight."

Gooden showed that his great rookie year had provided only a glimpse of what he could do. In his second year he reeled off 14 straight wins, built up a sizable lead in strikeouts and ERA, and became the youngest pitcher in baseball history to win 20 games in a season. It was Gooden's arm that carried the Mets through the first half, with Strawberry injured and Hernandez and Carter struggling at the plate.

Not that the Mets regretted The Big Trade. They may have given the Expos three everyday players in Hubie Brooks, Herm Winningham, and Mike Fitzgerald, but everyone in the Mets front office would make the trade again. Carter provided solid defense behind the plate and power, particularly down the stretch, despite playing with an injured knee. The Trade appeared to be one of those truly rare deals that helps both teams.

The Mets' other off-season acquisition, Howard Johnson, struggled early at the plate, but proved surprisingly sound in the field. Johnson seemed to snap out of his slump when facing former American League pitchers, a group that included such stars as Rick Sutcliffe and LaMarr Hoyt, leading the Mets to hope that his performance would improve as his familiarity with the circuit's pitchers grew.

As with any Mets team, though, the pitching would be the key. Ron Darling continued to improve, and joined Gooden on the all-star team. Ed Lynch pitched effectively, and worked more innings in the first half of the season than he had in all of 1984, putting to rest questions about his durability. Sid Fernandez, summoned from the minors in May, won back his status as the number four starter, and pitched well despite hard luck. In the bullpen, rookie Roger McDowell took on some of the responsibilities of both Jesse Orosco and Doug Sisk, sometimes serving as set-up man, sometimes as stopper. McDowell's 90 mph sinker gave Dave Johnson another option in his search for the hot hand in the pen.

With the addition of right-handed pinch hitter Tom Paciorek and infielder Larry Bowa, both acquired for the stretch drive, the Mets looked deep, poised, and every inch a contender. Whether they won the pennant or not, they would need only the slightest fine-tuning to stay a contender for years to come.

Despite the big deals, big signings, and big decisions, perhaps the most important development of the baseball winter of 1984 was the one that didn't happen: substantive negotiations toward a new basic agreement between the players and owners. Negotiations stalled in March with the owners' claims of severe economic problems. Peter Ueberroth ordered the owners to open their books to the players, but that only made the arguments more statistical. The owners' examiners saw $26 million in losses industry-wide; the players' experts saw several million dollars in profits.

The players voted in mid-July to authorize a strike date of August 6. In the weeks prior to the deadline, a variety of minor matters were settled, leaving the focus squarely on the most important areas: the players' demands that the owners substantially increase their contribution to the players' pension plan, and the owners' demands that the players help slow the salary spiral by placing some restrictions on arbitration awards and eligibility. The owners hoped to accomplish this by raising the time of service required before a player could go to arbitration from two years to three, and putting a lid on the amount a player's salary could increase in arbitration. A player would be able, at most, to double his salary. These conditions were unacceptable, and the strike began as scheduled on the sixth.

It ended on the seventh. The players accepted a far smaller pension fund contribution than they had sought. The owners dropped their demand for a cap on arbitration awards, but received two important concessions. First, the service requirement for arbitration would change to three years, this taking effect in 1987. Second, free agent salaries could not be used as precedents in setting arbitration awards. Since many players have been given contracts, like Darryl Strawberry's, that guarantee them high pay in exchange for taking them out of the arbitration jungle, it is not clear to what extent this provision will be effective. Presumably, those contracts will still have value to agents in making their arguments.

The owners also agreed to raise the major league minimum salary from $40,000 to $60,000, and they agreed to open up the free agent market by eliminating both the reentry free agent draft and compensation for type A free agents.

The rules of the game were changed, but only marginally. Player salaries will continue to rise. A Bruce Sutter will still be able to command pay that seems more like a gross national product than a salary. A Ted Turner will be able to hold onto a Donnie Moore despite the foolish no-trade clauses he gave a Rick Camp or Terry Forster. The next Fernando Valenzuela will still be able to seek a million dollars in arbitration; he'll just have to wait another year to do it. That extra year also means that there will be more players in Dwight Gooden's position (well, sort of), in which their only negotiating tool is a threatened holdout.

The rich, smart organizations will still be able to build perennial contenders. The poor, foolish clubs will still find every year an adventure. The events of the offseason will continue to influence and, in many cases, dictate the fortunes of the teams during the season.

Index